CLUSTERING

AND

AGGREGATION

IN

ECONOMICS

☐

CLUSTERING AND AGGREGATION IN ECONOMICS

WALTER D. FISHER

THE JOHNS HOPKINS PRESS, BALTIMORE

TO MARJORIE

PREFACE

In this book the aggregation problem of economics is studied with the purpose of recommending specific procedures to the econometric investigator. A theory of clustering and aggregation is developed from the notion that voluminous detail is costly, as well as sacrificed information. The theory is applied to basic types of economic problems. For three problems—a reduced form, an input-output matrix, and a linear programming problem—numerical data are used to determine solutions in the form of near-optimal groupings. A recommended step-wise clustering procedure to solve the problems is described, with brief outlines of computational programs.

Readers will find this approach somewhat novel, although not in conflict with the previous work of others. While the suggestion to use decision theory with aggregation problems in economics was made by me and others in the early 1950's, no systematic application of the suggestion has been made. The approach is used, or implied, in the groupings of input-output sectors made by Skolka in 1964, in the industrial clusters based on stock prices suggested by King in 1966, and in some previous work of mine. Being somewhat of a pilot study, the present work contains some unfinished business; I am acutely aware of this, and the reader will be also.

This work was supported by Grants GS–52 and GS–830 of the National Science Foundation, as well as by earlier fellowships awarded the author by the John Simon Guggenheim Memorial Foundation and the Social Science Research Council. Financial support was also received from the Bureau of General Research of Kansas State University, as well as from the Kansas Agricultural Experiment Station. I am indebted to the following individuals for collaboration, stimulation, and tangible assistance: E. Vaughn Brown, Larry A. Cammack, Philip DeMoss, Leonard Fuller, Paul L. Kelley, James Letourneau, H. Neudecker, S. Thomas Parker, Stanley Reiter, Rose M. Rubin, Jeanne Sebaugh, and Linda L. Woolf.

About one-quarter of the text has appeared previously in my published articles. The second example of Chapter 1 and most of section 2 of Chapter 5 came from "On grouping for maximum homogeneity," in the *Journal of the American Statistical Association* (December, 1958). The theoretical material in Chapter 2 came from "Optimal aggregation in multi-equation prediction models," in *Econometrica* (October, 1962); the rest of Chapter 2 on prediction models, along with the first example of Chapter 1 and the first two sections of Appendix G, came from "Simplification of economic models," in the July, 1966, issue of the same journal. Appreciation and thanks are expressed to the editors of these journals for permission to reproduce this material in the present form. The input-output example in Chapter 3 represents a portion of the doctoral dissertation of Rose M. Rubin (Kansas State University, 1968). Figure 9 and seven appendix tables come from this work, with Mrs. Rubin's permission. The linear programming example in Chapter 4 is the result of research conducted jointly by Dr. Paul L. Kelley, of Kansas State University, and me; certain unpublished data and results are being used here with the kind permission of Dr. Kelley. The research for section 1 of Chapter 6 and the writing of it was done by my wife, Marjorie Fisher, this specific contribution being just one of many.

W. D. F.

CONTENTS

LIST OF FIGURES

LIST OF TABLES

1

PURPOSE AND SCOPE

1. The Need for Simplification

With the growth and increasing quantification of the social sciences has come a need for systematic and scientific simplification. Human abilities to absorb, comprehend, and manage large volumes of data, or large numbers of concepts derived from data, are limited. Electronic computers must be programmed by human beings, and their output must ultimately be read and understood by human beings. Even at the level of theoretical analysis and exposition the theorist is required to, first, partition the universe into those parts which he will and will not deal with; and second, deal with the one part by means of a limited number of concepts—carefully selected and defined.

The econometric investigator is faced with a more serious simplification problem than the pure theorist. The theorist may assume, for example, that the consumer is choosing among n goods; he may not be inconvenienced in carrying through an analysis with large n. The econometrician, on the other hand, for obvious reasons would like to make n reasonably small. It may not be obvious how to select a small number of goods, or combinations of goods, from the large number originally available.

A simplification or aggregation problem is faced by a research worker whenever he finds that his data are too numerous or in too much detail to be manageable and feels the need to group or combine the detailed data in some manner. He will want to compute aggregative measures for his groups. Very often such grouping is performed at an early stage of the research without adequate analysis of the effects of the grouping on the substantive results. Often alternative methods of grouping are available but are ignored. Often a decision must be made as to the number of groups that are to be used; a smaller number is more manageable but causes more of the original information to be lost. The research worker seeks a solution of this aggregation problem that will best serve his objectives, or those of some decision-maker who will use his results.

The basic purpose of this book is to provide solutions to this simplification problem as it arises in a number of typical economic problems. Emphasis is given first to the development of a criterion by which alternative procedures may be judged, and second, to specifie procedures for selecting a "good" grouping in terms of the criterion. While the "aggregation problem" has been widely recognized and much discussed in the literature, not many specific suggestions have been made for "good" methods of grouping. To provide such suggestions is the main objective of the present contribution.

The two simple examples of the next section are intended to give the reader a feel for the type of problem to be dealt with in this book. The first example is from a research study in which the need for simplification was felt by the original investigator. The second is a textbook illustration. After these examples a more general definition of the problem will be given.

2. TWO EXAMPLES

Clustering of Productivity Coefficients

As an illustration of the use of economic analysis in the choice of alternative "systems," McGuire [1960] presents an optimization problem involving the aggregation of missions or "channels" to be performed by aircraft. The basic problem considered is to choose numbers of aircraft of alternative types that will perform specified tasks at minimum total cost. The simplification or aggregation part of the problem is described by McGuire as follows:

> Our object is to aggregate the 40 channels into a smaller number of groups without losing too much detail. From the standpoint of a given pair of aircraft, one channel differs from another only to the extent that the substitutability of the two aircraft on one channel is different from their substitutability on another channel. Their substitutability on a particular channel depends upon the ratio of their productivities (defined above as tonnages carried per flying hour). Therefore, the ratio of productivities for two aircraft will be called their substitution ratio. Channels with almost the same ratio can be treated as a single channel, and their requirements can be added together.[1]

Since four different types of aircraft are dealt with, three independent productivity ratios are available for each channel. The detailed data for

[1] McGuire [1960, pp. 151–52].

TABLE 1. AIRCRAFT PRODUCTIVITY RATIOS

(Tons per flying hour)

Channel	HC–400 C–97	HC–500 C–97	HC–600 C–97
57	1.96	4.08	5.25
59	1.97	4.62	5.27
61	1.33	3.48	3.57
5	2.60	3.98	6.83
11	2.54	3.77	6.66
25	2.56	4.08	6.90
27	2.54	4.08	6.91
29	2.50	3.99	6.82
31	2.53	4.04	6.86
47	2.56	3.84	6.72
9	2.12	4.17	5.89
13	2.14	4.47	5.97
45	2.13	4.38	5.95
33	2.05	4.19	5.62
43	2.02	4.20	5.78
23	2.22	4.17	6.20
35	2.24	4.06	6.29
41	2.33	4.15	6.36
17	2.04	5.52	5.64
7	2.44	4.37	6.41

Source: McGuire [1960, Table 16, p. 148].

twenty of these channels may be tabulated as three columns of figures with twenty figures in each column, as is done in Table 1, and may also be thought of geometrically as a set of twenty points in three-dimensional space.[2] "Similarity" of substitution ratios may be thought of as "closeness together" of points. It is desired to group together points that are close to each other. McGuire plots the twenty points on two graphs, using two dimensions at a time, and shows a partition of the points into nine subsets or "aggregate channels," which are used throughout the remainder of his analysis. The partitioning is apparently based on visual inspection of the two diagrams.[3] The two diagrams are reproduced in Figure 1.

A more objective criterion for the grouping, and one that is well known, is to require that the sum of the squared Euclidean three-dimensional distances of the individual points from the centers of gravity of the clusters to which they are assigned be a minimum.[4] That such a grouping exists is

[2] The remaining twenty channels are represented by points that are so close together as to be difficult to plot and play no significant role in McGuire's channel-aggregation problem.

[3] McGuire does not specifically state this, but implies it. He states: "All of our circles have diameters sufficiently small to avoid introducing distortion into the problem." (McGuire [1960, p. 152]).

[4] In mechanical terms, the sum of the moments of inertia around the cluster centroids is to be a minimum. An algebraic formulation is given in equation (1.8).

FIGURE 1. AGGREGATION OF AIR CARGO CHANNELS

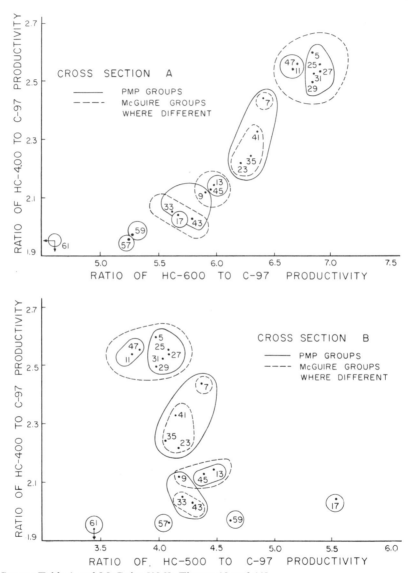

Source: Table 1 and McGuire [1960, Figures 10 and 11].

obvious, but to find it by a computational algorithm is not a simple matter. An algorithm that is believed to come close to the desired grouping is
described in Chapter 5 and Appendix G. By use of it a grouping was

found that is similar to but not identical with McGuire's. The sets are shown in Figure 1 by solid lines. McGuire's sets are shown by dotted lines. The value of the sum of squared deviations for McGuire's partition is .24; for ours .18. The true minimum is not yet known. If squared distance is considered a proper criterion, our partition serves the purpose well.

This problem is essentially equivalent to that described as "cluster analysis" in certain literature of other scientific disciplines.[5] The squared distance criterion used here and the method of finding the desired partition differs, however, from most of the methods used in these other studies, although there are close similarities. As will be seen in later chapters, this problem is a special case of more general problems. But some of its crucial traits carry over.

Admittedly there is some arbitrariness in the squared distance criterion, even though it is more objective than visual inspection of the two-dimensional scatter. One would naturally wish to develop a criterion in terms of the objectives of finding minimum total cost in McGuire's basic problem, which is one of linear programming. It is shown in Chapter 4 that a squared distance criterion of the type used here is a useful approximate criterion in the problem of aggregating constraints or activities in a linear programming problem.[6] Other approximate criteria might also have been used.

There is some arbitrariness in McGuire's choice of coordinates. Productivity is expressed in tons per unit of "aircraft," which is an arbitrary unit. If this unit is changed, this has the effect of subjecting one or both of the dimensions to a stretch transformation which will alter the distance relations between the points. Put in other words, the solution to the problem is not invariant with respect to differential changes of scale (or with respect to other nonorthogonal transformations of either the row-space or column-space of the matrix represented by Table 1). Since in this problem the productivity ratios are to be compared with ratios of money costs, a more logical scaling of the productivity coefficients would seem to be in money terms (tons per dollar rather than tons per aircraft).[7] This difficulty raises a fundamental point which will recur a number of times: if use is to be made of a scalar criterion, or measure of discrepancies of results caused by different methods of simplification, that criterion must reflect, in part, value judgments of the investigator (or decision-maker) as

[5] See Chapter 6.
[6] See Chapter 4, section 1.
[7] The problem was rerun with this rescaling, using costs for McGuire's Period I from his Table 17, and a somewhat different partition of the points resulted, which is shown in W. D. Fisher [1966, Figure 2].

to the relative importance of discrepancies in different "variables," or "dimensions" of the problem. Different judgments will lead to variation in method. The point is similar to that of postulating cardinal ulitity.[8]

Clustering with a Side Condition

In the preceding example the investigator, in solving the grouping problem, was at liberty to place any points in any group without restrictions or side conditions. In many practical problems side conditions are imposed. To take a simple example, involving in this case only a one-dimensional distance, consider the time series of ninety-six years giving the level of Lake Michigan–Huron, as shown in Table 2 and Figure 2. Wallis and Roberts in their text [1956] use these data to illustrate runs and moving averages. But suppose it is desired to subdivide the entire time-span into four epochs within each of which the variation in lake level is small. More precisely, say that it is desired to minimize the sum of squared deviations from mean levels within epochs.

This problem would be a simple one-dimensional analogue of the aircraft-channel clustering problem if we could put together any years that we wished to, irrespective of chronological order. The years could be reordered according to lake level, and a fairly good partition of the entire set of years into four subsets could probably be made by visual inspection of the resulting diagram. The problem is not so trivial when the partition has to be determined subject to the condition, which may be regarded as a side condition, that the members of a subset must be chronologically ordered years. This problem has been solved by means of a computer program written by me in 1956.[9] The optimal grouping into four groups is indicated in Figure 2 by the heavy lines intersecting the time-series graph. In Table 3 the solutions are listed for varying numbers of groups from ten down to one. This table shows also how the value of the criterion, which may be thought of as a cost, increases as the aggregation becomes more severe.

Other types of side condition may be imposed in aggregation problems. It may be required that the solution "respect" some partial ordering of the elements, rather than a complete ordering, or some restrictions on the location of these elements in some space other than the space used to de-

---

[8] In the McGuire problem the point arises in a somewhat different form with respect to the use of a particular aircraft (the C–97) for the denominator of the productivity ratios. The use of a different aircraft for the denominator essentially means the premultiplication of the matrix represented in Table 1 by a diagonal matrix. Again, the distance relations among the points would be altered; the criterion function might well require reconsideration.

[9] See Chapter 5.

Table 2. Lake Michigan–Huron Highest Monthly Mean Level for Each Calendar Year, 1860–1955

(Height in feet above 500)

Year	Level	Year	Level	Year	Level	Year	Level	Year	Level
1860	83.3	1880	82.1	1900	80.7	1920	81.0	1940	79.3
1	83.5	1	82.2	1	81.1	1	80.5	1	79.0
2	83.2	2	82.6	2	80.8	2	80.6	2	80.2
3	82.6	3	83.3	3	80.8	3	79.8	3	81.5
4	82.2	4	83.1	4	81.5	4	79.6	4	80.8
5	82.1	5	83.3	5	81.6	5	78.5	5	81.0
6	81.7	6	83.7	6	81.5	6	78.5	6	81.1
7	82.2	7	82.9	7	81.6	7	79.6	7	81.1
8	81.6	8	82.3	8	81.8	8	80.6	8	80.8
9	82.1	9	81.8	9	81.1	9	82.3	9	79.7
1870	82.7	1890	81.6	1910	80.5	1930	81.2	1950	80.0
1	82.8	1	80.9	1	80.0	1	79.1	1	81.6
2	81.5	2	81.0	2	80.7	2	78.6	2	82.7
3	82.2	3	81.3	3	81.3	3	78.7	3	82.1
4	82.3	4	81.4	4	80.7	4	78.0	4	81.7
5	82.1	5	80.2	5	80.0	5	78.6	5	81.5
6	83.6	6	80.0	6	81.1	6	78.7		
7	82.7	7	80.9	7	81.9	7	78.6		
8	82.5	8	80.8	8	81.9	8	79.7		
9	81.5	9	81.1	9	81.3	9	80.0		

Source: Wallis and Roberts [1956, Table 566].

FIGURE 2. LAKE MICHIGAN–HURON HIGHEST MONTHLY MEAN LEVEL, 1860–1955

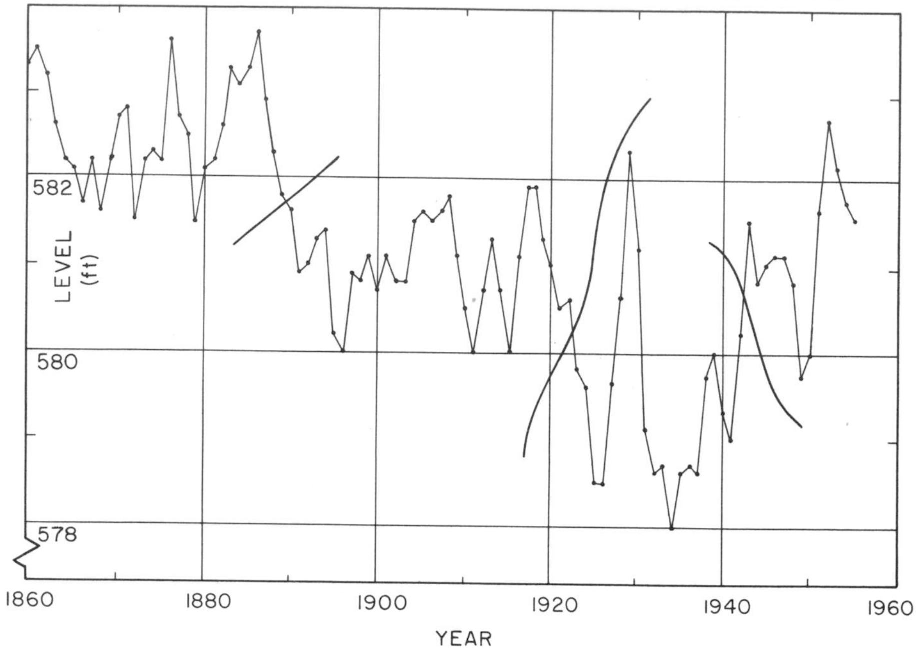

Source: Wallis and Roberts [1956, p. 567].

fine the criterion.[10] Or, the inclusion of certain specified elements in the same subset of a partition may be required, or forbidden, a priori.[11]

The two examples in this section are intended only to introduce concepts and aspects of a more general type of problem, which will be formulated in the next section and illustrated by more realistic economic examples in Chapters 2, 3, and 4.

3. THE PROBLEM: OPTIMAL SIMPLIFICATION

The Problem Formulated

Let us assume that an investigator has at hand a batch of *detailed data*, which will be designated X. The batch X comprises a finite number of elements, which are real numbers; and the batch itself may be thought of as a vector or a matrix. Indeed, X may be thought of as a member of some set of possible batches that might have been available, or might be in the future, and hence an element of a vector space.

---

[10] See the example discussed in W. D. Fisher [1953, section II].
[11] Forbidden inclusions are specified in the example in section 3 of Chapter 3.

TABLE 3. SOLUTION TO LAKE MICHIGAN–HURON PROBLEM FOR VARYING
NUMBER OF GROUPS

Number of groups	Value of criterion	Boundaries of groups[a]								
1	16,614									
2	8,673	31								
3	7,400	30	61							
4	4,969	30	63	83						
5	4,463	30	63	71	82					
6	3,580	30	63	68	71	82				
7	3,080	30	63	68	71	82	91			
8	2,857	23	29	63	68	71	82	91		
9	2,559	3	23	29	63	68	71	82	91	
10	2,359	3	23	29	63	68	71	78	82	91

[a] Serial number of the latest year in a group, all years being numbered from 1 to 96.
Source: W. D. Fisher [1958b, p. 794].

The investigator plans to compute and make use of another batch of *simplified data*, $\tilde{X}$, which is derivable from the detailed data by some procedure or *simplification function, f.* That is,

(1.1) $X \xrightarrow{\quad f \quad} \tilde{X}$.

One way of constructing a simplification function is by an *aggregation-disaggregation sequence.* We shall say that such a sequence is defined when $\tilde{X}$ comprises the same number of elements as X, and when there exists another reduced batch of *aggregated data,* $\bar{X}$, comprising a fewer number of elements than X, and also two additional functions, g and h, such that g is a function from the set of X to the set of $\bar{X}$, and h is a function from the set of $\bar{X}$ to the set of $\tilde{X}$.[12] Thus

(1.2) $X \xrightarrow{\quad g \quad} \bar{X}$, $\bar{X} \xrightarrow{\quad h \quad} \tilde{X}$.

Then we say that the composite function gh, which is also the function f, is the aggregation-disaggregation sequence. While $\tilde{X}$ has the same number of elements as X, in general some of the original detail of X is lost in $\tilde{X}$.[13]

A special case of the aggregation-disaggregation sequence that is of primary concern in this book is when the function h is of the class of *partitioned disaggregation*—that is, when h defines a certain *element-to-subset correspondence* from the elements of $\bar{X}$ to the elements of $\tilde{X}$. That is, for any particular pair of batches $(\bar{X}, \tilde{X})$ defined by the function h, in

[12] The function g is many-to-one onto. The function h is one-to-one but not "onto."

[13] When aggregation, but not disaggregation occurs, one could, of course, refer to the aggregate data $\bar{X}$ as "simplified data." But to avoid confusion we shall, whenever feasible, use the term "simplified data" only to refer to batches $\tilde{X}$ that have the same number of elements as X. An exception is the discussion of linear programming in Chapter 4.

which the elements of the batches are ordered, it will be true that with each element of $\bar{X}$ is associated a certain non-empty subset of the elements of $\tilde{X}$.

Thus

(1.3)
$$\bar{X}_i \xrightarrow{\quad h \quad} \tilde{X}_i \ ,$$

where $\bar{X}_i$ is an element of $\bar{X}$ and $\tilde{X}_i$ is a non-empty subset of $\tilde{X}$. This association indeed defines a partition of the elements of $\tilde{X}$.[14]

The simplification function involves two essential aspects: (1) degree of simplification, (2) method of weighting; it may also involve a third: selection of a partition; prior restrictions may be placed on the class of permitted simplification functions if desired.

A cost function is postulated on the product of the sets of X and of $\tilde{X}$ specifying the effects of using the simplified data in place of the original data:

(1.4)
$$c = \varphi(X, \tilde{X}) \ .$$

This function is assumed to take into consideration the purposes of the investigator or decision-maker (including whatever gain or utility functions are relevant), the relative seriousness of losses of information about various detailed subsets of the observed data (including considerations of relative quality of the data as indicators of population characteristics), and the increased difficulty and cumbersomeness of managing, handling, and understanding detailed data, as opposed to aggregative data. These latter costs may be called "costs of detail." It will be assumed that the cost is an increasing function of the amount of detail (number of distinct elements) remaining in the simplified data, given the discrepancies (to be defined rigorously later) between the original and the simplified data, and also an increasing function of such discrepancies, given the amount of detail.

The general problem is then, given the observed data X, to select a simplification function f, subject to whatever prior restrictions are placed

---

[14] For example let X be a row vector $(x_1 \ x_2 \ x_3)$, $\bar{X}$ be the aggregated vector $(\bar{x}_1 \ \bar{x}_2)$ and $\tilde{X}$ be the simplified vector $(\tilde{x}_1 \ \tilde{x}_2 \ \tilde{x}_3)$. Let the functions g and h be defined such that $\bar{X} = XA'$ and $\tilde{X} = \bar{X}B$, where A and B are each matrices of full rank of size 2 by 3. An aggregation-disaggregation sequence is thus found to be the matrix $A'B$. If, moreover, B has the form $B = \begin{pmatrix} b_1 & b_2 & 0 \\ 0 & 0 & b_3 \end{pmatrix}$, then we have partitioned disaggregation, with the first element $\bar{x}_1$ of $\bar{X}$ corresponding with the subset $(\tilde{x}_1 \ \tilde{x}_2)$ of $\tilde{X}$, and $\bar{x}_2$ corresponding with $\tilde{x}_3$. We also could have defined an analogous concept of "partitioned aggregation" by placing a similar requirement on the aggregating function f. In most cases discussed in this book we choose not to specify such a requirement, but rather shall allow the elements of $\bar{X}$ to depend on all of the elements of the original batch of data X.

on f, such that cost c is a minimum. It is assumed that the minimum exists. For simplified data with a specified number of degrees of freedom the problem involves searching for a method of simplification that entails minimum discrepancies, or "distance" in some sense, between X and $\tilde{X}$. When degrees of freedom of the simplified data are allowed to vary, the problem then also involves the weighing of the costs of loss of information (entailed by using few degrees of freedom) against the cost of detail (entailed by using many degrees of freedom). It is assumed that a balance can be struck. This assumption is supported by the observation that in many fields of quantitative inquiry averages are computed and found useful; yet group averages are often more useful than one grand average computed for the entire universe of study. This problem may be called optimal simplification.

The aircraft channel example of section 2 may be formally placed in this framework in the following way. With respect to some partition of the columns of some matrix X, let a grouping matrix T be defined as

$$(1.5) \qquad T = \begin{bmatrix} 1 & \cdots & 1 & 0 & & \cdots & & 0 \\ & 0 & & 1 & \cdots & 1 & & 0 \\ & & \cdot & & & \cdot & & \cdot \\ & & \cdot & & & \cdot & & \cdot \\ & & \cdot & & & \cdot & & \cdot \\ & 0 & & 0 & & \cdots & 1 & \cdots & 1 \end{bmatrix},$$

where the number of 1's in a row is the number of columns of X that is to be put into some subset and where a 0 stands for a row of scalar zeros.[15] Now let X be the 3 by 20 matrix obtained by transposing Table 1. Let T have 9 rows and 20 columns. Then let $\bar{X}$ be the aggregated matrix of size 3 by 9 conditional on the partition

$$(1.6) \qquad \bar{X} = XT'(TT')^{-1} .$$

It may easily be verified that $\bar{X}$ gives the coordinates of the centroids of the clusters of points defined by the partition. Let $\tilde{X}$ denote the 3 by 20 matrix formed by repeating columns of $\bar{X}$

$$(1.7) \qquad \tilde{X} = \bar{X}T = XT'(TT')^{-1}T .$$

This matrix $\tilde{X}$ may be thought of as a disaggregation of $\bar{X}$ or as a simplified version of X.

[15] Matrices of the structure of T will recur repeatedly in this study. When used as a premultiplier, T adds rows within subsets; when used as a postmultiplier, it repeats columns. Its transpose adds columns when used as a postmultiplier and repeats rows when used as a premultiplier. Except in a trivial limiting case, T is not square.

The requirement that the sum of squared distances of the points from their cluster centroids be minimized is found to be equivalent to the minimization of the cost function

$$(1.8) \qquad\qquad c = \text{tr}(X - \tilde{X})(X - \tilde{X})' \ .$$

Therefore the problem is to find a partition (it may not be unique) over the domain of partitions of 20 elements into 9 subsets that will give an $\tilde{X}$ that will make cost c a minimum.[16]

The Lake Michigan example would be formulated in the same way, except that X and $\tilde{X}$ would be 1 by 96 row vectors, $\bar{X}$ would be a 1 by 4 row vector, and the simplification function would be obtained subject to the side condition that the partition "respect" the chronological ordering of the elements of X.

In neither of these two examples has the cost of detail been specifically introduced. The degree of detail (number of subsets in the partition) has been preselected as another side condition. It would be possible to generalize these examples by allowing the degree of detail to be a variable and introducing the cost of detail into the cost function. It must be admitted, however, that such a generalization would require much more information, including a rather specific pinpointing of objectives. A cruder and more flexible approach would be to obtain optimal simplifications for various degrees of detail, as was done in the Lake Michigan problem, and allow the decision-maker to inspect these and later decide which solution or solutions are relevant to him. In practice such a decision would very likely be based in large part on introspection and hunch.

Stochastic Formulation

The formulation of the preceding section started with the set of detailed data X. No questions were raised as to where these data came from. Now it will be shown that these data may be derivable from a decision problem in a Bayesian stochastic setting.[17]

Consider that the state of the world relevant to a decision-maker is assigned the symbol s, which is an element of some set of states S. Let the decision itself be d, which is an element of set D. It is assumed that d has a finite number of elements (or that the decision space D has a finite

[16] This example has been formulated in a somewhat more restrictive manner than needed by the prior specification of the conditional $\tilde{X}$ as the coordinates of *centroids*. It would have been sufficient to allow the detailed specification of the cluster centers to be determined by the minimization process, and centroids would have turned up anyway because of the simple quadratic cost function postulated by (1.8).

[17] Alternative non-Bayesian formulations are indicated below in Chapter 2, section 2.

number of dimensions). Let a *loss function* be defined over the product of sets S and D

$$(1.9) \qquad\qquad L = \theta(s, d)$$

which determines the loss or negative utility to the decision-maker of making decision d when state s exists. L is assumed to be a non-negative scalar.

Now assume that the decision-maker has arrived at a *posterior probability distribution* over the set of states S. This distribution will be written $p(s)$. It may be discrete, continuous, or partly discrete and partly continuous. It may be assumed to have been derived via Bayes Theorem from a prior probability distribution (based on subjective notions, previous research, or a combination of these factors) and possibly from an observed sample, if one was available.[18]

The posterior risk, or simply risk r, is defined as the expected value of the loss. That is,

$$(1.10) \qquad\qquad r = E(L) = E[\theta(s, d)] \ ,$$

where E is a mathematical expectation operator with respect to the posterior distribution $p(s)$. Thus r is a function of the decision d.

A *detailed optimal decision d^** is defined as a decision that minimizes the risk r with no simplification conditions. It is assumed that the minimum r exists. We may write then

$$(1.11) \qquad\qquad d^* = \Psi(p, \theta)$$

to indicate that this detailed optimal decision depends on the characteristics of the posterior distribution and of the loss function, including parameters, moments, and whatever.

A *simplified decision $\bar{d}$*, is defined as a decision that is subject to restrictions on either (a) the assumed posterior distribution $p(s)$ or (b) the domain of possible decisions D. In either case (a) or case (b) the restrictions are used to obtain easier decisions. Under case (a) we include situations where the $p(s)$ is deliberately mis-specified in order to attain fewer variables or simpler mathematics.[19] Let us call such a modified distribution $\bar{p}(s)$. The same type of motivation occurs in case (b), only here the restrictions are placed on the space of possible actions (decisions). In fact the motive of simpler arithmetic or manageability will probably dictate the choice of whether case (a) or case (b) is used in a particular problem. In some prob-

---

[18] As a limiting case, when no sample is available, the posterior distribution is equivalent to the prior distribution.

[19] This case has been described by Reiter [1957], as leading to a "surrogate" decision problem.

lems correspondences exist between restrictions of the two different types.

In some cases $\tilde{d}$ may be a function of the posterior distribution and the loss function but different from Ψ:

$$(1.12) \qquad \tilde{d} = \tilde{\Psi}(p, \theta) \ .$$

Previously a set of detailed data X was postulated as input to the simplification problem. We may associate the X of that formulation with the detailed optimal decision of the present formulation and write

$$(1.13) \qquad d^* = X \ .$$

We are assuming that both d^* and X contain a finite number of elements. We may do the same for $\tilde{d}$ and $\tilde{X}$ and write

$$(1.14) \qquad \tilde{d} = \tilde{X} \ .$$

Then, from (1.10) we have for the differential risk between the dwo d's:

$$(1.15) \quad r(\tilde{d}) - r(d^*) = E[\theta(s, \tilde{d})] - E[\theta(s, d^*)] = E[\theta(s, X)] - E[\theta(s, \tilde{X})] \ .$$

The cost of the restrictions (simplification) is a function of the above difference in the r's, and of the change of detail or degrees of freedom resulting by using $\tilde{X}$ rather than X. Then cost is

$$(1.16) \qquad c = \varphi(X, \tilde{X}) \ .$$

In applications the suggested association between d^* and X is sometimes not very satisfactory because it implies that the detailed decision problem must be solved before the simplification or aggregation problem can be started. In some applications it may be possible to write (1.12) as

$$(1.17) \qquad \tilde{d} = \tilde{\Psi}(p, \theta) = \tilde{\tilde{\Psi}}(\tilde{p}, \tilde{\theta}) \ ,$$

where (p, θ) is representable as a vector and $(\tilde{p}, \tilde{\theta})$ as a vector in a lower dimensional space. Then we may assign

$$(1.18) \qquad (p, \theta) = X \ ; \qquad (\tilde{p}, \tilde{\theta}) = \tilde{X} \ ,$$

that is, assigning X to be "more original givens" than d^*. Then (1.16) will still hold with a different interpretation of the symbols, and possibly a more complicated function φ, but with the possibility of using a simpler function to approximate φ.

Some of the examples to be presented in the following chapters are based on the decision-theory approach outlined above. The manner in which X and $\tilde{X}$ are deduced from economic problems will depend on the particular problem considered.

Variants of the Problem

The reader may have had some difficulty in making a transition between the general problem just formulated and problems familiar to him. In order to be more specific let us postulate a kind of model used in economics, and probably also in other fields. This model is assumed to consist of a set of *variables*, and a set of *relations* between some or all of these variables.

One of the relations is an equation, called *objective function* or *criterion*, which expresses one scalar quantity, the "objective," as a function of other variables. The purpose of the investigator is either to maximize or minimize the objective. The other relations are either equations or inequalities. They may contain parameters that have to be estimated.

The set of variables may consist of some or all of the following classes: *predetermined variables*, whose values or probability distributions at the time of decision are determined outside of the model; *endogenous variables*, whose values or probability distributions are determined by the model; *disturbances*, which are random scalar variables, one of which may be assigned to each relation. The predetermined variables are divided into two subclasses: *decision variables* (or *instruments*) whose values are under the control of the investigator or decision-maker, and *uncontrolled predetermined variables* that are not under such control.

The decision variables together constitute the "decision" of the previous section. The objective function implies the loss function. The other elements of the model constitute the "state of the world" *s*. If the necessary probability distributions are known, or can be assumed, the decision problem can be solved.

In some applications the aim of the investigator is to predict values of the endogenous variables. His decision variables are called "estimates" or "predictions" of the endogenous variables. His objective function, which is the same as the loss function, will be an increasing function of "errors of prediction," which will be measured by some sort of distance between his predictions and the true values of the endogenous variables. In general it will be necessary as a by-product of obtaining estimates of the endogenous variables to obtain also estimates of the unknown parameters in the relations of the model. It may be assumed that the objectives of the investigator in making predictions with small errors are somehow related to some economic objectives of other parties who will use these predictions, but the nature of this relationship is unspecified. Or the investigator may be assumed to be pursuing "pure" and disinterested research. This type of problem will be called a *prediction problem*, and the associated model a *prediction model*.

In other cases the objective function represents true economic objectives or "utility" of decision-makers in a more proper or restricted sense. These decision-makers control the decision variables. The objective function is regarded as a function, directly or indirectly via the model, of the decision variables. This type of problem is called *decision-proper*.

The simplification-aggregation problem may, then, arise in either of these two contexts. Formally and methodologically, it may be regarded as the same problem, but the practical meaning of the terminology is different in the two cases. The classification of the optimal simplification problem into these two variants, prediction and decision-proper, is based on application, and for the economic problems each variant will be discussed separately.[20]

In making the dichotomy between prediction models and decision-proper models, no explicit recognition is given to the aggregation of "data," or of "observations," as a separate problem. This problem is, of course, of great practical importance and has been discussed by Prais and Aitchison [1954], Morgan and Sonquist [1963], Malinvaud [1966, pp. 242–46], and others. The leading example of the problem is perhaps grouping of households or firms in cross-section studies in order to facilitate regression analysis and to obtain a picture of differences between subgroups of a population.

In our treatment of the simplification problem we shall allow this problem to be classified either under the heading of prediction or decision-proper, depending upon the purposes of the particular investigation at hand, and we regard the aggregation of data as a kind of aggregation of variables or vice versa. It seems difficult semantically and unnecessary logically to make a general distinction between "data" and "variables." Who is to say whether x_{ij} and x_{ik}, the measures of consumption of cheese by households j and k respectively, are two observations on the same economic variable, consumption, or two different economic variables representing different kinds of consumption, with one observation on each? The type of simplification procedures to be recommended will not depend on this choice. The reader will, indeed, perceive the similarities between procedures to be recommended in later portions of this book and those suggested in the literature just cited.

4. The Problem Related to Inexact and Exact Simplification

Inexact Simplification

The problem as formulated in section 3 will have application to most real problems only when there is some discrepancy between the detailed

[20] The distinction between these two variants is similar to that discussed in W. D. Fisher [1962a].

data X and the simplified data $\bar{X}$. This case will be called *inexact simplification*. It is possible as a special and limiting case that the simplified data $\bar{X}$ will be identical with the detailed data X. This case will occur when either (1) there is something rather special about the detailed data (e.g., certain elements are equal to or proportional to each other), or (2) the simplification function f is the identity transformation. This case will be called *exact simplification*. The $\bar{X}$ sets associated with these two cases, if they exist, will be referred to as the cases of *inexact* and *exact aggregation*, respectively.

With the assumptions made about the nature of the cost function it can be seen that, given the degree of detail, the case of exact simplification represents one of minimal cost. It is a situation greatly to be desired, if it can be attained, as is also testified by the large proportion of literature on the aggregation problem in economics that is devoted to discussing it.[21] But it is a very special case. Thus the theory of optimal simplification depends on the recognition of inexact simplification, as well as measures of the discrepancies arising from it.

Ordinary averages are examples of simplified data. So are index numbers.[22] The important and pioneering work of Theil [1954] raised the question of the consequences of inexact aggregation in a stochastic model of simultaneous equations. Theil derived relationships between estimated parameters in detailed and aggregated models, when the parameters are estimated by linear unbiased methods.[23] In later work Theil extended this type of analysis to linear structural models fitted by the two-stage least-squares method [1959] and to input-output models [1957]. In a penetrating treatise on the aggregation problem in economic models Malinvaud [1956] emphasized the importance of inexact simplification, and also the differences between prediction and decision models.[24]

With regard to decision-proper models of the two-person game type, a rather general theorem was given regarding the effects of aggregation (exact or inexact) by Kemeny, Morgenstern, and Thompson [1956, Sec. 9]. Analysis of a special kind of linear programming problem to be considered in Chapter 4, called the "representative firm" problem was made by Hartley [1962], and empirical estimation of the effects of inexact aggre-

---

[21] See next section. Most of the literature does not make specific use of a cost or loss function. For surveys of the aggregation literature in economics see Green [1964], Malinvaud [1956], Nataf [1960], Peston [1959], and Theil [1962].

[22] See I. Fisher [1922], Frisch [1936]. For a recent survey of index numbers see Banerjee [1961, 1963].

[23] See especially Chapters 5 and 6.

[24] And also discussed the application of decision theory to these problems (see below). Studies of economic prediction models from the point of view of inexact aggregation have been made by Boot and DeWit [1960], Mundlak [1961], Lave [1964], Balderston and Whitin [1954], Ghosh [1960], and Moroshima and Seton [1961]. The last three of these were directed to input-output models.

gation for this type of problem has been made by a number of agricultural economists.[25] With regard to the classical problem of allocation of consumer's income, which is included in our rubric of a decision-proper model, there is a rapidly growing literature which will be considered in greater detail in other portions of this book. Examples that seem to recognize most specifically the problem of examining discrepancies of simplified from detailed structure are Pearce [1961a, 1961b, 1964], Barten and Turnovsky [1966], and Barten [1967].

In measuring the discrepancies from inexact simplification, a question arises as to whether the measures should be computed for sets of the size of the detailed data X, or between sets of the size of the aggregated data $\bar{X}$. This question, which will be discussed in more detail later on, arises especially in prediction models. Crudely speaking, the answer depends on what one wants to predict, and will lead either to a recommended procedure to use some sort of aggregate $\bar{X}$ or an aggregation-disaggregation sequence ending in a $\tilde{X}$. In the literature this distinction has not always been made clear; an excellent discussion of the distinction is given by Fei [1956] and Malinvaud [1956].

Exact Simplification

As stated above the term "exact simplification" is used here to describe the situation where the detailed data X and the simplified data $\tilde{X}$ coincide and there is no loss. Up to the present time a major portion of the economic literature dealing with aggregation has been concerned with this case and has dealt with one or another facet of the following problem: given an economic model in detail, what conditions must that model and the simplification function satisfy (or what must be the relationships between the two) in order to achieve exact simplification? More briefly, under what conditions will we lose no information whatever by simplification? The adjectives "consistent," "intrinsic," and "perfect" have also been used to describe this case.

One of the earliest and most productive investigators of this problem is Nataf.[26] One case dealt with is that of the exact aggregation of strict functional relationships derived from economic theory, such as utility and production relations, where the variables in these relations are subject to no side conditions (except possibly non-negativity).[27] A more important case

---

[25] See Abou-el-Dahab [1965], Frick and Andrews [1965], Miller [1967], Sheehy [1964], and Sheehy and McAlexander [1965].

[26] See writings cited in this and the next paragraph. Nataf has also discussed the inexact case [1958].

[27] Nataf [1948], Arrow [1951], May [1954], Samuelson [1947, Ch. 6], Solow [1956], and Strotz [1956].

is that of functional relations where some or all of the variables are subject to side conditions, such as the marginal conditions of consumer or producer equilibrium, or relations specifying proportional incomes or budget and accounting constraints.[28] Under these extra constraints on the variables in the models, it is found that the aggregation conditions are somewhat less severe. Other studies have dealt with systems of simultaneous relations containing stochastic elements,[29] with Leontief input-output models,[30] and with linear programming models.[31]

Most of the conditions for exact simplification obtained in these works essentially derive from, or may be derived from, certain mathematical theorems on separable functions.[32] The general conclusion arrived at is that the conditions for exact simplification are very severe and extremely unlikely to occur in any real economic context, or else that the simplification procedure must be custom-made to each concrete problem, using knowledge of the detailed relations of the model.[33] Despite this generally negative result, studies of the conditions for exact simplification have been instructive and have inspired and guided research into the simplification problem under more general and realistic specifications.

"Almost Exact" Simplification

This heading is intended to describe a small group of studies in which the requirement of exact simplification is not strictly imposed, but rather, in a sense is approached.[34] Two theoretical studies, one by Simon and Ando [1961] and one by Ando and F. M. Fisher [1963], characterize the dynamic behavior of an economic system, consisting of many sectors, that is arbitrarily close to some ideal simplified system. In the first study the ideal system is described by a block-diagonal matrix; in the second study the matrix is block-triangular. The theorems deduced are to the effect that the "almost" ideal systems have properties which come "as

[28] F. M. Fisher [1965], Gorman [1953, 1959a, 1967a], Green [1964, Chs. 6–8], Nataf [1953a, 1953b, 1958], Rajaoja [1958], Stigum [1967], and Strotz [1957, 1959].
[29] Klein [1946a, 1946b], May [1946, 1947], Shou Shan Pu [1946], and Theil [1954, Ch. 7].
[30] Ara [1959], Barna [1954], Hatanaka [1952], Malinvaud [1954], and McManus [1956a, 1956b].
[31] Day [1963], Lee [1966], and Miller [1966].
[32] See, for example, Goldman and Uzawa [1964], Leontief [1947a, 1947b], and Sono [1961].
[33] For example, Theil's "perfect aggregation" is a prescription to use aggregation weights based on ratios of certain microparameters in the particular detailed linear model at hand. See [1954, Ch. 7] and [1957, Sec. 11].
[34] There may be more studies of which I am unaware than the five to be referred to that belong in this class.

near as desired" to those of the ideal system, in the sense of a mathematical limiting process.

In three empirical studies of consumer demand for many commodities— by Frisch [1959], Houthakker [1960], and Barten [1964]—it is assumed that the Hessian matrix of the relevant utility function is block-diagonal, or at least "near enough" to block-diagonal. In the first two cases the ideal matrix is taken as pure-diagonal. The empirical work is conducted while maintaining these assumptions. Essentially the system assumed in each study is "almost" of an ideal simplified type.

All five of these studies are extremely interesting and valuable contri- butions. From the viewpoint of the optimal simplification problem con- sidered in this book, however, the conclusions deduced seem to have limited relevance. The issue is not raised as to how "close" some *given* economic model has to be to the ideal type in order for the theorems to apply, or for estimation to be possible; nor are any measures of "close- ness" proposed that would help answer such a question; nor is any guid- ance given as to how one might select some particular model of the ideal type among available alternatives as a surrogate for a given model at hand that is not ideal. With respect to these points the cited studies might just as well have postulated ideal simplified models as "almost" ideal simplified ones.

Optimal Simplification: Historical Note

The characteristic of the optimal simplification problem that distin- guishes it from other formulations just described is the systematic mini- mization (or approximate minimization) of a cost function that is defined over both exact and inexact simplifications. Within a short span of time in the early 1950's three economists formulated problems of this type. In an unpublished paper dealing with aggregations of inventories J. Marschak [1951] suggested that the problem be treated as one of cost minimization. In a paper presented to the Boston meeting of the Econometric Society in December, 1951, Hurwicz proposed that variables and equations in a stochastic economic model be aggregated on the principle of cost mini- mization (or utility maximization) including cost of detail by use of statis- tical decision functions.[35] The simpler and more specialized problem of aggregating K independent random variables was solved independently by W. D. Fisher [1953] using a statistical decision function with a Bayes prior distribution.[36] It is undoubtedly no coincidence that the Hurwicz

---

[35] The paper is abstracted in Hurwicz [1952].
[36] In an earlier unpublished paper W. D. Fisher [1951] had performed similar types of aggregations on various classes of retail stores, using a cruder principle.

and Fisher papers followed so shortly after the publication of Wald's book *Statistical Decision Functions* [1950].[37]

The suggestion to use this approach in simplifying economic models was expanded by Malinvaud [1956] in his treatise referred to earlier. In the following decade a number of theoretical elaborations, as well as empirical explorations of optimal simplification, have been made with a number of different kinds of economic models.[38] This work will be considered in more detail in the following chapters. There is undoubtedly other work not known to me. Some disciplines other than economics will be reviewed briefly in section 1 of Chapter 6. Some recent work of Theil in information theory [1967] has close relationships with optimal simplification as will be shown in section 2 of Chapter 6.

5. SCOPE AND PLAN

And so the objective of this book is to show how this basic problem, called optimal simplification, can be solved, or approximately solved, to yield useful simplified models in a wide variety of economic settings. The book is directed mainly to the econometrician: while theory is used to specify models and obtain loss or cost functions, the analysis is pursued to the point of encountering live samples of real numbers, and developing computational routines that yield specific solutions for the numerical examples.

The examples include both prediction and decision-proper models; both stochastic and nonstochastic problems are represented. In some examples the detailed data X represent solutions of economic problems, and in others they represent original data to these problems. No claim is made, however, that all relevant economic problems have been included in the study; consideration is limited to a few basic types of problems believed to be relevant.

No attempt has been made to develop cost as a function of degree of aggregation in the cases to be studied; the degree of aggregation is allowed to vary some, and the reader, or final decision-maker, has to select the optimal degree of aggregation by use of some intuitive cost function in his own mind. This is not, however, an unrealistic procedure.

[37] Reference should also be made to a statistical article that appeared at the same time by Dalenius [1950], which dealt with selection of optimal strata for sampling surveys. The stratification discussed may be regarded as a type of aggregation, where the variance of the central estimator is the cost function.

[38] W. D. Fisher [1958a, 1958b, 1962b, 1966], W. D. Fisher and Kelley [1968], King [1966], McCarthy [1956], Parks [1966], Rubin [1968], Skolka [1964], and Theil [1960]. Schneeweiss [1965] has shown that Theil's procedure for obtaining "best linear index numbers" proposed in the last cited work may be considered a special case of a type of optimal simplification, subject to rank restrictions described in W. D. Fisher [1962b].

As the use of the word "clustering" in the title of the book suggests, detailed discussion and examples are limited to simplification functions implying an aggregation-disaggregation sequence with partitioned dis-aggregation, which as will be seen, leads to a type of "clustering" of the detailed data. Most types of factor analysis, for example, are not included. This limitation corresponds with the most prevalent usage of the word "aggregation" in the economic literature.

In the examples a quadratic function will be repeatedly used to approximate the cost function, which may originally not be quadratic. This practice may be defended, in this stage of research, on the ground that precise utility or loss functions seldom exist, or if they do they are only imperfectly known, but the concept nevertheless does have fundamental relevance.

In Chapters 2 and 3 prediction models in economics will be analyzed, including multi-equation models in the reduced form and then Leontief input-output models. Decision-proper models are considered in Chapter 4, including those of the linear programming type (and hence, also the rectangular game type) as well as more conventional optimizing models such as that of the consumer-utility maximizer. In Chapter 5 an account is given of the computational methods found useful in solving the problems, while Chapter 6 consists of a brief survey of analogous problems in disciplines other than economics and of related methods not otherwise dealt with in the book.

2

□

PREDICTION MODELS

1. AN ERROR CRITERION

A prediction model was defined as an economic model that has two characteristics: (1) the decision variables are intended to be "estimates" or "forecasts" of some or all of the endogenous variables of the model; (2) the loss function is an increasing function of "errors" or discrepancies between values of the endogenous variables as determined by the model and the forecasts of them. In a broad sense a prediction model is a type of decision model, but different from the type we have designated "decision-proper" that will be considered in Chapter 4. While errors in the prediction model are assumed to be costly, no explicit economic theory is adduced to explain just why.

It should not be surprising then that in this model a conventional error function is resorted to, since no theory is available for subverting convention and mathematical convenience supports it. Let y denote a vector of G endogenous variables in some stochastic economic model. Let $\tilde{y}$ denote a corresponding vector of forecasted endogenous variables. Let C denote a given symmetric positive semi-definite matrix of size G by G. The following loss function is postulated:

$$(2.1) \qquad L = (\tilde{y} - y)'C(\tilde{y} - y) .$$

This is a quadratic form in the errors; positive and negative errors are assumed to be equally serious; the matrix C assigns relative weights to the squared errors of the separate variables in y and to possible interactions between these errors. In the special case where there are no such interactions and we will settle for a sum of squared errors, C is diagonal. Note that this loss function has for arguments the detailed endogenous variables—not aggregated variables. It is assumed that the forecaster desires to make forecasts of the original variables; if aggregation procedures are used to combine variables, then some sort of disaggregation procedure must also be used in order to recover the original number of elements— that is, in order to obtain a $\bar{y}$ of the same order as y, as specified. This specification will sometimes be referred to as a *micro-prediction* approach, as contrasted with a *macro-prediction* approach, where the loss, explicitly or implicitly, is assumed to be a function of errors in aggregated variables.[1] An investigator should ask himself which approach he really wants. It depends on his purposes or his assessment of the probable purposes of those who will use his work. The micro-prediction approach seems more reasonable for most applications, at least when the aggregation grouping is not specified a priori, or when outcomes relevant for policy are functions of the original endogenous variables.

2. The Reduced Form

The Cost Function

In this section we take as point of departure the reduced form of a simultaneous equation model that has already been estimated in complete detail, and which will be used for forecasting purposes. It is assumed that some savings will result, both conceptually and computationally, by reducing or simplifying the model. These assumptions imply that substantial costs of detail have already been invested into computing the detailed estimates. It is assumed that there will still be the possibility of saving additional costs of detail via simplification. Examples of such costs would be the costs of publishing the model in detail; the conceptual difficulties to readers of the publication in comprehending the detailed model; and costs of estimating, predicting from, and using "similar" models, which might be simplified in a manner resembling extrapolation of the given model.

The reduced form that is to be considered in the following discussion may be postulated to arise from a set of structural behavior equations. It is convenient, however, in the prediction problem here considered, to deal directly with the reduced form.[2]

Assume that it is known that the true reduced form is given by

$$(2.2) \qquad\qquad\qquad y = \Pi z + v \; ,$$

where y is a G by 1 vector of endogenous variables, z an H by 1 vector of

---

[1] For example Theil [1954, 1957, 1959, 1967] defines "aggregation bias" in terms of macro-variables, which implies a macro-prediction approach. The present writer used a macro approach in [1958a].

[2] For a recent and interesting discussion of the relevance of reduced forms, see Klein [1960].

predetermined variables,[3] v a G by 1 vector of random disturbances, and Π a G by H matrix of unknown parameters. It is assumed that the random vector v satisfies

(2.3) $$E(v) = 0 \; ; \qquad E(vv') = V \; ;$$

where V is some unknown positive semi-definite symmetric matrix.

It is usual to treat the prediction problem in linear models under the assumption of given, nonstochastic predictors. For example, in least-squares regression, after the regression coefficients have been estimated, the standard error of forecast of the endogenous variables depends on the values of the predetermined variables in the prediction period.[4] The prediction period would therefore seem to be important in any appraisal of alternative methods of estimation or of the simplification of models based on the criterion of small errors in endogenous variables. But what if a series of predictions is contemplated? Then simplification should be related to the anticipated range of variation to be experienced in the predetermined variables for the entire series of prediction periods. So we shall assume that z is also a random vector, having a domain of variation and a probability density that is independent of v and relevant for the predictions that will be made. Assume that the first two moments of z are known:

(2.4) $$E(z) = \hat{z} \; ; \qquad E(zz') = M \; ,$$

where M is a symmetric positive semi-definite matrix.

The available knowledge of the detailed reduced-form parameters is assumed to be in the form of the first and second moments of a Bayesian posterior distribution. So, for unity of treatment, let us now postulate a joint Bayesian distribution $f(v, z, \text{ and } \Pi)$, where v, z, and Π are all independent of each other;[5] where the unconditional means and second moments of v and z are given by (2.3) and (2.4) respectively, and those of Π are given by

(2.5) $$E(\Pi) = P \; , \qquad E\{\text{col}(\Pi - P)[\text{col}(\Pi - P)]'\} = V_{\Pi} \; ,$$

where V_{Π} is an unknown GH by GH positive semi-definite symmetric matrix and where $\text{col}(\Pi)$ is the GH by 1 column vector formed by placing the columns of Π in a single column end-to-end in order.

The Bayesian posterior mean P may be given a more specific interpre-

---

[3] The adjective "predetermined" rather than "exogenous" is used advisedly. After estimation of a reduced form has been accomplished, a forecaster will handle all predetermined variables—exogenous and lagged endogenous—in the same way.

[4] See for example Klein [1960], and Hooper and Zellner [1961].

[5] It is operationally immaterial whether v, or z, is regarded as a "random vector" or as an "unknown parameter vector with a Bayesian distribution." The same can be said about y. If y is considered as an unknown parameter, $\hat{y}$ could be said to be an "estimate" of y.

tation if additional assumptions are made regarding prior restrictions, the prior distribution and the data distribution. The writer has shown elsewhere[6] that if a suitable assumption of uniform prior ignorance is made, involving a limiting process, with no a priori restrictions on the matrix Π and if the usual data assumptions are made, including normally distributed disturbances, independent observations and a positive definite M, then P is identical with the matrix of classical least-squares regression coefficients of the reduced form. The reader may find it convenient in what follows to think of P in this way. Another special case would be that where the covariance matrix of Π approaches the zero matrix (perhaps as the result of very large samples) so that the true matrix Π is virtually known with certainty. We could then regard the problem as one of complete certainty. The aggregation aspects of the problem would not be altered.

With the Bayesian approach, the imposition of prior restrictions on the unknown parameters would have the effect only of modifying the prior distribution of an unrestricted Π, and hence also the posterior distribution, by specifying certain regions of the complete parameter space where Π occurs with zero probability. We can compute the posterior mean P, and the analysis will proceed from that point forward in exactly the same way—restrictions or no restrictions. The relationship of such a P to conventional statistical estimates is, however, not always clear.[7]

Now a cost function in the sense of formula (1.4) in Chapter 1 will be derived conditional on a given degree of detail. Say that on any particular forecasting occasion when the vector of predetermined variables z is known, the forecaster will obtain the vector of forecasted endogenous variables $\tilde{y}$ by means of the linear formula

$$(2.6) \qquad\qquad \tilde{y} = \tilde{P}z ,$$

where $\tilde{P}$ is a simplified estimate of the unknown parameter matrix Π, this estimate to be conditional on a given degree of detail.[8]

----

[6] W. D. Fisher [1962a, section 4].

[7] One may, if one wishes, use a P without a Bayesian interpretation. See the discussion immediately following Theorem 1.

[8] It may be imagined that a forecaster will routinely forecast the values of a set of endogenous variables, using on each forecasting occasion a set of given values of predetermined variables, and a simplified model $\tilde{P}$. The values of the predetermined variables will, in general, be different on each forecasting occasion, but the value of the simplified model $\tilde{P}$ will be the same for all occasions. This simplified model will be supplied by another man who may be called an "aggregator." The forecaster's knowledge about the true model Π may be assumed to be limited to the $\tilde{P}$ that is given him by the aggregator. The aggregator, on the other hand, knows the Bayesian moments of Π, but his knowledge about the predetermined variables z is limited to the moments $\hat{z}$ and M. (It may be imagined that he has to make his decision as to what $\tilde{P}$ to give the forecaster before the forecaster actually goes to work.) Successful "aggregating and forecasting" is measured by low Bayes risk. The problem is to prescribe how the aggregator is to select the $\tilde{P}$ so that risk will be minimized when the $\tilde{P}$ must satisfy certain "simplifying" restrictions to be discussed below.

THEOREM 1. In the stochastic prediction model (2.2)—(2.5) with the quadratic loss function (2.1) and the linear forecast (2.6) the cost of simplification is:

$$(2.7) \qquad c = \text{tr}(\tilde{P} - P)'C(\tilde{P} - P)M \ .$$

PROOF. First, an expression for the posterior risk as given by (1.10) will be obtained. From (1.10) and the rules for conditional expectations, we have

$$(2.8) \qquad r = E(L) = \underset{\Pi}{E} \left\{ \underset{z,\,v}{E} [L|\Pi] \right\} = \underset{\Pi}{E} \left\{ \underset{z,\,v}{E} [E(L|\Pi,z)|\Pi] \right\} \ ,$$

where a symbol under an expectation sign denotes variation of that variable, and a symbol following vertical straight line denotes the condition that that variable is being held constant. From (2.1), (2.2), (2.6), and (2.3) we have

$$(2.9) \qquad \underset{v}{E}(L|\Pi,z) = z'(\tilde{P} - \Pi)'C(\tilde{P} - \Pi)z + \text{tr}CV \ .$$

Then taking the expected value of the above while allowing z to vary, but still holding Π constant, we have, using (2.4)

$$(2.10) \qquad \underset{z,\,v}{E} [L|\Pi] = \text{tr}(\tilde{P} - \Pi)'C(\tilde{P} - \Pi)M + \text{tr}CV \ .$$

Then, allowing Π to vary and using (2.5), we have the posterior risk

$$(2.11) \qquad r(\tilde{P}) = \text{tr}(\tilde{P} - P)'C(\tilde{P} - P)M + \text{tr}(M \otimes C)V_\Pi + \text{tr}CV \ ,$$

where $\otimes$ denotes the Kronecker product operation.[9]

The matrix $\tilde{P}$ corresponds to the simplified decision d defined on page 13. If there were no simplification requirements on $\tilde{P}$, and we were free to choose it so that $r(\tilde{P})$ in (2.11) were made a minimum, this choice, call it P^*, would correspond to the detailed optimal decision d^* defined by formula (1.11) in Chapter 1 and is obviously

$$(2.12) \qquad P^* = P \ ,$$

which gives the value of the risk:

$$(2.13) \qquad r(P^*) = \text{tr}(M \otimes C)V_\Pi + \text{tr}CV \ .$$

Since we are holding the degree of detail constant, the cost may be taken as

[9] This last step is made as follows. The expectation of the first trace in (2.10) becomes:
$$E[\text{row}(\tilde{P} - \Pi)'(M \otimes C)\text{col}(\tilde{P} - \Pi)] = \text{row}(\tilde{P} - P)'(M \otimes C)\text{col}(\tilde{P} - P) +$$
$$E[\text{row}(P - \Pi)'(M \otimes C)\text{col}(P - \Pi)] = \text{tr}(\tilde{P} - P)'C(\tilde{P} - P)M + \text{tr}(M \otimes C)V_\Pi$$

(2.14) $c = r(\tilde{P}) - r(P^*)$.

By substituting (2.11) and (2.13) into (2.14), (2.7) is obtained, which was to be proved.

If an investigator wishes to avoid the Bayesian approach and to suppress assumption (2.5), but will still go along with the other assumptions of the model, including (2.4), relating to the distribution of the predetermined variables, he may go with us as far as formula (2.10). Then he may use some other kind of estimate for the unknown Π in (2.10), and let this formula represent his cost of simplification. It differs from our formula only by a constant. For example, he could use the maximum-likelihood estimate of Π as his P. His analysis of the simplification problem would be the same as ours except that he could not make the claim that his cost function is the expected value of his original loss function.

Simplified Partitioned Models

It will be presumed, without entering into a detailed theory of the costs of detail, that smaller models are easier to comprehend and to work with than larger ones, as are also models that are "blown up" from smaller ones by arbitrarily simple disaggregations such as repeating rows and columns, or adding rows or columns that are proportional to those in the small model. Hence, if an aggregator starts off with a given large model, he may want to lower cost by first reducing its dimensions (aggregating), and then on the basis of the aggregated model constructing a simplified counterpart of the original large model. This is the type of simplification that will be assumed here.

It will, moreover, be assumed that the *degree* of aggregation—i.e., the dimensions of the small model—are given.

DEFINITION 1. With respect to a given matrix P of size G by H, an *aggregated matrix* $\bar{P}$ is a matrix that is a function of P and of size F by J, where $F \leq G$ and $J \leq H$.

DEFINITION 2. A simplified matrix $\tilde{P}$ is *disaggregated from* $\bar{P}$ if

(2.15) $\tilde{P} = S'\bar{P}T$,

where S is a full-rank matrix of size F by G and T is a full-rank matrix of size J by H.[10]

DEFINITION 3. A full-rank matrix A with no more rows than columns is a *partitioning operator* if it is in the block-diagonal form

---

[10] Note that in general $\tilde{P}$ is not of full rank. Note also that (2.15) is equivalent to placing homogeneous linear restrictions on the elements of $\tilde{P}$. See Appendix B.

(2.16)
$$A = \begin{bmatrix} a_1 & 0 & & 0 \\ 0 & a_2 & & 0 \\ & & \cdot & \\ & & & \cdot \\ 0 & 0 & & a_G \end{bmatrix} ,$$

where each of the a_i is a row vector with positive elements.

DEFINITION 4. A simplified matrix $\tilde{P}$ is in *block-homogeneous form* if it satisfies (2.15) where S and T are each a partitioning operator.

Some comments on these definitions may be in order. Note first that if $\tilde{P}$ represents some simplified matrix of coefficients of a reduced form system, as in (2.6), and if $\tilde{P}$ is also disaggregated from some aggregated matrix $\bar{P}$ according to Definition (2.15), we may write

(2.17) $\qquad \tilde{y} = \tilde{P}z = (S'\bar{P}T)z = S'[\bar{P}(Tz)] .$

That is to say, we could, if we wished, write

(2.18a) $\bar{z} = Tz$; $\qquad$ (2.18b) $\bar{y} = \bar{P}\bar{z}$; $\qquad$ (2.18c) $\tilde{y} = S'\bar{y}$.

The forecasting of the endogenous variables by use of the simplified model (2.17) is thus found equivalent to the following procedure: (a) aggregate the H predetermined variables z into J aggregated predetermined variables; (b) using some reduced aggregated model $\bar{P}$ forecast the values of F aggregated endogenous variables; (c) disaggregate from the aggregated endogenous variables to obtain the forecast $\tilde{y}$. It also follows from footnote 10 that if $\tilde{P}$ is to be estimated from observed data, certain linear homogeneous restrictions must be satisfied as side conditions.

It can be seen that the smaller are F and J in comparison with G and H, the more severe are the aggregations (or the linear restrictions on $\tilde{P}$).

The definitions have implied simultaneous operations on rows and on columns of the matrix P, or, in other words, aggregations both of endogenous and predetermined variables. It is convenient to handle the problem in this general way, taking account of the possibility of the investigator desiring to make either or both types of aggregation. If the investigator wishes to consider aggregation of endogenous variables only, i.e., a reduction in the number of linearly independent equations in the model, but no reduction in the number of predetermined variables, the matrix $\bar{P}$ will have order F by H—a reduced number of rows but full number of columns. The matrix T will be specified H by H nonsingular (the identity matrix for convenience). This situation may be referred to as *row-wise aggregation*.

If it is desired to consider aggregation of predetermined variables only, leaving the original equations and endogenous variables unchanged, the matrix $\bar{P}$ will have order G by J—a reduced number of columns but a full number of rows, and the matrix S will be specified as the identity matrix of order G. This situation may be referred to as *column-wise aggregation*.

If P is square, and it is desired to handle the rows and columns in the same way, set $G = H$, $F = J$, and $S = T$. This situation will be called *corresponding row-column aggregation*.

The numerical example in section 3 is one of column-wise aggregation, and the input-output case discussed in Chapter 3 is one of corresponding row-column aggregation.

The case of block-homogeneous form is especially important. As may be easily seen, it implies *partitioned disaggregation* in the sense of the definition given on page 9.[11] The aggregated element may, however, depend on any elements of the original data. Nor is any particular functional form of the aggregating function g specified at this point—for example, it is not required a priori that the aggregations be linear.

Within the case of block-homogeneous form four subcases arise, depending upon the type of knowledge or assumption that the investigator is prepared to make about the partitioning operators S and T. In the following discussion the non-zero elements of S and T are referred to as "weights."

(1) Fixed partitions and fixed weights. The S and T matrices are completely known.[12] The simplification restrictions (2.15) are then linear restrictions on $\tilde{P}$.

(2) Unknown partitions and fixed weights, conditional on the partitions. For example, the weights could be specified as equal within the same subset, or as having specified ratios to each other. Then, *conditional on a*

---

[11] This can be seen as follows. Since S and T are full-rank matrices, the matrices SS' and TT' are also of full rank, and hence have inverses. Premultiply (2.15) by $(SS')^{-1}S$ and postmultiply it by $T'(TT')^{-1}$. The result is

(2.15a) $$(SS')^{-1}S\tilde{P}T'(TT')^{-1} = \bar{P} \ .$$

Moreover, by definition of block-homogeneous form, both S and T are partitioning operators and have the special form of (2.16). This special form, along with (2.15a) implies

(2.15b) $$s_{ii}^{-1}s_i\tilde{P}_{ij}t_j't_{jj}^{-1} = \bar{p}_{ij} \qquad (i = 1 \ldots F, j = 1 \ldots J) \ ,$$

where $\tilde{P}_{ij}$ is some submatrix of $\tilde{P}$ whose rows are selected by the position of the row vector s_i in the operator S and whose columns are selected by the position of the column vector t_j' in the operator T', and where s_{ii} is the scalar s_is_i', t_{jj} is the scalar t_jt_j', and $\bar{p}_{ij}$ is a scalar element of $\bar{P}$. (In special cases either S or T could be the identity matrix.) Now associate P, $\bar{P}$, and $\tilde{P}$ with X, $\bar{X}$, and $\tilde{X}$ (pages 8–10). Then (2.15b) defines the correspondence between an element of $\bar{X}$ and a subset of $\tilde{X}$ needed to come under the definition of partitioned disaggregation.

[12] One partition is associated with S and one with T.

partition, the S or T matrix is specified and the restrictions are linear. The solution to the problem of optimal simplification then implies a search for an optimal partition. Most of the discussion of this chapter, and in fact in this book, is concerned with this case. As stated previously, we shall assume that the degree of aggregation—here the integers F and J—are given, or that a series of them is given.

(3) Fixed partitions and unknown weights. Although the assumption of a known partition avoids a combinatorial search problem, the remaining mathematical problems associated with the determination of an optimal simplified model are not simple. The problem is discussed briefly in W. D. Fisher [1962b, pp. 763–65]. In special cases (where the C and M matrices have the appropriate kind of block-diagonality) the problem can be decomposed into a set of independent problems each of which involves a characteristic root problem. The "best index number" problem of Theil [1960] is of this type. The problem of McManus [1956a] in an input-output setting is closely related.[13]

(4) Unknown partition and unknown weights. This case can be formulated as a set of problems of type (3). The computational burden seems to be extremely formidable, even with high-speed computers and sophisticated programming aids, and is beyond the scope of this book.

The following discussion deals with the first two of these four cases—that is where weight structure is known or assumed, at least conditional on a partition.

It will be shown in Chapter 5 that there is a certain relationship between the operators S, T, and the matrices C, M, and P that can keep the problem invariant. Certain transformations of S and T may be made—such as multiplication by a diagonal matrix, and invariance of the problem maintained—provided that certain compensating changes are made in the other matrices.

Optimal Simplified Models with Fixed Weights

At this point we mean by an optimal simplified model a coefficient matrix $\tilde{P}$ that is subject to the requirements of type (1) or (2) of the previous section and which minimizes the cost function as given by (2.7). More specifically, it is assumed that the detailed coefficient matrix P, the matrix of the loss function C, and the moment matrix M of the predetermined variables are given. Conditional on two partitions, one of the

---

[13] If the requirement of partitioned form is completely dropped, the matrices S and T becoming completely variable, the problem becomes one of finding an optimal simplified model P of rank no greater than F or J, whichever is lower. See W. D. Fisher [1962b, pp. 755–56] and Appendix C.

indices of the rows of P and one of the indices of columns, the matrices S and T are also given. By an *optimal partition* we mean one of a pair of partitions, one for rows and one for columns, with numbers of subsets F and J given, such that, when $\tilde{P}$ is optimally selected, cost c as given by (2.7) is a minimum.

The minimization may be performed conceptually in two steps. First, one may ask what is the optimal simplified model $\tilde{P}$, conditional on the two partitions? This is the problem of type (1) above. Then one may ask: with $\tilde{P}$ always being optimally selected, what is a pair of optimal partitions?[14]

The first step is that of minimizing a quadratic function subject to linear constraints. Its solution depends upon the following theorem.[15]

THEOREM 2. A simplified matrix $\tilde{P}$ that minimizes the quadratic simplification cost as given by (2.7) and also satisfies the linear restrictions (2.15) for specified S and T, but unknown $\bar{P}$, is obtained when in (2.15)

$$(2.19) \qquad \bar{P} = \bar{C}^g SCPMT'\bar{M}^g \ ,$$

where $\bar{C}$ and $\bar{M}$ are aggregations of C and M respectively, defined by

$$(2.20a) \quad \bar{C} = SCS' \ , \qquad\qquad\qquad (2.20b) \quad \bar{M} = TMT' \ ,$$

and where $\bar{C}^g$ and $\bar{M}^g$ are generalized inverses of $\bar{C}$ and $\bar{M}$ respectively.[16] The minimum cost is given by

$$(2.21) \qquad c = \mathrm{tr} P'CPM - \mathrm{tr}\bar{P}'\bar{C}\bar{P}\bar{M} \ .$$

PROOF. Assign temporarily the symbols X and Y for $\tilde{P}$ and $\bar{P}$ respectively. X and Y are then variable matrices to be determined so that

$$(2.22) \qquad c = \mathrm{tr}(X - P)'C(X - P)M$$

is a minimum subject to the condition

$$(2.23) \qquad\qquad X = S'YT \ .$$

Equations (2.22) and (2.23) are rewritings of (2.7) and (2.15) respectively. By substituting (2.23) into (2.22), performing the multiplications, and

---

[14] In all of the specific examples to be considered below, it will be assumed either that one partition is fixed (actually with identity operator), or that the two partitions are the same, so that only one optimal partition is sought for.

[15] In W. D. Fisher [1962b] this theorem was proved for the case where $\bar{C}$ and $\bar{M}$ are both nonsingular and hence positive definite. (Apparently this assumption for $\bar{M}$ was not explicitly stated, but was implied by the presumed existence of $\bar{M}^{-1}$ in [equation (4.4) of 1962b].) This nonsingular case is handled in the Corollary which follows. The singular case is relevant in some applications.

[16] "Generalized inverse" is taken in the sense of Penrose [1955], and is defined in the proof of the theorem.

using the theorem that $\text{tr}(AB) = \text{tr}(BA)$, as well as the theorem that $\text{tr}(A + B) = \text{tr}A + \text{tr}B$, one gets

(2.24) $$c = \text{tr}\,Y'\bar{C}Y\bar{M} - 2\text{tr}\,Y'SCPMT' + k \ ,$$

where $\bar{C}$ and $\bar{M}$ are defined by (2.20a) and (2.20b) and $k = \text{tr}CPMP'$. Let s denote the rank of $\bar{M}$ and let q denote the rank of $\bar{C}$. Then since these matrices are symmetric positive semi-definite, there exist full-rank matrices V of size s by J, and U of size q by F, such that

(2.25a) $\quad \bar{C} = U'U \ ,$ $\hspace{4cm}$ (2.25b) $\quad \bar{M} = V'V \ .$

Let W be an arbitrary unknown q by s matrix. Now specialize Y in the following way. Let Y be required to satisfy

(2.26) $$UYV' = W \ .$$

W is then a matrix of a reduced set of scalar unknowns, each of which is a linear combination of the original unknown elements of Y. In particular, take Y as

(2.27) $$Y = U^g W V^{g'} \ ,$$

where

(2.28a) $\quad U^g = U'(UU')^{-1} \ ,$ $\hspace{3cm}$ (2.28b) $\quad V^g = V'(VV')^{-1} \ .$

It is easily verified that $UU^g = I$, $VV^g = I$, and that Y as taken in (2.27) satisfies (2.26). Substituting (2.25a), (2.25b), and (2.27) into (2.24), one obtains, after manipulating the arguments of the traces and simplifying,

(2.29) $$c = \text{tr}\,W'W - 2\text{tr}\,W'K + k \ ,$$

where

(2.30) $$K = U^{g'}SCPMT'V^g \ .$$

Since W is arbitrary, it may be taken as a full-rank matrix. Hence $W'W$ is positive definite and c is shown by (2.29) to be a strictly convex function of W. Hence this function possesses a unique minimum, and a unique solution for W exists that provides this minimum. To obtain the solution, one can take partial derivatives of c with respect to each element of W, and equate the derivatives to zero. Using matrix notation for the partial derivatives,

(2.31) $$\frac{\partial c}{\partial W} = 2W - 2K = 0 \ ,$$

from which, using also (2.30), the solution for W is

(2.32) $$W^* = K = U^{g\prime}SCPMT'V^g ,$$

from which, using also (2.27), one possible solution for Y is

(2.33) $$Y^* = U^g U^{g\prime}SCPMT'V^g V^{g\prime} .$$

Now let

(2.34a) $$\bar{C}^g = U^g U^{g\prime} = U'(UU')^{-2}U$$

and

(2.34b) $$\bar{M}^g = V^g V^{g\prime} = V'(VV')^{-2}V .$$

Then

(2.35) $$Y^* = \bar{C}^g SCPMT'\bar{M}^g = \bar{P} ,$$

which establishes (2.19), and from which, using also (2.29) and (2.26), the minimum cost is found to be

(2.36) $$c = \mathrm{tr}CPMP' - \mathrm{tr}\bar{C}\bar{P}\bar{M}\bar{P}' ,$$

which establishes (2.21) and proves the theorem.

The matrices U^g, V^g that are used in the above proof, as well as $\bar{C}^g$ and $\bar{M}^g$, are generalized inverses in the sense of Penrose [1955]. See Appendix D for more details. Since the ordinary inverse of a nonsingular matrix, as Penrose shows, may be regarded as a special case of the generalized inverse, we have the following corollary.

COROLLARY TO THEOREM 2. When $\bar{C}$ and $\bar{M}$ are positive definite, the $\bar{P}$ that provides for minimum c in Theorem 2 is unique and is given by

(2.37) $$\bar{P} = \bar{C}^{-1}SCPMT'\bar{M}^{-1} .$$

The proof, which is given in W. D. Fisher [1962b, Theorem 4.1], is omitted. Note that the premise of this corollary holds, a fortiori, when the original C and M matrices are each positive definite. It cannot be emphasized too strongly that in the original case, on the other hand, when $\bar{C}$ or $\bar{M}$, or both, are singular, there is not a unique solution for $\bar{P}$ (and hence neither for $\tilde{P}$), but rather an infinite set of solutions, and that the particular solution displayed in (2.19) is only one out of many possibilities.

Note that Theorem 2 holds for *any* specified S and T operators, and does not require the assumption that these matrices are partitioning operators. But if they are, such partitioning operators are used also in the aggregation process prescribed by (2.19).

The solution for $\tilde{P}$ given by (2.19) and (2.15) may be interpreted geometrically as a certain minimal-distance projection in the GH dimensional vector space of the matrix P. Let the matrices P_1 and P_2 denote two points in this space, with corresponding elements as coordinates, and define the distance between P_1 and P_2 as

$$d(P_1,P_2) = \sqrt{\operatorname{tr}(P_1 - P_2)'\, C(P_1 - P_2)M}\ .$$

Consider the FJ dimensional linear subspace of points satisfying the restrictions (2.15). Then $\tilde{P}$ is the image of a projection of P onto this subspace, where the projection is taken in a direction that minimizes distance in the sense of this definition.[17]

Note that the optimal aggregated matrix $\bar{P}$ is shown by (2.19) or (2.37) to consist of elements that are certain weighted averages of the elements of P, the averaging being done both row-wise and column-wise. Note also that the averaging of the rows of P depends only on the matrices S and C, while the averaging of the columns depends only on T and M. This means that these two operations are independent of each other in the sense that if S or C were changed, this would not affect the column operations, and that if T or M were changed, this would not affect the row operations.

The application of Theorem 2 is only to the first step of the two-step minimization of cost described above. The second step—that of finding the optimal partitions—must still be undertaken. This problem has a combinatorial character. A search technique is needed for scanning a relatively large number of possible partitions, and finding one that has a minimum value, or a near-minimum value, of the desired cost function. The computation of the quadratic function itself is quite simple. The difficult part is the development of a systematic and practical procedure for searching, including a procedure for mass screening of irrelevant alternatives, since the total number of possible partitions, even for fairly small problems, is too large to be tested individually by even the fastest digital computers available or conceivable.

For certain cases of the economic problems described in this book I have developed a technique of finding near-optimal partitions by a stepwise procedure of merging two elements at a time into a common subset. This procedure, called Progressive Merger Procedure, or PMP for short,

---

[17] This can be seen as follows. Let col(P) denote the column vector obtained by placing the columns of P end-to-end in order. Let col($\tilde{P}$) denote a corresponding vectorization of $\tilde{P}$. The result (2.19) together with (2.15) may be shown to be expressible in the form: $\tilde{P} = APB'$, where A and B' are certain idempotent matrices of ranks F and J respectively. Then this equation is equivalent to: col($\tilde{P}$) = $(A \otimes B)$col(P), where $\otimes$ denotes the Kronecker product operator and where $A \otimes B$ is found to be idempotent of rank FJ. Since an idempotent matrix of rank FJ represents a projection into an FJ dimensional subspace, the last equation represents a transformation of this character. That it is the minimal distance projection described in the text follows from the result of Theorem 2 that $\tilde{P}$ minimizes c as given by (2.7), $\sqrt{c}$ being also $d(\tilde{P}, P)$.

is described in detail in Chapter 5; it is used for many of the examples of economic aggregation problems.

In section 3 of this chapter a specific example of an economic prediction model is described, where the original coefficient matrix of the reduced form was estimated in complete detail, but later the investigator wished to reduce the model by certain aggregations of the predetermined variables. This problem thus becomes a special case of the simplification problem described in this section, where only column-wise aggregation and simplification is considered (the rows being unchanged and hence the S operator being defined as the identity matrix). The problem leads then, to a search for an optimal partition of the columns of the P matrix of coefficients of the reduced form.

In Chapter 3 another special case, but an important one, of the prediction model is considered: that of Leontief input-output analysis. Here the endogenous variables are "gross outputs," the predetermined variables are "final demands," and the P matrix is the "Leontief inverse" matrix, and is square. It is required, moreover, that in making aggregations, the same partition be used over the rows as over the columns since both rows and columns refer to the same industrial sectors. This is the case of corresponding row-column aggregation in the framework developed above, and leads to a search for a partition that will be applied to both rows and columns. This requirement forces a variation in computational program that is described in Chapter 5.

I have not yet developed a computational program that will search simultaneously for two different optimal partitions—one over rows and one over columns—which would implement the most general case described in the present section. Such a program would not, however, be difficult, and would be a logical development from the special programs to be described below.

3. Example: Partition of Predetermined Variables

One-Way Simplification

As before, let the coefficient matrix of a reduced form be denoted by P, of size G by H. That is, the model contains G endogenous and H predetermined variables. Consider the special case of the preceding section where it is desired to aggregate the predetermined variables only. That is, it is desired to partition the columns of P into J disjoint subsets but to leave the rows as they are. Then the operator S is the identity matrix, $\bar{P}$ is of size G by J, and $\bar{C} = C$. Let us assume further that both C and M are positive definite. Then, from Theorem 2 and its Corollary, we have, whatever the partition,

(2.38) $$\bar{P} = PMT'\bar{M}^{-1} ,$$

(2.39) $$c = \text{tr}CPMP' - \text{tr}C\bar{P}\bar{M}\bar{P}' .$$

Recall that the weighting matrix C expresses the ideas of the investigator regarding the relative seriousness of errors in forecasts of particular endogenous variables and their interactions. As a further special case assume that the consequences of error are regarded as adequately expressed by a simple unweighted sum of squared errors in each endogenous variable. This would be true only if, among other things, units of measurement of these variables were considered "comparable." This might be true if money units were used for each variable. This is not a trivial issue, and requires some attention to the matter of scaling. But if this further special assumption can be made, the C matrix may be set equal to the identity matrix of order G. Then (2.39) becomes

(2.40) $$c = \text{tr}PMP' - \text{tr}\bar{P}\bar{M}\bar{P}' .$$

Even if this assumption cannot be made at the outset, note that it is possible to accomplish the same thing by defining a new set of endogenous variables as a certain linear transformation of the original ones. Let D be a matrix such that $D'D = C$. This is always possible if C is positive semidefinite. Then define the set of variables w by

(2.41) $$w = Dy ,$$

and then the loss function (2.1) in the first section of this chapter becomes

(2.42) $$L = (\tilde{w} - w)'(\tilde{w} - w) ,$$

which implies an identity matrix for the transformed C. The entire analysis could be carried through in terms of these transformed endogenous variables, which would then imply formula (2.40). These transformed variables may not, however, have any economic meaning and should be converted back again to the original variables for interpretation. To summarize: the solution to the problem of optimal partitioning of the predetermined variables depends on what loss function of the endogenous variables is assumed.[18]

Then the second step of the cost minimization involves the search for the optimal partition over the columns of the P matrix, using formula (2.39) or (2.40) as the criterion. It has been found convenient to designate the Progressive Merger Procedure when applied to this case as the "One-way PMP."

---

[18] If, in addition, the matrix M is also taken as the identity matrix, then we get back to a problem like the clustering of aircraft productivity coefficients of Chapter 1, which is equivalent to a simple clustering of points with a simple Euclidean distance function.

With a couple of further assumptions a definite connection may be made between the above analysis and ordinary least-squares estimation. By its original definition the matrix M is the moment matrix of the predetermined variables in the prediction period. Say that this same matrix pertains to the sample period also—i.e., the sample period is "typical" of the prediction period. Then, if Z is the matrix of size N by H and of rank H containing the sample data for N observations on the H predetermined variables, we have

(2.43) $M = Z'Z$.

Say also that the matrix P, originally defined as a Bayesian posterior mean, is equivalent to the classical least-squares regression coefficients. (This is true only under special assumptions, as mentioned above in section 2.) Then P may be expressed by the familiar least-squares formula

(2.44) $P = Y'Z(Z'Z)^{-1}$,

where Y is the data matrix of size T by G of the endogenous variables.

Let $\bar{Z}$ be the matrix of sample data for a set of aggregated predetermined variables obtained by simple summation of the original predetermined variables within the subsets of the partition. Then

(2.45) $\bar{Z} = ZT'$.

Then, by substituting (2.44) and (2.45) into (2.38), and also using (2.20b) and (2.43), we have

(2.46) $\bar{P} = Y'\bar{Z}(\bar{Z}'\bar{Z})^{-1}$.

That is, under these additional assumptions the optimal aggregated coefficients $\bar{P}$ are obtained by computing a set of least-squares regressions of the endogenous variables on the aggregated (summed) predetermined variables. Then, from (2.40) the simplification cost is obtained as the difference between the sums of two sets of "explained sums of squares": one set explains the variation in the endogenous variables when the detailed predetermined variables are used; the other set does the same when the aggregates are used.

If there is only one endogenous variable in the model, P is a row vector, there is only one least-squares multiple regression equation, the trace symbols are not needed in (2.40), and the simplification cost is expressed as the difference between two scalar "explained sums of squares."

It should be realized that the equivalence of P with ordinary least-squares as given by (2.44) and the interpretation of (2.40) just given does not necessarily hold for any reduced form. For example it does not hold in the illustration to be presented in the next section, where the reduced form is subject to overidentifying restrictions of a structural model.

It is still necessary to find the optimal partition—i.e., the manner of grouping the predetermined variables so that simplification cost is as small as possible.

Klein–Goldberger Data

In his follow-up analysis of certain characteristics of the Klein–Goldberger model, Goldberger presents the reduced form of a linearized version of the model.[19] This is a table of coefficients of forty-three predetermined variables in twenty-one equations (each equation associated with one endogenous variable) and requires five printed pages of rather closely spaced numbers. A reader might well be somewhat chagrined to read that "the reduced forms of the K–G model, derived in this chapter, constitute the foundation on which all of the subsequent analysis is built."[20]

Goldberger himself is interested in reducing the size and complexity of the model, such reduction being essential to his further analysis. In later chapters he examines the quantitative importance of the forty-three predetermined variables to the sample variation in the endogenous variables, discarding unimportant ones, and in fact settles on a simplified reduced form using only six predetermined variables.[21]

Say that it is desired to simplify the reduced form by replacing the coefficient matrix P by another of the same dimensions, $\tilde{P}$, where certain columns of $\tilde{P}$ are required to be identical with each other. If P had G rows and H columns, and if J is the number of columns of $\tilde{P}$ that may be different, this may be formally expressed by specifying

$$(2.47) \qquad\qquad \tilde{P} = \bar{P}T \; ,$$

where $\bar{P}$ is some G by J matrix and where T is given by (1.5) of Chapter 1. Note that from (2.17) this specification is equivalent to forecasting the endogenous variables by using the aggregated matrix $\bar{P}$ along with aggregated predetermined variables $\bar{z}$ which are certain simple sums.

Assume that the rows of the reduced form refer to endogenous variables in which we are especially interested, and that we make no simplification requirements on the rows. This is already implied by (2.47). Assume further that it is desired to choose the simplified matrix $\tilde{P}$ in such a way that the unweighted sum of the mean-square errors in the G endogenous variables is a minimum. By mean-square error is meant $E(y - \bar{y})^2$,

---

[19] [1959, Table 3.2].
[20] [1959, p. 15].
[21] [1959, pp. 119–20].

where y is the true value of an endogenous variable, and $\tilde{y}$ is the value as predicted from the simplified reduced form. Note the assumption here that the effect of errors in each of the variables is equally serious. Then, it follows that whatever partition T is based on, the desired $\bar{P}$ in (2.47) is in the form of $\bar{P}$ as given by (2.38), where $\bar{M}$ is given by (2.20b), and that the magnitude of the sum of the mean-square errors is given by the c of (2.39). (We again mention that the C and S are here each the identity matrix.) The progressive merger procedure can then be applied to find an optimal partition of the columns of the detailed reduced form coefficient matrix P, provided that a suitable M matrix can be found.

As a starting point for the procedure we use as P a 4 by 14 submatrix of Goldberger's reduced form. The four endogenous variables—Consumption, Depreciation, Private Wage Bill, and Gross National Product—were selected because they play an important role in Goldberger's analysis. The fourteen predetermined variables used are listed in Table 4. They were selected as those that appeared to be at least moderately important in each of the four equations involving the four endogenous variables just named.[22] The list was limited to fourteen to avoid singularity of the M matrix that was based on data from only 18 observations.

The M matrix was computed from data on annual changes of the predetermined variables over the sample period.[23] The assumption behind the use of this matrix is that the variations and correlations from year to year during the sample period are typical of those to be expected during the periods of prediction from the simplified model. The matrices are displayed in Table A1.

In addition to the problem just described, four additional problems were considered: namely, the selection of an optimal partition of the same fourteen predetermined variables when each of the four endogenous variables is considered separately in turn. In these last four problems we seek "custom-made" simplifications for each separate endogenous variable, rather than one "over-all" simplification that is optimal in an average sense; the P matrices used are just the row vectors of the P matrix shown in Table A1, and the M matrix is the same.

[22] In [1959, Table 4.4] Goldberger presents data on "contributions" of each of the forty-three predetermined variables to each of the twenty-one endogenous variables of his reduced form. (These are not marginal contributions as the term is usually understood in multiple regression analysis but rough approximations thereto. The reduced form coefficients were not obtained by unrestricted least-squares, but from a structural model estimated by the limited information method and subsequently linearized.) The fourteen predetermined variables used here were selected as the set union of the top eight or nine contributors to each of C, D, W_1, and Q, according to this table. (There is one inadvertent exception: time t should have been included as a significant variable in the W_1 equation—as a constant term in the first difference equation.)

[23] [1959, Table 4.1].

TABLE 4. VARIABLES USED IN SIMPLIFICATION OF REDUCED FORM

Endogenous variables

1	C	Consumption
2	D	Depreciation
3	W_1	Private wage bill
4	Q	Gross national product

Predetermined variables

1	T_w	Wage taxes (less transfers)
2	G	Government expenditures and exports
3	$W_?$	Government wage bill
4	N_p	Population
5	C_{-1}	Consumption, lagged
6	D_{-1}	Depreciation, lagged
7	$(W_1)_{-1}$	Private wage bill, lagged
8	$(R_1)_{-1}$	Farm income, lagged
9	$(L_1)_{-1}$	Household liquid assets, lagged
10	$(L_2)_{-1}$	Business liquid assets, lagged
11	K_{-1}	Capital stock, lagged
12	P_{-1}	Nonwage farm income, lagged
13	$(T_E)_{-1}$	Indirect taxes, lagged
14	$(T_c)_{-1}$	Corporate taxes, lagged

Note: All variables are in units of billions of 1939 dollars except N_p which is in millions of persons.
Source: Goldberger [1959].

Results and Appraisal

For each of these problems from two to six chains were run by the progressive merger procedure.[24] The last portion of one chain for each problem is shown as a branching diagram in Figure 3. The chain diagrammed in each case is the chain that gave the final chained partition at $J = 6$. The number 6 was chosen because Goldberger uses 6 predetermined variables in his simplified reduced form,[25] namely, the variables G, C_{-1}, D_{-1}, $(W_1)_{-1}$, K_{-1}, and P_{-1}. The branching diagrams show the progressive mergers from $J = 7$ down to $J = 2$, and also show the cost in terms of $\sqrt{c}$ after each merger. The final chained partitions at $J = 6$ are spelled out in terms of the original variable symbols in Table 5.

From Table 5 it can be seen that there is considerable similarity in the optimal partitions into six subsets for the different endogenous variables. In four out of the five problems lagged capital stock, K_{-1}, appears as a separate variable by itself. The combination of lagged depreciation, lagged farm income, and lagged profits appears together in all five problems. The combination of four lagged variables—including private wage bill, indirect taxes, and the two liquid asset variables—appears intact in three

[24] For the meaning of "chain" see Chapter 5. The number of chains varies because a threshold consequence rule, admittedly somewhat arbitrary, was used for stopping the formation of new chains. More details are given in Chapter 5.

[25] See [1959, pp. 119–20]. Goldberger does not give complete details on how he selected his particular variables.

42

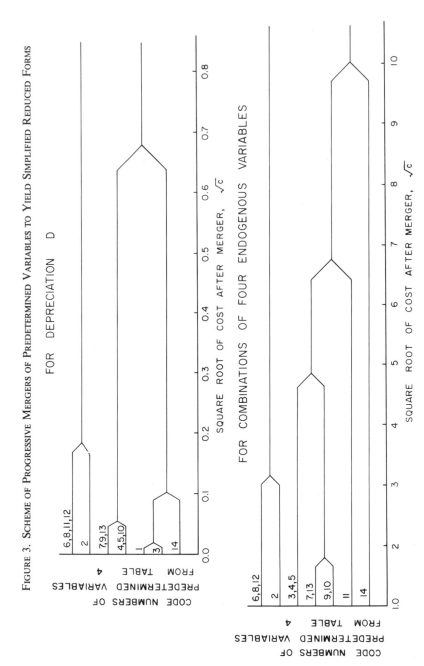

FIGURE 3. SCHEME OF PROGRESSIVE MERGERS OF PREDETERMINED VARIABLES TO YIELD SIMPLIFIED REDUCED FORMS

FOR DEPRECIATION D

SQUARE ROOT OF COST AFTER MERGER, $\sqrt{c}$

CODE NUMBERS OF
PREDETERMINED VARIABLES
FROM TABLE 4

FOR COMBINATIONS OF FOUR ENDOGENOUS VARIABLES

SQUARE ROOT OF COST AFTER MERGER, $\sqrt{c}$

CODE NUMBERS OF
PREDETERMINED VARIABLES
FROM TABLE 4

Source: W. D. Fisher [1966, pp. 575–76].

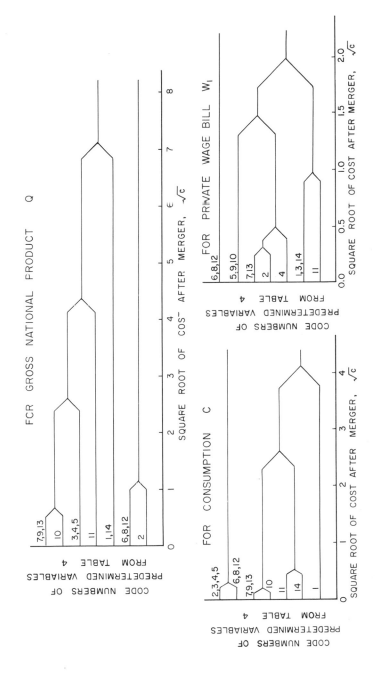

Figure 3. (continued)

TABLE 5.　BEST PARTITIONS INTO SIX SETS OF PREDETERMINED VARIABLES FOR REDUCED FORM

Endogenous variable	Associated sets of predetermined variables					
Combination of four endogenous variables listed below	T_w $(T_c)_{-1}$	G	W_2 N_p C_{-1}	D_{-1} $(R_1)_{-1}$ P_{-1}	$(W_1)_{-1}$ $(L_1)_{-1}$ $(L_2)_{-1}$ $(T_E)_{-1}$	K_{-1}
Consumption C	$(T_c)_{-1}$	T_w	G W_2 N_p C_{-1}	D_{-1} $(R_1)_{-1}$ P_{-1}	$(W_1)_{-1}$ $(L_1)_{-1}$ $(L_2)_{-1}$ $(T_E)_{-1}$	K_{-1}
Depreciation D	$(T_c)_{-1}$	G	N_p C_{-1} $(L_2)_{-1}$	D_{-1} $(R_1)_{-1}$ K_{-1} P_{-1}	$(W_1)_{-1}$ $(L_1)_{-1}$ $(T_E)_{-1}$	T_w W_2
Private wage bill W_1	T_w W_2 $(T_c)_{-1}$	G $(W_1)_{-1}$ $(T_E)_{-1}$	N_p	D_{-1} $(R_1)_{-1}$ P_{-1}	C_{-1} $(L_1)_{-1}$ $(L_2)_{-1}$	K_{-1}
Gross national product Q	T_w $(T_c)_{-1}$	G	W_2 N_p C_{-1}	D_{-1} $(R_1)_{-1}$ P_{-1}	$(W_1)_{-1}$ $(L_1)_{-1}$ $(L_2)_{-1}$ $(T_E)_{-1}$	K_{-1}

Note: The variables are defined in Table 4.
Source: W. D. Fisher [1966, p. 574].

out of the five problems, and three members of this combination appear together in the remaining two problems. The "over-all" partition is precisely the same as the one for gross national product and almost the same as the one for consumption.

Some of these groupings can be traced to the existence of identical coefficients in all four equations—see, for example, columns 6 and 8 in the P matrix of Table A1. Combination seems obviously called for here.[26] In other cases—for example, the two liquidity stock variables—combination seems reasonable. In no case do the combinations suggested by the partitions seem outrageous on a priori grounds.

The magnitude of the simplification costs involved in the reduction to these six aggregates is shown in Table 6, along with some related measures. Recall that the $\sqrt{c}$ is the quadratic mean error of an endogenous variable attributable to the simplification.[27] This $\sqrt{c}$ is found to range from .2 to .7 per cent of the sample mean and from .6 to 1.8 per cent of the sample standard deviation. Although ratios are to some extent arbitrary,

[26] These equalities result from a priori restrictions imposed on the parameters of the structural equations of the Klein–Goldberger model.

[27] It does not include additional errors attributable to sampling errors in P or to random disturbances, which we have not attempted to estimate and which are represented by the last two traces in equation (2.11).

TABLE 6. SIMPLIFICATION COST AND RELATED MEASURES FOR SEPARATE
ENDOGENOUS VARIABLES

| Endogenous variable | Cost $\sqrt{c}$ at six groups | Sample measures | |
| | | Arithmetic mean | Standard deviation |
	Billions of 1939 dollars		
Consumption	.21	75.9	21.7
Depreciation	.02	11.4	3.3
Wage bill	.32	46.9	17.6
GNP	.68	105.6	36.8

these costs of aggregation appear to be quite small when compared with these two measures.[28]

Since all of the six predetermined variables included by Goldberger in his simplified reduced form are also included in our list as well as some others, the simplified reduced forms found by our procedure are less drastic simplifications than his and entail lower simplification costs, given the assumption that the M matrix used reflects adequately variations in the predetermined variables during the prediction period.[29]

The branching diagrams can be used to decide whether and to what extent more drastic simplification (use of fewer subsets of predetermined variables) may be resorted to. For example, the diagram for consumption in Figure 3 shows that very little extra cost will be entailed by proceeding down to four subsets by continued mergers, but a very large increase in cost will occur by proceeding down to three. Final conclusions on this question can be reached only by examining more chains, however, since it is possible that a better partition into three subsets can be reached in a manner other than by progressive mergers of the best six subsets.

It is believed that meaningful simplified models of Goldberger's reduced form have been obtained, which have caused only a small percentage of the original information to be lost, and yet involve far fewer variables than the original model, thus providing greater manageability and ease of comprehension. The proposed progressive merger procedure seems to be practically useful; although it does not guarantee the selection of an optimal partition, it comes close. While the size of the example is small in terms of economic models that have been estimated, the handling of much larger sizes is feasible with available computers.

[28] They would appear to be larger, for example, if we had based them on first differences of the variables.

[29] It is unfortunately not possible to obtain a valid numerical comparison between these costs and those that would pertain to the simplified reduced form published by Goldberger [1959, pp. 119–20], since the $\bar{P}$ matrix of that reduced form is not computed by our definition. It is just a submatrix of the original P unadjusted for the omission of significant and correlated predetermined variables.

3

□

INPUT-OUTPUT ANALYSIS

1. The Simplification Problem in Input-Output Analysis

The Problem As Prediction

One of the most important, as well as most discussed, applications of the simplification-aggregation problem in economics is that of input-output analysis. From the early days of research on interindustry relationships, investigators have recognized the importance of the "aggregation problem" and the fact that the results of the research depend upon the particular procedures used to combine industries. During the last fifteen years a large number of writers have been concerned with both theoretical and practical aspects of this subject.[1]

The potential user of input-output analysis often needs to reduce a table to smaller size. A large table—say 200 by 200 or even 50 by 50—is cumbersome for many purposes. The theorist finds it too detailed to understand, and the econometrician finds himself swamped with output tabulation sheets from his computer. The same considerations of cost of detail that have been discussed earlier in this book also lead to the reduction of input-output tables.

One frequent objective of input-output analysis is the prediction of output of particular industries, given a set of final demands. It would be too strong to claim that this is the only objective, but it is certainly one of the most important. In some applications it is desired to predict the output of only a single industry. For example, the steel industry may want to know what its expected output will be, given estimated final demands for the various industrial products of the United States. In other applications it may be important to consider more than one industry, or even all industries, in an economy. This would be the case with problems of general economic planning or mobilization.

[1] See references in next section.

The aggregation problem will in general be different in these two cases. In making a special-purpose prediction of the output of one industry, the objective in aggregation would be to combine other industries in such a way that error in predicting this output would be small. If the method of aggregation that gave this result happened to involve large errors in predicting outputs of other industries, this would not matter. But in making predictions for many industries simultaneously, a criterion of minimizing errors in all industries would be used. Some sort of compromise or weighting would have to be made among the various criteria for aggregation that would be most useful for each industry separately. This brings back a point, emphasized earlier, that the purposes of an inquiry will influence the simplification methods selected.

For the purposes of this chapter it is assumed that an economy is adequately represented by a static, open, Leontief input-output model of H industries, for which the input (or technical) coefficients are known exactly. The usual assumptions of the model include: just one commodity produced by each industry, strict complementarity among inputs, and constant returns to scale. This is our detailed model, and the industry classifications used for it will sometimes be referred to as "small industries" or "small sectors." It is further assumed that an investigator, having certain prediction objectives sharp enough to be described by a mathematical loss function, wants to simplify the detailed model by means to be defined so that loss, or expected loss, is minimized. This formulation admittedly bypasses many problems connected with the validity of the detailed model and the procedures to be used in its estimation. Attention is directed to the use of the model rather than its construction, following a distinction in problems pointed out by Malinvaud [1954].

It has been shown by Klein [1953, pp. 208–10] that this classic scheme, when augmented by random disturbances, may be considered as a special case of a reduced-form system of equations in which the gross industrial outputs are the endogenous variables, the final demands are predetermined variables, and the Leontief inverse matrix $(I - A)^{-1}$ is the coefficient matrix of the reduced form, which in this case is square.[2]

The input-output model may then be handled as a part of our general prediction model when considering the simplification problem. The assumptions (2.2) through (2.6) of the last chapter can be used, as well as the quadratic loss function (2.1). Theorems 1 and 2 then apply.

A special situation now occurs with respect to the requirements to be

---

[2] Klein also pointed out that this correspondence makes clear that there are a number of possible ways to estimate the technical coefficient matrix A, other than the traditional method of using interindustry flows for a single base year. Later Arrow and Hoffenberg [1959] used time series for this purpose.

placed on the simplified coefficient matrix $\tilde{P}$. In input-output theory this matrix is not only square but a correspondence exists between the rows and the columns: they both apply to the same industrial sectors. It seems reasonable to require that when $\tilde{P}$ is specified as block-homogeneous form, the same partition be made over rows as over columns. That is, the partitioning operators S snd T should use the same partition. With this specification, (2.20a), (2.20b), and (2.21) may be used.

What about the weights (non-zero elements) contained in S and T? There is some choice here, and there is some arbitrary element in any system of fixed weights. The simplest alternative is to specify that $S = T$, and that each contain all weights of unity. In the case where C and M are positive definite, this leads to the prescription to choose a partition of rows and columns so as to minimize cost, as given by (2.21), where now

(3.1a) $\quad \bar{C} = TCT'$, $\qquad\qquad\qquad$ (3.1b) $\quad \bar{M} = TMT'$,

(3.2) $\qquad\qquad\qquad \bar{P} = \bar{C}^{-1}TCPMT'\bar{M}^{-1}$,

and where T has the special unitary form of (1.5). This is the selection that is used for the example in section 3. Other possible choices for S and T are discussed on pages 54 to 56.

Historical Note

This approach varies from most approaches to the aggregation problem of input-output analysis in three essential respects: (1) it is an optimizing approach; (2) the "rules of consolidation" derive in part from the expected variation in final demands during the prediction period (via the M matrix) and from the relative a priori seriousness of errors in the forecasts of specific endogenous variables as assessed by the investigator (via the C matrix) rather than from a consolidation of sectors based on proportions from a flow table for one particular base year; (3) we are dealing here with *micro-bias* in the predictands rather than macro-bias—i.e., bias or error in the detailed endogenous forecasts after use of an aggregation-disaggregation sequence, rather than bias in the aggregated endogenous forecasts after aggregation alone.

The treatments of the aggregation problem in input-output analyses that have taken the optimal simplification approach and that are known to me are those of McCarthy [1956], Skolka [1964], Rubin [1968], W. D. Fisher [1958a], and Neudecker [1968]. The first three of these studies used criteria which may be regarded as closely related to the micro-bias approach. McCarthy sought to find a simplified coefficient matrix of lower rank than the original, such that the sum of squared deviations between corresponding coefficients in the two matrices was minimized. Skolka sought an aggregated coefficient matrix in partitioned form, such that a certain measure of information loss was minimized.[3] Rubin in some experiments with numerical applications used the squared-prediction error of small industries suggested here.[4] W. D. Fisher in [1958a] used a macro-bias approach, employing a criterion of minimizing expected squared-prediction errors in the large (aggregated) industries. Recently Neudecker has extended this approach.

Of other treatments of the input-output aggregation problem—i.e., those not taking a specific optimizing approach—those of Fei [1956] and Ghosh [1960] evaluate the effects of simplification in terms of micro-bias. Fei's article is a theoretical formulation of the effects of a certain aggregation-disaggregation sequence. That of Ghosh evaluates the prediction errors in final demands, given gross outputs, of certain simplification schemes that are closely related to notions of strong separability and block-diagonality of the coefficient matrix.[5] Other treatments take the approach of evaluating macro-bias, or testing consistency, of measures on large industries. In a majority of these a conventional consolidation is assumed.[6]

2. FURTHER TRAITS OF THE PROBLEM

Variation in Final Demands

Implied in the simplification theory that we are using is the proposition that the optimal aggregation partition will depend, in part, on the pattern of variation of final demands, as well as on the structure of the coefficient matrix. This proposition follows immediately from the presence of the moment matrix of predetermined variables in formula (2.21), as well as the specification that the final demands are the predetermined variables in the input-output model. It seems, moreover, intuitively plausible that when, for example, final demands for two small industrial sectors are positively correlated with each other there is a presumption that, other things being equal, they would be placed together in a subset of a partition. Indeed this type of conclusion also emerges within the framework of exact or consistent aggregation.[7]

[3] The relationship between this measure of information loss (which is also used in Theil [1967]) and prediction error is discussed in section 2 of Chapter 6.

[4] Some of these examples are presented in section 3.

[5] See section 2 of Chapter 4 for a discussion of this type of simplification.

[6] Fixed-weight aggregation of quantity flows seems to be assumed in Ara [1959], Balderston and Whitin [1954], Barna [1954], Hatanaka [1952], Holzman [1953], Leontief [1951], Malinvaud [1954], McManus [1956b], and Theil [1957, 1967]. In at least two studies—those of McManus [1956a] and Moroshima and Seton [1961]—some variant of the procedure is used.

[7] See, for example, Malinvaud [1954] or Theil [1957].

A practical problem, however, is that of estimating or assuming a specific M matrix for a particular aggregation problem. In input-output analysis the situation is usually more difficult than in other prediction problems, such as the Goldberger example in section 3 of Chapter 2, where time series on all predetermined variables were available. One usually has some estimates of final demands for detailed sectors for some data year and can usually make the assumption that final demands are non-negative—in some sectors perhaps always zero—but that is about all. Some relevant properties of the M matrix can, nevertheless, be deduced from these assumptions.

If $\hat{z}_i$ denotes the expected value of final demand for small sector i, var z_i the variance of this final demand,[8] then the coefficient of variation is

$$(3.3) \qquad\qquad k_i = \sqrt{\operatorname{var} z_i / \hat{z}_i} \ .$$

If $\operatorname{cov}(z_i, z_j)$ denotes the covariance between final demands in small sectors i and j, if r_{ij} denotes the simple correlation coefficient between these final demands, and if m_{ij} denotes the corresponding element of the M matrix, then, from (2.4) and (3.3)

$$(3.4) \qquad\qquad m_{ij} - \hat{z}_i \hat{z}_j + \operatorname{cov}(z_i, z_j) - \hat{z}_i \hat{z}_j (1 + k_i k_j r_{ij}) \ ,$$

where, as usual,

$$(3.5a) \quad r_{ii} = 1 \ , \qquad\qquad\qquad (3.5b) \quad -1 \le r_{ij} \le 1 \text{ for } i \ne j \ ,$$

and where the correlation matrix (r_{ij}) is positive semi-definite. We also assume that $\hat{z}_i$ and $\hat{z}_j$ are non-negative; hence k_i and k_j are also non-negative. If reasonable assumptions can be adduced regarding means, coefficients of variation, and correlations among the various final demands, then formula (3.4) can be employed to develop a reasonable M matrix. This is done for the example in section 3.

The consequences of assuming that M is a diagonal matrix will now be examined. If $m_{ij} = 0$ for $i \ne j$, it follows from (3.4)

$$(3.6) \qquad\qquad k_i k_j = -\frac{1}{r_{ij}} \ , \qquad i \ne j \ ,$$

which implies that, since all k_i are assumed non-negative, all r_{ij} must be non-positive for $i \ne j$. Moreover, since, from (3.5b), $|r_{ij}| \le 1$, we have

$$(3.7) \qquad\qquad k_i k_j \ge 1 \ , \qquad i \ne j \ ,$$

which implies that each k_i must be greater than or equal to 1, except possibly for one small industry.[9]

[8] More precisely, we are referring to the marginal distribution of final demand i.

[9] From (3.7) and the bounds on r_{ij} it is impossible that any two different k's be each smaller than 1. The theoretical possibility exists that a single k say k_o could be smaller than 1 if all of the other k's are sufficiently large (i.e., satisfy $k_i \ge [k_o(-r_{io})]^{-1}$ for all other i).

The above considerations, then, have put a lower bound of unity on the coefficients of variation if M is to be diagonal. In fact, more stringent (higher) lowest bounds are implied by the requirement that no r_{ij} can be positive, plus the requirement that the matrix of r's be positive semi-definite. While precise mathematical expression of this requirement in the general case is cumbersome, the impact of the requirement can be seen by considering the special case of a correlation matrix where all off-diagonal elements are negative and of the same value. It turns out that the absolute value of the off-diagonal elements cannot be greater than $1/(n-1)$, where n is the order of the matrix.[10] This in turn places on the k's the requirement

$$(3.8) \qquad\qquad k_i k_j \geq n - 1 \ ,$$

which implies that the individual k's must be of the same order of magnitude as the square root of the order of the input-output matrix. These bounds seem very unrealistic, especially when the additional requirement is specified that the domain of the final demands is non-negative.[11]

We conclude that the implications of assuming the moment matrix M to be diagonal in the input-output model are such that this assumption is highly implausible. This conclusion seems warranted by the requirement that every correlation coefficient between a pair of final demands be negative; the additional implications of the assumption on the size of coefficients of variation make it even more so. This conclusion does not follow in the general-prediction model where predetermined variables may take on negative, as well as positive, values.

Proportional Final Demands

Another extreme case, but an instructive one, is when the final demands move strictly in proportion. That is, if (z_i, z_j) is a pair of final demands for two small industries, the ratio z_i/z_j is fixed for all possible observations, and similarly for any pair of final demands. Or, in other words, all possible vectors of final demand are proportional. It is seen that for this case all pair-wise correlation coefficients are unity, and all coefficients of variation are identical.[12] Denote the common coefficient of variation by k.

[10] See Appendix F. The gist of the matter can be seen intuitively by realizing that if $r_{12} = -1$ and $r_{13} = -1$, r_{23} cannot also be -1; in fact it must be $+1$. For the three r's to be all negative and equal their common absolute value cannot exceed $\frac{1}{2}$.

[11] The non-negativity requirement means that the marginal distributions of final demands must be extremely skew with long right tails in order to produce such high coefficients of variation. If the marginal distributions were symmetric, coefficients of variation could not *exceed* unity.

[12] Proof of the last statement: Let the relationship between final demands i and j be $z_i = az_j$, where a is a constant. Then the mean of z_i is equal to the constant times the mean of z_j and the standard deviation of z_i is equal to the constant times the standard deviation of z_j, so the two coefficients of variation are the same.

Then from (3.4) we have

$$(3.9) \qquad m_{ij} = (1 + k^2)\hat{z}_i\hat{z}_j \ ,$$

or the moment matrix can be represented by the form

$$(3.10) \qquad M = (1 + k^2)\hat{z}\hat{z}' = zz' \ ,$$

where $\hat{z}$ is the column vector of expected final demands (assumed to have at least one positive element), and z is another column vector proportional to same. Thus M is of rank one.

Theorem 2 will now be specialized to handle this case.[13] When M is of the form given by (3.10), we have from (2.20b) and (2.25b)

$$(3.11) \qquad \bar{M} = Tzz'T' = V'V = \bar{z}\bar{z}'$$

say, where $\bar{z}$ is defined as

$$(3.12) \qquad \bar{z} = Tz \ ,$$

so that in this case V is the 1 by J row vector

$$(3.13) \qquad V = z'T' = \bar{z}' \ .$$

Then the generalized inverse $\bar{M}^g$ is, from (2.28b) and (2.34b)

$$(3.14) \qquad \bar{M}^g = \bar{z}(\bar{z}'\bar{z})^{-2}\bar{z}'$$

Now define the column vectors y and $\bar{y}$ as

$$(3.15a) \quad y = Pz \ , \qquad\qquad\qquad (3.15b) \quad \bar{y} = \bar{C}^g SCy \ .$$

Note that these may be interpreted as detailed and aggregated endogenous variables, respectively. Then, using (2.19), (3.12), (3.14), and (3.15b), the aggregated matrix $\bar{P}$ is found to be

$$(3.16) \qquad \bar{P} = \bar{y}(\bar{z}'\bar{z})^{-1}\bar{z}'$$

which has rank one.[14] Then, conditional on a given degree of detail, the minimal cost is obtained from (2.21), after manipulation of the traces, as

$$(3.17) \qquad c = y'Cy - \bar{y}'\bar{C}y \ .$$

The problem has been reduced to one of finding a single optimal partition of the row vector of endogenous variables y, using the loss matrix C as a weighting matrix. The techniques referred to at the end of Chapter 2 as "one-way progressive merger procedure" may be used to search for the

---

[13] This specialization of Theorem 2 does not depend upon the assumptions of this chapter other than M being of rank one. Thus, it could have been made for the general linear prediction model when exogenous variables are collinear and when P is not necessarily square. A similar result could be derived for collinear C.

[14] In the general prediction model with two-way aggregation $\bar{P}$ is of size F by J. In the input-output case it is of size J by J.

optimal partition. This reduction of the problem to a one-way problem in one dimension has been the result of assuming that the final demands are known (up to a constant of proportionality). The P matrix in the usual input-output application is the Leontief inverse matrix $(I - A)^{-1}$, and then the y vector is the vector of detailed sector gross outputs. If the final demand vector z is taken for some base year, then the gross output vector y will also apply to that base year. The aggregation problem of input-output analysis is then no longer that of reducing a square matrix, but rather that of reducing a vector. The final demand vector has served essentially the function of weights to form a linear combination of the columns of the coefficient matrix.

Further obvious specializations of these results may be made—for example, by assuming the S matrix to be equivalent to the T matrix, or by assuming the C matrix to be the identity matrix.

Relation to Conventional Consolidation

We now return to the more general formulation of the input-output model and ask: What is the relationship of our procedure to that aggregation procedure most frequently used and discussed in the literature?

After an aggregation partition is determined, the conventional consolidation prescribes simple summation of base-year flows within large sectors. If X is the detailed flow matrix for the base year, A is the detailed technical coefficient matrix, and W is a diagonal matrix whose elements are the base-year detailed outputs y_i, then

$$(3.18) \qquad\qquad\qquad X = AW \ ,$$

and the conventional consolidation prescribes the following aggregates:

$$(3.19a) \quad \bar{X} = TXT' \ , \qquad (3.19b) \quad \bar{W} = TWT' \ , \qquad (3.19c) \quad \bar{A} = \bar{X}\bar{W}^{-1} \ ,$$

where T has the unitary form of (1.5). With a macro-prediction approach no disaggregation is performed. With a micro-prediction approach one must specify a disaggregation operator. One may form a simplified coefficient matrix $\tilde{A}$ by a procedure that has been used in the literature—for example, by Fei [1956]—and amounts to repeating columns of $\bar{A}$ and allocating rows of $\bar{A}$ according to some preselected proportions. More specifically, let V be some positive diagonal matrix (which may or may not be the same as W), and set

$$(3.20) \qquad \tilde{A} = VT'(TVT')^{-1}\bar{A}T = VT'(TVT')^{-1}TAWT'\bar{W}^{-1}T \ ,$$

where use has been made of (3.18) and (3.19) in the right-hand equation.[15] A correspondence may be made with our micro-prediction theory by making the substitutions:

$$(3.21) \qquad P = A \ , \qquad M = W \ , \\ S = TV \ , \qquad C = V^{-1} \ .$$

Then it follows that

$$(3.22) \qquad TVT' = SCS' = \bar{C} \ ; \qquad T = SC \ ;$$

and (3.20) becomes

$$(3.23) \qquad \tilde{A} = S'\bar{C}^{-1}SCPMT'\bar{M}^{-1}T \ ,$$

which is exactly in the form of our simplified model $\tilde{P}$ for the case of non-singular C and M, as can be seen by looking back at (2.15) and (2.37).

For what sort of prediction problem would this simplified matrix be used? In the usual problem the coefficient matrix is the Leontief inverse, the endogenous variables are the gross outputs, and the predetermined variables are the final demands. Here, we simplified the original coefficient matrix. The relevant prediction problem when the coefficient matrix is A is to predict intermediate outputs $y - z$, given the gross outputs y. Consideration of the usual accounting equations of input-output analysis will give the system

$$(3.24) \qquad y - z = Ay \ ,$$

where $y - z$ are now endogenous and gross outputs y are now predetermined.

If this is the prediction problem to be considered, then (3.20) gives a formula for a simplified coefficient matrix according to our theory, using the definitions (3.21). But a serious problem arises: The M matrix defined in (3.21) is diagonal, and this matrix is supposed to represent the raw second moments of the predetermined variables. On pages 51 to 52 it was shown that such a moment matrix is highly implausible. That argument was applied to final demands, but could equally well be applied to gross outputs. For either the prediction problem now being suggested, or the inverse problem, when $P = (I - A)^{-1}$, the M matrix in (3.23) should be a nondiagonal matrix.

Looking at the weighting system applied to the *rows* of $\tilde{A}$ by the matrix $VT'(TVT')^{-1}$ in (3.20), a choice for V must be made. Our choice would be, if we were considering this prediction problem, to set $V = I$, so from (3.21)

---

[15] By setting $\tilde{A}$ equal to Fei's A_*^*, and also setting $VT'(TVT') = H_w$, $WT'\bar{W}^{-1} = H$, $T = G$, we have $A_*^* = H_wGAHG$, which is Fei's simplified matrix after both his aggregation and disaggregation operators have been applied to the original A matrix. See Fei [1956, equations (1.4), (1.18), (A5)]. The V here is not the V of Chapter 2.

$S = T$ and $C = I$. This has the advantage of simplicity. But it is somewhat arbitrary, and the question presents itself: Could our theory be applied by using a "half-way" conventional consolidation and accepting the multiplying matrix on the left of $\bar{A}$ in (3.20) as the specified disaggregation procedure, using some V other than the identity matrix and then using some nondiagonal M on the right? A possible choice for the diagonal elements of V would be the base-year values of the endogenous variables—i.e., the intermediate outputs in the base year. This choice is also suggested by the information-content approach discussed in section 2 of Chapter 6. This choice could be defended as being less arbitrary; it also employs more of the detailed data.

Following this line of thinking to the inverse problem, it seems that one could use an S matrix containing positive elements proportional to the gross outputs y_i, rather than the unitary S matrix.

To summarize, the conventional consolidation is a well-known method for aggregating flows or a coefficient matrix. To evaluate it one must know for what purpose it is to be used. With suitable amendment, including a disaggregation operation and a plausible M matrix, it can be brought into correspondence with the micro-prediction error theory.

If one wants to predict gross outputs with $(I - A)^{-1}$ for coefficient matrix, and also to solve an optimal simplification problem, one has to invert a large matrix at the outset, or use an approximation. Our suggestion is that one may avoid the inversion by using $I + A$ as an approximation for $(I - A)^{-1}$, or else use a larger number of terms from the power series suggested by Waugh [1950]:

$$(3.25) \qquad (I - A)^{-1} = I + A + A^2 + \ldots$$

The first-order approximation $I + A$ is used for some of the experiments in section 3.

The Lockstep Routine

In the input-output model, apart from the special case of proportional final demands, an optimal partition is sought that applies both over the row and column indices of the coefficient matrix (or its inverse). If rows alone were being partitioned, the optimum would undoubtedly be different than if columns alone were being partitioned; a compromise is necessary. This requirement introduces a new variant into the computation problem of searching for the optimal partition. The situation has been called earlier "corresponding row-column aggregation." Since the two partitions, one over rows and the other over columns, are tied together, the computing routine used is called the "lockstep" progressive merger procedure.

This computing routine is described in Chapter 5 and in Appendix G. It was developed specifically for the case of input-output analysis and was used for the example of the next section.

3. Example: The Morgenstern Matrix[16]

Data and Procedure

Numerical experiments were undertaken in finding partitions of a well-known 18 by 18 input-output matrix representing the United States economy in 1939, based on the criteria developed in this chapter. This matrix, published by Morgenstern and his associates,[17] represents already a considerable aggregation from much larger tables previously compiled by the U.S. Bureau of Labor Statistics. A certain amount of experimentation in aggregation has previously been performed on it.[18] The technical coefficient matrix and its Leontief inverse is reproduced in the appendix as Tables A4 and A5. A schematic diagram of the Leontief inverse, intended to give the reader a visual impression of where the largest numbers are, is shown in Figure 4. The industry numbers and code names are given their complete titles in Table 7. This Leontief inverse, often referred to as $(I - A)^{-1}$, is the P matrix of the problem, but experiments were also conducted while setting $P = (I + A)$, purportedly a "first-order" approximation to $(I - A)^{-1}$ according to the power series in equation (3.25).[19]

The loss matrix C is assumed to be the identity matrix. This assumption reflects a judgment that the cost of making forecast errors is adequately represented by a simple sum of squared errors in the various endogenous variables.

An assumed moment matrix M was constructed from formula (3.4) and the following additional assumptions: The expected final demands $\hat{z}_i$ are proportional to recorded final demands for the base year (these are shown in Table 8);[20] all coefficients of variation k_i are unity;[21] correlation coefficients r_{ij} are randomly chosen but subject to the condition that they form a positive definite matrix. The correlations were obtained by first drawing a series of decimals in the range from -1 to 1 from a table of random

[16] The research described in this section was accomplished by Rose M. Rubin as a part of her doctoral dissertation [1968] at Kansas State University.

[17] Morgenstern [1954], Balderston and Whitin [1954].

[18] Especially by Balderston and Whitin [1954] and W. D. Fisher [1958a].

[19] Experiments in using $P = A$ were also conducted by Rubin, but the results showed little resemblance to those for $(I - A)^{-1}$.

[20] Sector 16, Trade, originally had a final demand of zero; this was changed to 600; this number was selected as a conveniently rounded number that was still relatively small, but would serve to avoid singularity of the M matrix.

[21] Examination of time series from the Netherlands compiled by Tilanus [1964] showed this assumption to be reasonable.

FIGURE 4. SCHEMATIC DIAGRAM OF MORGENSTERN INVERSE MATRIX

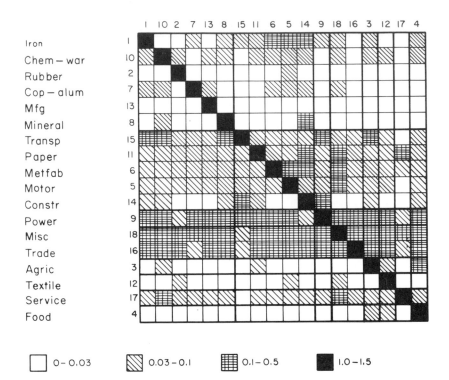

| | 0 – 0.03 | | 0.03 – 0.1 | | 0.1 – 0.5 | | 1.0 – 1.5 |

(0.5 – 1.0 interval is empty)

TABLE 7.   SMALL INDUSTRIES CLASSIFICATION AND CODE FOR THE 18 BY 18 MATRIX

Industry number	Industry code	Classification title
1	Iron	Ferrous metals
2	Rubber	Rubber
3	Agric	Agriculture and fishing
4	Food	Food, tobacco and kindred products
5	Motor	Motor vehicles, industrial and heating equipment
6	Metlfab	Metal fabricating
7	Cop-alum	Nonferrous metals and their products
8	Mineral	Nonmetallic minerals and their products
9	Power	Fuel and power
10	Chem-war	Chemicals, including munitions
11	Paper	Lumber, paper and their products; printing and publishing
12	Textile	Textiles and leather
13	Mfg	All other manufacturing
14	Constr	Construction
15	Transp	Transportation
16	Trade	Trade
17	Service	Business and personal services
18	Misc	Undistributed

Source: Balderston and Whitin, [1954, p. 115].

TABLE 8. BASE YEAR FINAL DEMANDS AND GROSS OUTPUTS FOR SMALL INDUSTRIES

Industry number	Industry code	Final demand	Gross output
		Millions of 1939 dollars	
1	Iron	197	3,887
2	Rubber	398	1,170
3	Agric	5,259	12,473
4	Food	16,061	18,790
5	Motor	3,245	7,672
6	Metlfab	2,417	8,582
7	Cop-alum	529	2,957
8	Mineral	352	2,734
9	Power	5,455	13,493
10	Chem-war	1,741	5,017
11	Paper	2,110	8,893
12	Textile	8,085	12,031
13	Mfg	1,189	2,360
14	Constr	7,358	10,089
15	Transp	2,020	7,615
16	Trade	600[a]	18,610
17	Service	15,710	20,567
18	Misc	872	21,240

[a] This figure was changed from 0 in the original data. See footnote 20.
Source: Balderston and Whitin [1954, p. 116].

numbers to form a symmetric matrix; the result of these drawings is shown in Table A2. This matrix was then squared (to insure positive definiteness) and the resulting matrix normalized by dividing by a certain scalar so that all nondiagonal elements would have absolute values less than unity.[22] The M matrix resulting from these manipulations is shown in Appendix A, Table A3, and a schematic diagram of the matrix is shown in Figure 5.[23] It was used for all of the experiments.

For one of the experiments two alternative assumptions about the correlation coefficients were made; (1) that each off-diagonal r_{ij} is zero, and (2) that each off-diagonal r_{ij} is .5. Another experiment was made on the assumption that all $r_{ij} = 1$ (constant final demands case).

The S and T matrices were taken to be of the "unitary" form of (1.5), which requires that the simplified $\tilde{P}$ be formed by repeating both rows and columns of the aggregated $\bar{P}$.

Two sets of side conditions in the form of forbidden merger pairs were used in order to test the effect of such conditions on the resulting partitions. These conditions will be described below.

[22] The range of the diagonal elements of the squared matrix was found to be from 6.77 to 12.07; the normalization was fudged slightly; each off-diagonal element was divided by 10 (for convenience) and each diagonal element changed to 1. This implied "rounding" of the diagonal elements might have spoiled the positive-definite character of the matrix, but, in the course of inverting it later on, this possibility was found not to have occurred.

[23] In both Figures 4 and 5 the rows and columns have been arranged according to the first partition to be reported on below.

FIGURE 5. SCHEMATIC DIAGRAM OF ASSUMED MOMENT MATRIX

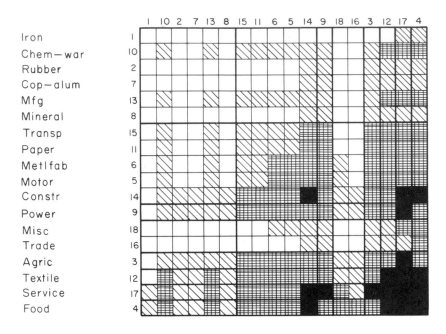

□ 0-200   ▦ 1,000 – 10,000

◩ 200 – 1,000   ■ 10,000 – 50,000

The lockstep progressive merger procedure was used in the seven problems to be reported on.[24] In all of these the terminal number of subsets was eight. Detailed results are shown in Tables A6 to A10. In three of the seven problems two different "branches" are shown; these pertain to the efforts of the computer to approach more closely to the true optimal partition, and will be explained in Chapter 5. For present purposes attention will be concentrated on the "least-cost" branches.

The First Solution

The first problem was run using the true Leontief inverse and making no restrictions on permissible partitions. The final partition into eight subsets arrived at by the computer is shown as a segmented bar graph in

[24] In Rubin [1968] some additional experimentation was made on the Morgenstern matrix and also a number of experiments with a 31 by 31 matrix compiled for the economy of Boulder, Colorado.

FIGURE 6. AGGREGATION PARTITIONS OBTAINED WITHOUT AND WITH FORBIDDEN MERGERS

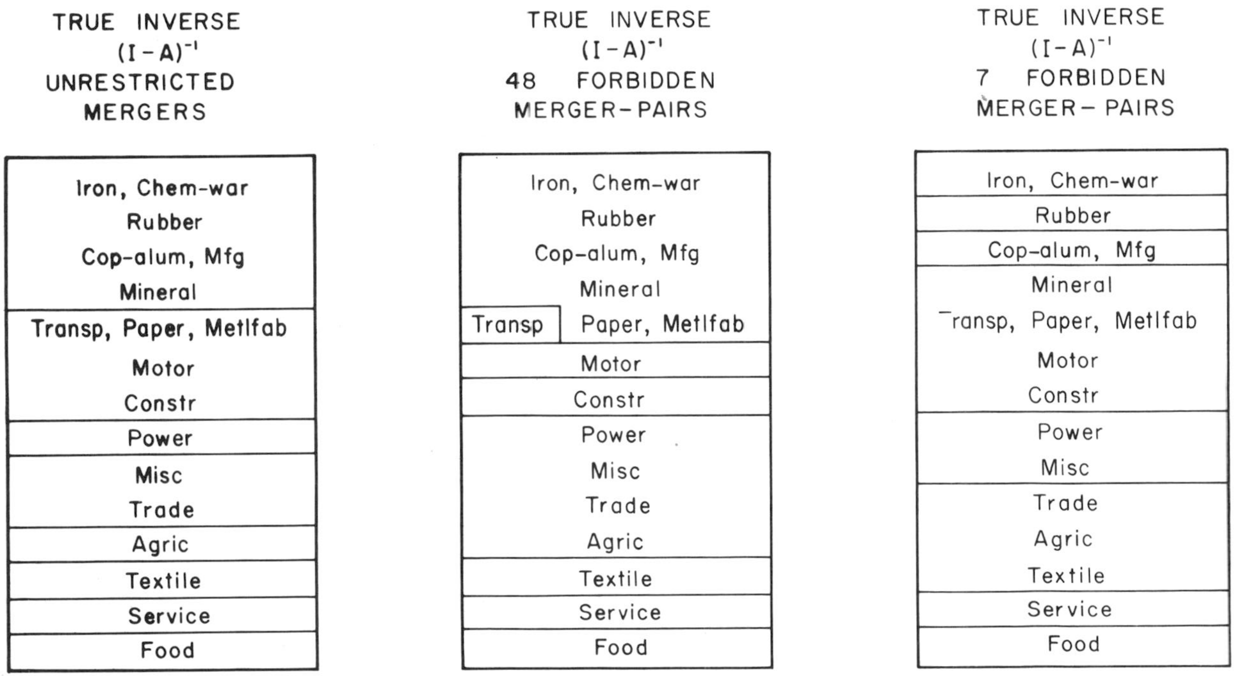

TRUE INVERSE
$(I - A)^{-1}$
UNRESTRICTED
MERGERS

Iron, Chem-war
Rubber
Cop-alum, Mfg
Mineral
Transp, Paper, Metlfab
Motor
Constr
Power
Misc
Trade
Agric
Textile
Service
Food

TRUE INVERSE
$(I - A)^{-1}$
48 FORBIDDEN
MERGER-PAIRS

Iron, Chem-war	
Rubber	
Cop-alum, Mfg	
Mineral	
Transp	Paper, Metlfab
Motor	
Constr	
Power	
Misc	
Trade	
Agric	
Textile	
Service	
Food	

TRUE INVERSE
$(I - A)^{-1}$
7 FORBIDDEN
MERGER-PAIRS

Iron, Chem-war
Rubber
Cop-alum, Mfg
Mineral
Transp, Paper, Metlfab
Motor
Constr
Power
Misc
Trade
Agric
Textile
Service
Food

Note: For full titles of code names see Table 7.

FIGURE 7. AGGREGATION PARTITIONS OBTAINED WITH TRUE
AND APPROXIMATE INVERSES

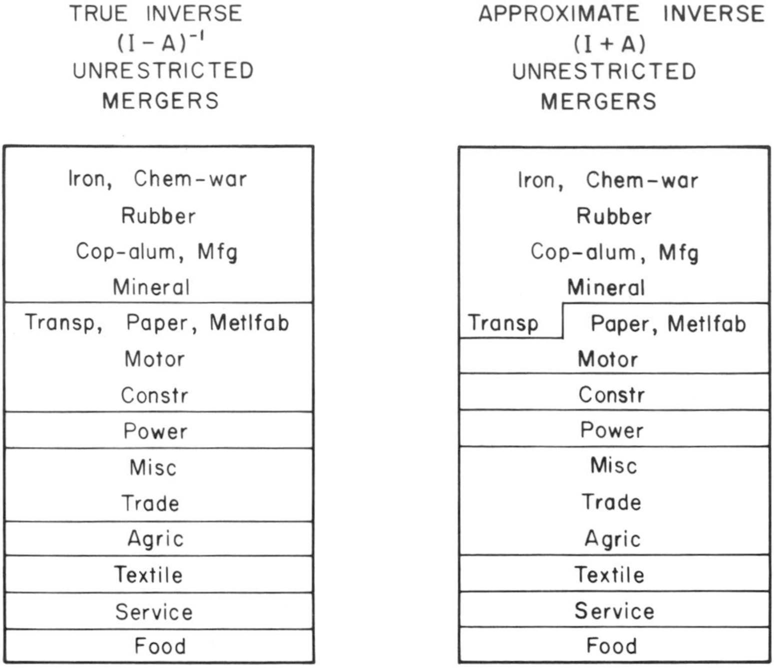

TRUE INVERSE
$(I - A)^{-1}$
UNRESTRICTED
MERGERS

APPROXIMATE INVERSE
$(I + A)$
UNRESTRICTED
MERGERS

Iron, Chem-war
Rubber
Cop-alum, Mfg
Mineral

Transp,	Paper, Metlfab

Motor
Constr
Power
Misc
Trade
Agric
Textile
Service
Food

Iron, Chem-war
Rubber
Cop-alum, Mfg
Mineral

Transp	Paper, Metlfab

Motor
Constr
Power
Misc
Trade
Agric
Textile
Service
Food

Note: For full titles of code names see Table 7.

Figure 6 (left bar). More details are given in the appendix; the aggregated $\bar{P}$ matrix is given in the upper section of Table A10, and the sequence of values taken by the cost function as the number of subsets of the partitions declined from eighteen to eight is shown in Table A8.

The groupings of industries shown in the bar graph appear to be quite reasonable. A group of six of the original small industries associated with metals, minerals, chemicals and munitions, rubber, and miscellaneous manufacturing forms one large sector. Another is formed of five industries: transportation, lumber and paper etc., metal fabricating, motor vehicles (with industrial and heating equipment), and construction. Trade and Miscellaneous are linked together. Five of the original industries remain segregated in the final partition: Food, Services, Textiles and Leather, Agriculture, and Fuel and Power.

Some explanation for this result can be found by looking back at the listing of the values of the final demands in Table 8, and at the diagrams of the P and M matrices in Figures 4 and 5. Of the eighteen industries listed in Table 8 the six having the largest final demands are Food, Services,

Textile, Construction, Power, and Agriculture. Five of these six (those except Construction) are the five that get placed in five separate subsets of the final partition. The dark shading in the lower right corner of Figure 5 shows the same thing; this matrix, recall, is constructed with the final demands used as diagonal elements; high numbers are associated together (the partitions are indicated in Figures 4 and 5 by heavy dividing lines). The smaller industries (in terms of final demand) are associated together in the larger groupings.

The industries Trade and Miscellaneous are associated together, probably mostly on account of their joint characteristic of having fairly large coefficients in the P matrix with respect to all other industries (see Figure 4).

To summarize: this eight-set partition was determined by the numerical data from the eighteen original industries. To some extent the numerical values were determined by economic considerations (food has a larger final demand component than has iron). To some extent also these values were determined by the accidents of arbitrary classification and aggregation at the lower levels.

Restrictions on Permitted Partitions

If one does not like what one receives from a computer, one can always give the computer new instructions. Indeed, in the type of partitioning problem considered here there are often legitimate reasons for placing side conditions on the prescription to find that partition that minimizes cost. Theoretical considerations, for example, or the desire to concentrate attention on certain industrial sectors, may lead to rules to bar certain partitions, or certain particular subsets.

In the progressive merger procedure provision is made for additional input parameters, if desired, in the form of a list of specific pairs of indices of rows or columns of the P matrix that will not be merged at any stage. These are referred to sometimes as "forbidden merger pairs." At each stage the computer scans the list against any proposed merger before effecting the merger.[25] The final partition attained by the computer is then, the optimal chained partition, subject to these forbidden merger rules. The final cost will be higher than without such rules.

Two lists of forbidden merger pairs were used in the experiments with the Morgenstern matrix and additional problems run in order to test the effects of these restrictions. One list of seven pairs was constructed as follows: six forbidden pairs were chosen to break up the combination of

---

[25] Although forbidden merger pairs were not considered in Chapter 2, this feature of the computer program is available for the one-way, as well as the lockstep, version.

small industries numbered 1, 2, 7, and 8 (iron, rubber, cop-alum, and mineral), and the pair (16, 18) (trade and miscellaneous) was also listed as forbidden. Another list of 48 pairs was constructed so as to completely isolate each of the small industries—5 (motor), 14 (construction), and 15 (transportation)—from all other industries.

The two right-hand bars on Figure 6 show the final partitions into eight subsets that were obtained for these two lists of forbidden pairs when using the true Leontief inverse matrix.[26] Although the restrictions have been observed, the general picture is not greatly changed in either case. In order to go from the unrestricted partition to the partition subject to the forty-eight forbidden pairs, one must shift six small industries from one large industry to another; in order to go from the unrestricted partition to the one that is subject to seven forbidden pairs (shown on the extreme right bar of Figure 6), one must shift seven small industries. It thus appears that the seven forbidden-pair requirement was more severe than the forty-eight forbidden-pair requirement.

This impression is confirmed by comparing the costs in the three cases, which are shown in Table 9. The unrestricted case shows lowest cost; the case of forty-eight forbidden pairs is substantially higher (over twice as high in terms of c), and the cost with seven forbidden pairs is higher still. This shows that the severity of the restrictions does not necessarily depend on the number of forbidden pairs, but rather on the relation of the particular pairs forbidden to the optimal unrestricted pattern.

It is also seen from Table 9 that the cost, when expressed as $\sqrt{c}$, is a higher percentage of the absolute level of total output (5 percent for the unrestricted case) than comparable percentages from the example of Chapter 2.[27]

The cost of each of these cases, when expressed as c, is plotted in Figure 8 as a function of the number of subsets in the partition. The path of rising cost with increasing degree of aggregation is evident.

TABLE 9. SIMPLIFICATION COST WITHOUT AND WITH RESTRICTED MERGERS

Forbidden mergers	Cost as c (dollars $\times 10^{18}$)	Cost as $\sqrt{c}$ (billion dollars)	$\sqrt{c}$ as percent of total output[a]
None	87.9	9.4	5.3%
48	207.7	14.4	8.1%
7	311.1	17.6	9.9%

[a] Total output of all eighteen small industries is 178.18 billions of 1939 dollars.

[26] Additional details are shown in Tables A6, A8, and A10.

[27] As mentioned in Chapter 2, there is an arbitrary element in such ratios. Here the total output of all eighteen small industries is used as a base in order to gain an impression of the importance of $\sqrt{c}$, which is in comparable units and expresses the quadratic mean-prediction error attributable to the simplification.

FIGURE 8. SIMPLIFICATION COST AS A FUNCTION OF NUMBER OF SUBSETS
WITHOUT AND WITH RESTRICTED MERGERS

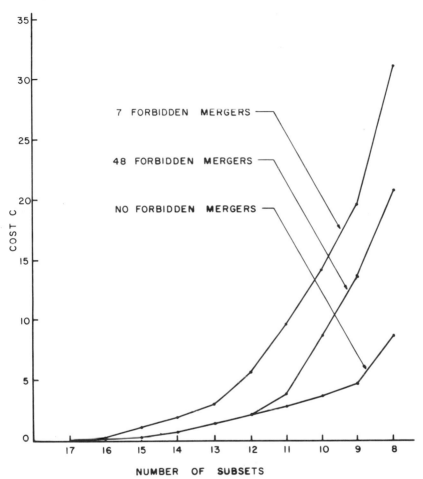

The same alternative side conditions in terms of forbidden merger pairs were used for additional problems using $(I + A)$ as the P matrix, with the same general conclusions regarding the relative severity of the two lists of pairs and the trends of simplification costs. Details of these additional results are shown in Tables A7, A9, and A10.

Sensitivity to Variations in Data

Additional problems on the Morgenstern matrix were run, using $(I + A)$ as an approximation to the Leontief inverse $(I - A)^{-1}$, recognizing that one of the frequent purposes of aggregation is to avoid inverting a large matrix. It was desired to test the extent to which use of this first-order approximation would affect the final partition. As stated above, variations of the moment matrix M were also introduced to see the effect on the results.

In the right bar of Figure 7 is shown the final partition that resulted when $(I + A)$ was used in place of $(I - A)^{-1}$ and when no restrictive side conditions were imposed. By comparison with the original partition (left bar), the change seems moderately small, although not insignificant. Three shifts of small industries are needed to go from one partition to the other.[28] When forty-eight forbidden pairs were used, the final partitions were the same. When seven forbidden pairs were used, the difference was six shifts of small industries.

In the results from the 31 by 31 matrix Rubin [1968] reported that when no restrictions were used the final partitions of fifteen subsets were exactly the same; when restrictions in the form of four and seven forbidden-merger pairs were introduced, differences of four shifts resulted each time between the $(I + A)$ case and the $(I - A)^{-1}$ case. Percentage-wise, these differences are smaller than in the 18 by 18 case. Further investigation revealed that the 31 by 31 $(I + A)$ matrix was a closer approximation to its Leontief inverse than was the 18 by 18 $(I + A)$ matrix.[29]

It seems that the first-order approximation $(I + A)$ to $(I - A)^{-1}$ is certainly a useful one in aggregation studies and that near to optimal partitions can be obtained by using the approximation. Complete reliance cannot be placed on this approximation in all cases, however, and it will sometimes be worth while to include more terms of the Waugh power series for the approximation.

The variants of the moment matrix M in which off-diagonal correlations were uniformly set at 0 and at .5 (rather than varying) were used in the unrestricted merger problem along with the true inverse $(I - A)^{-1}$. For each of these variants the final partition came out exactly the same as for the original problem. Although this evidence is not voluminous, it does provide some assurance that the solutions to the aggregation problem displayed here are not overly sensitive to the particular assumptions regarding the correlation coefficients of final demands, provided that some randomness in final demands is assumed.

When we drop the assumption of random final demands, and go to the assumption of perfectly correlated (proportional) final demands, the results are much different. One of the results of Rubin [1968] for this case is shown in Figure 9. It will be recalled that the optimal partitioning problem

[28] The costs between these two cases are not comparable.
[29] Rubin [1968, p. 72].

FIGURE 9. AGGREGATION PARTITION FOR THE CASE OF
PROPORTIONAL FINAL DEMANDS

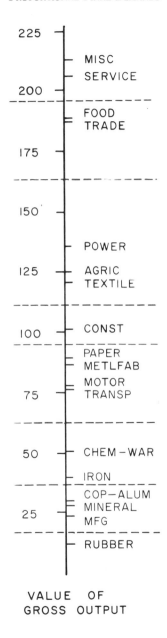

VALUE OF
GROSS OUTPUT

Source: Rubin [1968, Figure 1].

for this proportional final demand case reduces to the one-dimensional problem of partitioning the vector of gross outputs. If final demands are assumed to remain proportional to the values of the base year, then the vector of gross outputs in the base year may be used as input data for the optimal partitioning problem. From the data on gross outputs shown in Table 8, the optimal partition with no side conditions was obtained, and is shown by dotted dividing lines on the graph in Figure 9. The partition was obtained by the computer using the one-way progressive merger procedure, but could also be obtained, or at least closely approximated, by visual inspection of the linear scatter of points. It is seen that there are some substantial differences between this partition and the first unrestricted case discussed above. The type of M matrix (rank one) implied by the assumption of proportional final demands seems to induce more radical changes in the solution to the simplification problem.

Conclusions

Reasonable and useful results can be obtained by approaching the simplification problem in input-output analysis from the viewpoint of the micro-prediction error theory. The empirical experiments reported on are of a small scale and of the nature of an illustrative pilot study. They cannot be used to infer substantive conclusions about the structure of the United States economy. They indicate, however, that further application of the optimal simplification methods to larger matrices would be worth while.

4

DECISION-PROPER MODELS

The objective now is to show how the notion of optimal simplification can be applied to what are often called "decision models." This term appears to have been used first by Frisch [1950]. The idea has been developed theoretically and practically by Tinbergen [1952, 1956] and Theil [1958], and is now widely used in management science as well as in general economic policy-making. Simply stated, a decision model is an economic model of the type, considered on page 15, that contains decision variables and an objective function explicitly derived from economic criteria.

This last requirement—that the objective function be derived from economic criteria—defines the distinction between these decision models, which we here call "decision-proper" models, and what we have called "prediction models." For prediction models the objective function was taken as some function of the errors of prediction of endogenous variables; the relationship of this function to economic objectives, if it existed at all, was vague and intuitive. In decision-proper models we shall consider more directly economic objective functions such as profit and utility.

These two classes of economic model may be regarded as variants of a decision model in a broader sense—namely, that in each some sort of decision must be taken to optimize some sort of function. The distinction is then one of application rather than of mathematical structure of the problem. Indeed the reader must be warned now that before we are finished here we shall be making quadratic approximations to the objective functions adduced and shall be getting back to our former problem of selecting an optimal partition with respect to a quadratic function.

It is obvious that in this chapter it is impossible to discuss this question in a comprehensive manner, or even to mention all of the types of decision-proper models to which the suggested methods can be applied, or all of the various types of simplified assumptions that might be relevant. Two types of problems are considered: linear programming and conventional maximizing—the latter term denoting the case where the objective is a differentiable function and is maximized subject to constraints in the form of differentiable equations only. For the first type a relatively simple numerical example is presented.

1. LINEAR PROGRAMMING[1]

Problems in Game Form

Consider first the general linear programming problem: choose a non-negative vector x so that the linear form

$$(4.1) \qquad\qquad z = c'x$$

is a maximum subject to the linear constraints

$$(4.2) \qquad\qquad Ax \leq b \ ,$$

where A, b, and c are known. In a well-known application x represents activity levels related to goods, b the amounts of fixed resources available, c the net revenues accruing from one unit of activity level, and A the matrix of real costs, in the sense that the typical element a_{ij} denotes the amount of resource i that is needed to produce one unit of good j. It is clear that this problem is one employing a decision-proper model with the objective function $c'x$ being total profit from operating all activities. Because of this application we shall sometimes refer to A as the *cost matrix*; a_{ij} as a *cost coefficient*, b as the *resource vector*, and c as the *net revenue vector*.

Now consider the special problem that arises when the elements of A are all non-negative, and the elements of b and c are all unity. For reasons that are either obvious to the reader, or may appear so after explanations to be given presently, this special problem will be said to be in *game form* or in *normalized form*. It is convenient in what follows to deal with the problem in game form and to assume that an originally given linear programming problem has been converted into this form.[2] This may be done

---

[1] Theoretical analysis of qualitative aggregation effects in the type of model to be considered in this section has been made by Kemeny, Morgenstern, and Thompson [1956, sec. 9]. Exact aggregation theorems are given by Day [1963] and Miller [1966] and discussed by Lee [1966]. Reference should also be made to the literature on the decomposition principle in linear programming, a subject of some importance which is related to the approach taken here, but is not dealt with here. The basic articles are those of Dantzig and Wolfe [1960, 1961]. Recent work on the decomposition algorithm has also been done by Weil [1968].

[2] It is assumed that the constraint set defined by the original problem is bounded and that a solution to the problem exists.

by performing the following steps: (1) replace any zero elements in the b or c vectors by very small non-zero elements; (2) multiply any negative elements in these vectors by -1 and also multiply the corresponding rows or columns of A by -1 (in the latter case redefining an activity as the negative of the original activity); (3) remove any negative elements in the A matrix resulting after the preceding steps by adding a sufficiently large positive constant to all elements of A; (4) normalize the cost matrix A to A^*, where

(4.3) $a^*_{ij} = a_{ij}/b_i c_j$,

where the symbols on the right refer to the problem after transformation by steps (1), (2), and (3). The profit of the transformed problem can be made arbitrarily close to that of the original problem after adding to the original profit the constant mentioned in step (3); henceforth we shall use the symbol z to denote the new profit. The solution vector x of the transformed problem may be made arbitrarily close to that of the original problem after multiplication of the former by a certain known diagonal matrix involving the c_j and after further multiplication of the original x_j by ± 1. The new solution may be interpreted as a vector whose elements represent activity levels in terms of "dollars worth," and the new constraints may be imagined as statements in terms of "fractions of available resources."[3]

There is a well-known correspondence between this normalized problem and its dual on the one hand, and a zero-sum matrix game on the other hand, where the normalized cost matrix A is also the pay-off matrix of the game.[4] Let the dual problem be that of selecting a vector y such that the linear form $b'y$ be minimized subject to the constraints

(4.4) $A'y \geq c$,

where now both b and c have elements of unity. Then by the duality theorem of linear programming if the primal problem has solution x^*, the dual problem also has a solution, say y^*, and the solution for the value of the maximized z in the primal problem, say z^*, is also the solution for the value of the minimand of the dual problem.[5] Now let A be the pay-off matrix of a rectangular game where the maximizing player is to choose a mixed strategy, say x, over the rows of A and the minimizing

[3] So the normalized cost coefficient a^*_{ij} states the fraction of available resource i needed to produce one dollar's worth of good j, and the new b and c vectors have all unit elements.

[4] For the remainder of this section we shall omit the asterisk from the normalized A^* and its elements a^*_{ij}.

[5] See, for example, Gale [1960, p. 78.]

player chooses a mixed strategy, say y, over the columns of A, and where the value of the game is v. Then it can be shown that the solution of the rectangular game problem, say (x^0, y^0, v^0), is related to the solutions of the primal-dual linear programming problems as follows:[6]

(4.5a) $\qquad\qquad x^0 = x^*/z^*$,   (4.5b) $y^0 = y^*/z^*$,

(4.5c) $\qquad\qquad\qquad v^0 = 1/z^*$.

So, if one solves the linear programming problems, then one can solve the game problem, and the value of the game is the reciprocal of the profit. Moreover, proportionalities exist between the game solution and the programming solutions. This correspondence means that our discussion of simplification of linear programming problems will also carry over to rectangular games, if one is careful with the formulation and interpretation of objectives in each context.

An instructive and presently useful geometric interpretation of the solution to the primal linear programming problem can be given.[7] Let each resource (or its associated constraint) be represented by a Cartesian axis in M-space, where M is the dimension of the vector b; let each activity (or its associated good) be represented by a point in this space. Let the coordinates of each point be the cost coefficients (normalized). Then the normalized cost matrix A represents a collection of N points, where N is the dimension of the vector c. In Figure 10 the case of $M = 2$, $N = 5$ is represented by the five points P_1 to P_5. These may be called *activity points*. The fractions of available resources expended in operating any single activity j at x dollars can be read off the graph by finding the ray connect-

---

[6] See, for example, Gale [1960, pp. 217–18]. The proof runs as follows: Let j' be a row vector of 1's. Then in the primal linear programming problem $j'x^* = z^*$, and, from (4.5a) $j'x^*/z^* = j'x^0 = 1$, so x^0 is a mixed strategy since its elements sum to 1 with each element non-negative. In the dual problem the solution y^* must lie in the feasible set, and hence must satisfy

$$y^{*\prime}A \geq j' .$$

Hence, from (4.5a) and (4.5c) and the above, the game solution must satisfy

$$y^{0\prime}A \geq v^0 j' .$$

Hence, for any mixed strategy x,

$$y^{0\prime}Ax \geq v^0 j'x ,$$

or, using the definition of mixed strategy $j'x = 1$ and of value of the game, $v^0 = y^{0\prime}Ax^0$, we obtain

$$y^{0\prime}Ax \geq y^{0\prime}Ax^0$$

for any mixed strategy x. This last relation is the definition of an optimal, or solution strategy, x^0. By precisely symmetrical reasoning y^0 is found to be a solution strategy also.

[7] This interpretation follows closely those of Dorfman [1951, p. 44] and Waugh [1951, p. 304].

FIGURE 10. GEOMETRIC INTERPRETATION OF A NORMALIZED
LINEAR PROGRAMMING PROBLEM

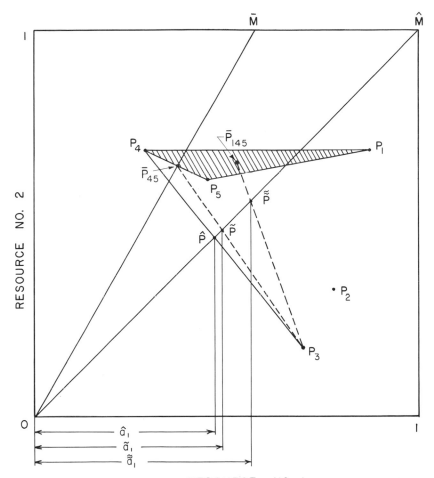

RESOURCE   NO. I

ing the origin with point P_j, going out on this ray a distance corresponding with x dollars (the point P_j itself is at a distance corresponding with
one dollar), and reading off the coordinates of the point at this distance.
(If a coordinate were to exceed 1, that would mean that more of this resource than is available would be required to operate the activity at that
selected level.) Likewise, the fractions of available resources expended in
operating any "composite activity" (two or more activities operated jointly
in specified proportions) at level x dollars may be found in a similar manner by using a point, say $\bar{P}_{jk...}$, that is the specified convex combination of
the original P's representing the activities being combined. For example,

$\bar{P}_{45}$ in Figure 10 is the composite activity point representing the activity of spending 50 cents on activity 4 and 50 cents on activity 5; its coordinates are the fractions of available resources expended by that particular composite.

Then it is seen that the optimal program is represented by the composite activity point that lies on the intersection of the "southwest frontier" of all activity points with the 45° ray,[8] and the profit from this program is the reciprocal of one of the coordinates of this point. In Figure 10 the optimal composite is shown as $\hat{P}$, and the profit associated with it is $1/\hat{a}_1$.[9] More generally we may say that the maximum profit, say $\hat{z}$, is given by the formula

(4.6)
$$\hat{z} = \frac{1}{\min_i(\max \bar{a}_i)} ,$$

where $\bar{a}_i$ is some convex combination of the elements a_{ij} in the ith row of the normalized cost matrix A, and the minimizing is over the entire set of such convex combinations.[10]

Aggregating Activities and Constraints

An excellent intuitive insight into the effects of aggregation on the linear programming solution can be obtained in the two-dimensional case. With reference to Figure 10, consider again the composite activity represented by $\bar{P}_{45}$. This could also be called an *aggregate activity*. Suppose that $\bar{P}_{45}$ replaces the individual points P_4 and P_5 in the diagram. The solution point to the problem is then $\tilde{P}$ instead of $\hat{P}$, and the profit is $1/\tilde{a}_1$ instead of $1/\hat{a}_1$. This is a lower profit, but the change is not great. Consider next the aggregate activity point $\bar{P}_{145}$, which is the centroid of the triangle $P_1P_4P_5$, and consider the effect of replacing these three points

---

[8] The 45° ray is defined as the straight line through the origin, making an angle of 45° with each coordinate axis.

[9] This can be seen as follows. The largest profit z that can be realized by operating any activity, original or composite, without violating constraints, is the highest level of that activity in terms of dollars (i.e., the largest multiplier of a unit level of one dollar) that is possible before the most restrictive constraint is violated. For example, the largest profit that can be realized from the activity represented by $\bar{P}_{45}$ in Figure 10 is the ratio $O\bar{M}/O\bar{P}_{45}$, which is equal to the reciprocal of the ordinate of $\bar{P}_{45}$ (since, for a larger multiplier more of Resource 2 would be required than is available). It follows that the optimal program—i.e., the one yielding highest profit—is represented by the point whose largest coordinate is the smallest possible and is still some convex combination of the original activity points (i.e., lies in their convex hull). The point in Figure 10 that meets this requirement is $\hat{P}$, which lies on the frontier segment $\overline{P_3P_4}$, and hence represents a combination of these two activities.

[10] This statement follows directly from the correspondence between the normalized linear programming problem and the rectangular game. The reciprocal of $\hat{z}$ is the optimized value of the game.

by their centroid. This is a more severe aggregation. The frontier is pushed back to the dotted line connecting $\bar{P}_{145}$ with P_3; the new solution point is $\tilde{\hat{P}}$, and the new profit is $1/\tilde{\hat{a}}_1$, a substantially lower profit than in the two previous cases. The reason for this larger decrease in profit is evidently the aggregation of points that are quite distant from each other.

Going back to the original points, suppose now that P_1 and P_2 had been aggregated. The frontier is still the line connecting P_3 and P_4, and maximum profit remains at $\hat{P}$. It is seen that the reason for this aggregation having no effect on the profit is that neither point aggregated was effective (i.e., was not on the relevant frontier segment and therefore was at zero level in the solution).

This analysis suggests that when convex combinations of original activity points (vectors) are used as aggregate activities to replace the original activities, the following effects occur: (1) the profit is either reduced or remains the same (and remains the same in the case that only ineffective activities are aggregated), and (2) the amount of reduction in profit will be small when the distances between the activity points aggregated are small.[11]

Now extend the analysis to N points in M-space, and extend the concept of aggregation as follows: define an *aggregation partition of activities* as a partition of the columns of the normalized cost matrix A into J disjoint and exhaustive subsets, where J is some integer less than N (geometrically, this partition groups the N activity points into clusters); then replace the original columns of A by J *aggregate activities*, each aggregate activity being a column vector that is some convex combination of the original column vectors of a subset of the partition (geometrically, these aggregate points are centroids, possibly weighted, of the clusters); call the new matrix an *aggregated cost matrix $\bar{A}$*.[12] The conclusions of

---

[11] The fact that the solution point of a linear programming problem may be regarded as a continuous function of the data (when the data are regarded as variables) is sufficient to insure that in the sense of a limiting process, "small" distances between the aggregate point and the original points aggregated will entail only a "small" displacement of the solution point. But this conclusion does not solve the problem of selecting among alternative finite distances, associated with alternative aggregates. Nor is it necessarily true that when the distances are large the decrease in profit will be large, since the conclusion regarding the profit depends also to some extent on the direction of the distances. (E.g., if P_3 and P_5 are aggregated, the reduction in profit is seen to be moderate, even though these points are quite distant from each other, and the reason for this is seen to be the fact that the direction of line P_3P_5 is almost the same as that of the P_3P_4 segment of the frontier.)

[12] The aggregation of A to $\bar{A}$ may be regarded as a case of the function g of equation (1.2) in Chapter 1. Here (in contrast with problems of previous chapters) we do not employ a disaggregation operator leading to, say, a singular matrix $\bar{A}$, obtained by inserting equal or proportional rows or columns into $\bar{A}$, because a linear programming problem would be unchanged by such insertions and it is simpler not to make them.

the preceding paragraph may be easily extended to this more general case.[13]

Now let us turn to the aggregation of constraints. Define an *aggregation partition of constraints* as a partition of the rows of A into F disjoint and exhaustive subsets, where F is some integer less than M. Define an *aggregate constraint* as a row vector that is some convex combination of the original row vectors of a subset of the partition. Geometrically, this definition may be conceived by inverting the roles of "points" and "coordinates" as previously defined, and considering now the *rows* of A as points in N-space. Then there are M original points, and F aggregate points.

But-by the duality theorem of linear programming if we consider the dual problem, with the roles of rows and columns of A interchanged, so that the rows are now *activities* and the objective function is to be *minimized*, the solution of the dual problem is precisely the profit solution of the primal problem. By applying our previous analysis of the effects of aggregating activities, but now to the dual problem, we conclude that the value of the objective function of the dual is *raised* (or remains the same) by aggregation. Therefore, the aggregation of *constraints* in the original problem has the same effect—i.e., *raises* (or leaves unchanged) profit. It would also seem that the magnitude of the effect will be small when the points defined by the rows of A are close together.

These conclusions conform to common sense. By aggregating constraints the number of constraints is reduced, and such reduction removes to some extent the limitations on the freedom of action of the decision-maker and, hence, possibly increases his profit. On the other hand, an aggregation of activities, and a reduction in their number, removes to some extent the alternative means of making profit, and so profit would be expected to be reduced.

We must now raise the question of who is doing the simplification and why. Suppose, first, that the decision-maker of the original linear programming problem is also the simplifier, or at least is the director of the man who is simplifying, and he is doing the simplification in order to avoid costs of detail. Now if the constraints of this original problem are given by nature, then of course they cannot be changed in fact, and this decision-maker does not really have the option of "aggregating his constraints." He does, however, have the option of aggregating his activities, which are under his own control, and he may choose to do so, advisedly accepting a lower value of z that will be more than offset by a still lower cost of detail (arising from economies of not having to fuss with so many

[13] Subject to the qualifications expressed in footnote 11 and the fact that one typically does not know a priori where the true frontier is.

detailed decisions). We do not pursue here the explicit theory of such costs. But given the degree of detail (e.g., the integer J), the problem of how to do the aggregating of activities (columns of A) is relevant to this decision-maker.

If there is an economically relevant dual problem, then the decision-maker associated with that problem will have control over the *rows* of A and not the columns.[14]

In the rectangular game problem the implications of the suggested simplifications are straightforward. The aggregation of the rows of A implies that the maximizing player is restricted in his choice of strategies in such a way that he must select certain elements of the strategy vector in prior fixed ratios. It is easy to show that such a restriction is equivalent to the player's using a combination in place of some individual rows to get an "aggregate" solution to the problem, and then disaggregating the solution in the prescribed a priori manner. It would be expected that such a procedure would lower the value of the game to the maximizing player, and this conclusion indeed follows from the reciprocal relationship between the value of the game and the profit of the primal programming problem—as shown in (4.5c)—along with the previous conclusion that the aggregation of the rows of A raises the profit. By symmetrical considerations, an aggregation of columns of A by the minimizing player—or an associated restriction on his strategies—would raise the value of the game and lower profit of the primal programming problem.

The "simplifier" could be an impartial investigator who was interested in determining the solution point of either of the three problems. His motive for simplifying would be to attain greater manageability and clarity, even at the cost of attaining only an approximate solution rather than the true one, and his loss would depend in some sense on the "distance" between the two solutions, or "bias." It is assumed in this chapter that such an investigator accepts as a measure of this distance the value of the objective function of the problem he is considering. But note he must still decide whether this problem is one of the programming problems or the game. The measures of the two are different, and equal arithmetic changes in one measure do not imply equal arithmetic changes in the other.

From this point on, therefore, we shall adopt the point of view of an investigator interested in the primal programming problem and accept the profit z as the relevant measure. We shall allow aggregations over both rows and columns of A in defining the aggregated matrix $\bar{A}$, and the loss function will be the absolute value of the difference between the true profit,

---

[14] It is not apparent that there will always be an economically relevant dual problem.

when matrix A is used, and the assumed profit, when $\bar{A}$ is used, that is, say,

(4.7) $$L = \delta z = |z(A) - z(\bar{A})| \ .$$

Sometimes the term *micro-programming* will be used to describe the use of the original matrix A in solving the linear programming problem, while the short-cut use of the aggregated matrix $\bar{A}$ will be described as *macro-programming*.

Minimal Distance Clustering

The reader who has followed us this far will probably perceive the direction we are going. We are going to suggest some sort of cluster analysis based on a partition of points, such as those that are plotted in Figure 10, so that points that are "near" to each other are placed in the same cluster, and then construct an aggregated matrix $\bar{A}$ associated with such a partition. To derive the details of a good procedure is, however, not a trivial matter; our explorations suggest that there is room for continued research in this field.

A preliminary remark should be made. The search for an optimal partition is a relevant problem only if the linear program has *not* already been solved; if it has, a trivial partition is immediately available at zero simplification cost. This partition divides the A matrix into four submatrices based on a division of its rows and columns into two subsets each; the rows are divided into effective and ineffective constraints; the columns are divided into effective and ineffective activities. This partition and the weights to be used in combining the effective rows and columns are provided by the solution to the linear programming problem; the weights for the remaining rows and columns do not matter. In other words, an activity like $\hat{P}$ in Figure 10 is itself an aggregate column, and a very fine optimal one. If we know what it is, let's close shop.

That observation suggests another. Let's not suggest any aggregation procedure that is more costly than the solution of the detailed linear programming problem, unless we are going to use the procedure for a series of problems that we believe have "similar structure" in some sense. A procedure is required that is relatively simple.

The analysis of Figure 10 suggests that distances within subsets created by an aggregation partition are significant in assessing the effect of aggregations on profit. Squared distances may be defended because of their symmetry with respect to positive and negative direction, their mathematical convenience, and their common usage. We are thus led to consider the squared-distance criterion stated on page 3, or one of its variants, and to establish subsets with small distances within.

The analysis of Figure 10 also indicated that when aggregation was one-way (e.g., only activities being merged), the direction parallel to the 45° ray was of significance in that it was the distances in this particular direction that had the effects observed. It may be possible to achieve considerable simplification of the problem by considering the distances, not in the M-space, but in the one-dimensional space of this ray by projecting the points on it and considering the projected points. This projection is a simple operation; the coordinate of a projected point is the arithmetic mean of the original coordinates. We would be led then to consider a partition that minimizes the quantity

(4.8)
$$D_{\bar{a}} = \sum_{j=1}^{N} (\bar{a}_j - \bar{\bar{a}}_j)^2 ,$$

where $\bar{a}_j$ is the simple arithmetic mean of a_{ij} for column j and $\bar{\bar{a}}_j$ denotes the mean of the $\bar{a}$'s that are assigned to the same subset as is $\bar{a}_j$. The problem is then reduced to a one-dimensional cluster analysis problem of a simple type. For one-way aggregations this possibility is quite attractive; to our knowledge it has not been experimented with.[15]

For two-way aggregations the criterion (4.8) is not adequate. We need also a similar measure, taken again with respect to a different set of points—i.e., those representing the rows, rather than columns, of A. In a case of corresponding, or partially corresponding, row-column aggregation, we would need to effect some sort of compromise between the partitions suggested by the two different criteria, as is done in the lock-step progressive merger procedure. I have not pursued this possibility further, but it is worth further pursuit.[16] Another possibility, and the one we have pursued, is to take the sum of the squared distances in the M-space. This has the desirable property of being the same scalar quantity as the sum of squared distances in the other space, the N-space, and is given by

(4.9)
$$D_a = \mathrm{tr}\,AA' - \mathrm{tr}\,\bar{A}\bar{I}_J\bar{A}'\bar{I}_F ,$$

where $\bar{I}_J$ and $\bar{I}_F$ are diagonal matrices of order J and F, respectively, whose diagonal elements contain the numbers of rows (or columns) in a subset of a partition. Partitions would be sought that make D_a small.

[15] My efforts have been concentrated on two-way problems, of which an example is discussed in section 2.

[16] In some situations one would consider the sum of two criteria such as (4.8), one defined over a partition of rows, the other over a partition of columns. These are essentially the "row effects" and the "column effects" of the classical analysis of variance decomposition of A. In cases where the interaction term of this decomposition is small, the sum of the row and column terms alone would approximate the sum of squared distances within sets to be defined next.

The criterion D_a seems reasonable when we look at the rectangular game problem, but somewhat less reasonable when we look at the primal linear programming problem, where the objective is to maximize profit, which is the reciprocal of the value of the game. It seems probable that a better measure for the programming problem is attainable when reciprocals of the cost coefficients are used, rather than the coefficients themselves. The reason is the following. Let $\hat{z}$ denote the profit under micro-programming and $\bar{z}$ the profit under macro-programming. Let the absolute aggregation error be

(4.10) $$\delta z = |\hat{z} - \bar{z}| .$$

It is conjectured that an upper bound for δz is the largest range of the reciprocals of the cost coefficients within any one submatrix of A created by the partitions. That is, let

(4.11) $$r_{gi} = 1/a_{gi} ,$$

and let f designate one subset of rows, and k one subset of columns of A, so the pair (f, k) designates one submatrix. Then we conjecture

(4.12) $$\delta z \leq \max_{f, k}[(r_{gi} - r_{hj})|g, h \,\epsilon\, f; i, j \,\epsilon\, k] ,$$

where it is understood that the maximization is over all submatrices.[17] This conjecture suggests that a distance metric in terms of reciprocals may be more efficacious in preventing large biases than one in terms of the original cost coefficients themselves. It is therefore suggested that the criterion

(4.13) $$D_r = \mathrm{tr}RR' - \mathrm{tr}\bar{R}\bar{I}_J\bar{R}'\bar{I}_F ,$$

where R is the matrix of detailed reciprocals and $\bar{R}$ is defined analogously to $\bar{A}$ as a convex combination of R, is preferable to D_a as given by (4.9). Then we seek to choose the partitions such that D_r is a minimum. This procedure may be referred to as the "method of cost reciprocals," while use of D_a may be called the "method of cost coefficients." A numerical test of the two methods is included in the example of section 2.

---

[17] The conjecture is obviously true for the special case where $\hat{z}$ and $\bar{z}$ are each strictly positive-convex combinations of only one and the same submatrix of the partitions. For then we have

$$\delta z = |\hat{z} - \bar{z}| = |1/\hat{a} - 1/\bar{a}| \leq 1/\min(a_{gi}) - 1/\max(a_{gi}) ,$$

where $\hat{a}$ and $\bar{a}$ are the values of the micro-game and macro-game respectively and min and max are over elements within the submatrix referred to.

The Matter of Weights

Suppose now that in one way or another a partition of the cost matrix A has been decided on. The question of settling on a particular method of weighting the elements of A for construction of the aggregate matrix $\bar{A}$, which is to be used in the macro-programming, must be determined. This has been deliberately left vague so far; on page 75, above, we defined an aggregate activity as simply being "some convex combination of the original column vectors of a subset" without specific definition of the weights to be used in such a combination.

The question is similar to that discussed with prediction models, only now we are specifying aggregating weights directly, without deriving them from disaggregating weights. We need to specify two positive diagonal matrices, say V and W, of orders M and N respectively, and then let

$$(4.14) \qquad\qquad \bar{A} = \bar{V}^{-1} T_F V A W T'_J \bar{W}^{-1} ,$$

$$(4.15a) \quad \bar{V} = T_F V T'_F , \qquad\qquad\qquad (4.15b) \quad \bar{W} = T_J W T'_J ,$$

where T_F and T_J are the unitary grouping matrices of (1.5) of sizes F by M and J by N respectively.

The particular selection of weights will depend on the problem. In some situations it will be appropriate to let V and W be the identity matrices, which amounts to taking simple averages of the normalized cost coefficients to construct the aggregate cost coefficients. In many economic contexts, however, this will not be appropriate. Recall that the normalized coefficients were computed from (4.3). The b_i and c_j appearing in the denominator on the right of (4.3) represent original data on resource availabilities and net revenues—that is, represent original information that is lost in the normalization and may indicate relevant weighting. For example, should a row with a large b_i, or a column with a large net revenue c_j, not be given a large weight in determining the aggregate data, when those aggregate data are to be inputs in a profit-maximization problem? Will an unweighted average of normalized cost coefficients not give undue weight to the more restrictive resources and the less efficient activities in the aggregate problem? These considerations will often lead to a decision to use as weights

$$(4.16a) \quad V = B , \qquad\qquad\qquad\qquad (4.16b) \quad W = C ,$$

where B and C have b_i and c_j as diagonal elements. In fact this type of weighting is used in our empirical example in section 2.

2. EXAMPLE: REPRESENTATIVE FIRMS[18]

The Problem As a Linear Program

When an "industry" in economics is regarded as consisting of a large number of firms, it is possible to derive industry behavior as the "summing up" of firm behavior, where the behavior of one firm is determined by the solution of a linear programming problem. For example, industry outputs of various commodities at a certain price constellation may be regarded as the sum of firm outputs, if a commodity is reasonably homogeneous among firms. In order to avoid the high computational costs of solving all the individual linear programming problems for each firm, the suggestion has been made to define strata and compile data for a "representative firm" for each stratum by taking averages of all of the actual firms in the stratum; then solve just one programming problem for each representative firm; then obtain the desired results for the industry by computing suitable weighted sums of the representative firms' solutions.[19] The computational economies will be substantial if the number of strata is a fairly small fraction—say one fifth or less—of the number of firms. The success of the representative-firm method depends on how closely the solution obtained by it approximates the true solution by the long method.

Assume that an industry contains K firms, each of which possesses exactly the same m fixed resources and produces exactly the same n goods, but the amounts of the resources and the net revenues obtainable from the goods differ by firm, as well as the real cost matrices. No change in the problem occurs if we regard the set of K linear programs for the separate firms as one large industry linear program whose data are arrayed as in Table 10 with the A matrix in block-diagonal form with Km and Kn columns. Or the data could be rearranged as in Table 11 by activity and constraints. (In Table 10 the subscripts in parentheses refer to firms; in Table 11 the subscripts refer to constraints and activities, and each of the matrices A_{ij} is a K by K diagonal matrix.)

The representative firm problem may be regarded as a special case of the aggregation problem discussed in the last section with $M = Km$ and $N = Kn$. We restrict the permissible partitions of the large A matrix to consist only of a class which we shall designate *firm-wise:* when the data

[18] I conducted the research underlying this section jointly with Dr. Paul L. Kelley of Kansas State University, with the assistance of James Letourneau, Linda Woolf, and Ming Wu, and was supported jointly by the Kansas Agricultural Experiment Station and the National Science Foundation. More details on the subject may be found in Fisher and Kelley [1968].
[19] Hartley [1962] and Day [1963].

TABLE 10. INDUSTRY LINEAR PROGRAMMING PROBLEM WITH DATA GROUPED BY FIRM

$c'_{(1)}$	$c'_{(2)}$	•	•	•	$c'_{(K)}$	
$A_{(1)}$	0	•	•	•	0	$b_{(1)}$
0	$A_{(2)}$	•	•	•	0	$b_{(2)}$
•	•	•	•	•	•	•
0	0	•	•	•	$A_{(K)}$	$b_{(K)}$

TABLE 11. INDUSTRY LINEAR PROGRAMMING PROBLEM WITH DATA GROUPED
BY ACTIVITY AND CONSTRAINT

c'_1	c'_2	•	•	•	c'_n	
A_{11}	A_{12}	•	•	•	A_{1n}	b_1
A_{21}	A_{22}	•	•	•	A_{2n}	b_2
•	•	•	•	•	•	
A_{m1}	A_{m2}	•	•	•	A_{mn}	b_m

are arranged as in Table 11, the partition of the rows and columns must be such that for each A_{ij} the partition of K firms into G strata is the same. More crudely described, we are not going to merge any constraints or activities within any firm; we are just going to merge firms, and by merging two firms we mean to merge every corresponding constraint and activity of the two. With this understanding we can proceed with the suggested minimal-distance clustering to determine the strata, and then average the data to form the data for the representative firms.

Now assume that the A matrix has been normalized by (4.3). We persist in withholding the asterisks from the normalized A for a little while longer.[20] When A has the special structure of Table 11 and the partitions over rows and columns of A have the special "firm-wise" structure described in the last paragraph, the method of cost coefficients leads to the criterion[21]

[20] Recall that the asterisks have also been withheld from the normalized matrix A in (4.9) and from its matrix of reciprocals R in (4.13).

[21] Let T_G denote the unitary grouping matrix of the form of (1.5) of size G by K that defines the firm-wise partitions (firms into strata) over each of the rows and columns of the diagonal matrices A_{ij} in Table 11. Then set

$$(4.18a) \quad T_F = \begin{bmatrix} T_G & & & \\ & \cdot & & \\ & & \cdot & \\ & & & \cdot \\ & & & & T_G \end{bmatrix}, \qquad (4.18b) \quad T_J = \begin{bmatrix} T_G & & & \\ & \cdot & & \\ & & \cdot & \\ & & & \cdot \\ & & & & T_G \end{bmatrix},$$

where T_G is repeated m times in T_F and repeated n times in T_J. (T_F is of size F by M, or Gm by Km, and T_J is of size J by N, or Gn by Kn.) Then with equal weighting $\bar{A}$ in (4.9) becomes

(4.17)
$$D_a = \sum_{i,j,k} \left[a_{ijk}^2 - 1/n_g^2 \Big(\sum_{k \in g} a_{ijk} \Big)^2 \right] ,$$

where i, j, k index resources, goods, and firms, respectively, and where n_g is the number of firms in stratum g. By the same algebra the method of cost reciprocals leads to the criterion

(4.24)
$$D_r = \sum_{i,j,k} \left[r_{ijk}^2 - 1/n_g^2 \Big(\sum_{k \in g} r_{ijk} \Big)^2 \right] ,$$

where r_{ijk} is the reciprocal of a_{ijk}.

While it is undoubtedly feasible to program a computer to select near-optimal partitions based on these criteria, we have found it convenient to use modified criteria that lead to an easy application of our one-way progressive merger procedure and probably are highly correlated with D_a and D_r. If we use n_g rather than n_g^2 in the denominator of the second term of the square brackets in (4.17) and (4.24), we obtain, say,

(4.25)
$$\tilde{D}_a = \sum_{i,j,k} \left[a_{ijk}^2 - 1/n_g \Big(\sum_{k \in g} a_{ijk} \Big)^2 \right] ,$$

(4.26)
$$\tilde{D}_r = \sum_{i,j,k} \left[r_{ijk}^2 - 1/n_g \Big(\sum_{k \in g} r_{ijk} \Big)^2 \right] ,$$

and choose a partition of the K firms into G subsets such that either $\tilde{D}_a$ or $\tilde{D}_r$ is a minimum, depending on which criterion is preferred. This amounts to doing a cluster analysis of K points in mn dimensional space, using the simple Euclidean distance criterion suggested in the first example of Chapter 1, section 2, and placing them in G clusters.[22] Now assume

---

(4.19)
$$\bar{A} = (T_F T_F')^{-1} T_F A T_J' (T_J T_J')^{-1} = [\bar{A}_{ij}] ,$$

where

(4.20)
$$\bar{A}_{ij} = I_G^{-1} T_G A_{ij} T_G' I_G^{-1} ,$$

and where

(4.21)
$$I_G = T_G T_G' .$$

Moreover, I_F and I_J in (4.9) may be represented as

(4.22a) $I_F = T_F T_F' ,$ (4.22b) $I_J = T_J T_J' .$

Then, by substituting (4.19), (4.22a), and (4.22b) into (4.9) and making use of (4.20) and the diagonality of A_{ij} we obtain

(4.23)
$$D_a = \sum_{i,j} [\operatorname{tr} A_{ij} A_{ij}' - \operatorname{tr} I_G^{-2} (T_G \cdot A_{ij} T_G')^2] ,$$

which, after expanding the traces further, becomes equivalent to (4.17).

[22] See Chapter 5, section 3. If mn is much larger than K, as it probably will be, the method of using the symmetric matrix $P'P$ as input instead of P can be used.

that the G strata have been determined and that it is decided to form the aggregates by the method of weighted means of normalized cost coefficients—i.e., the method of combination defined by (4.14), (4.16a), and (4.16b). Now, putting the asterisk back on the normalized A matrix in (4.14), this means that we specify

(4.27) $\bar{A} = (TBT')^{-1}TBA^*CT'(TCT')^{-1}$.

But the normalization procedure of (4.3) implies that

(4.28) $BA^*C = A$.

Hence, from (4.27) and (4.28),

(4.29) $\bar{A} = (TBT')^{-1}TAT'(TCT')^{-1}$,

where A is now the un-normalized cost matrix. The aggregated cost matrix $\bar{A}$ according to this method is then the normalization of the *un-weighted* sum of the *original* un-normalized A matrix. Since the profit solution of a linear programming problem is invariant with respect to normalization of the data of that problem, this method amounts to a prescription to form the representative firms by taking simple averages of the original data of the firms within the strata. Crudely described, the weighted average of the normalized costs is equivalent to the unweighted average of the original costs.

Data and Procedure

As mentioned in Chapter 1, empirical estimates of the effects of aggregation on the solutions of representative firm problems have been made by Abou-el-Dahab [1965], Frick and Andrews [1965], Miller [1967], Sheehy [1964], and Sheehy and McAlexander [1965]. These studies have included some comparisons between different methods. No study, to the present author's knowledge, has attempted to select the strata of firms by a systematic optimization procedure.[23]

In an investigation conducted by Kelley and Knight [1965] detailed data were developed for forty-nine dairy farms in the milkshed of Topeka, Kansas, and linear programming problems were solved for each individual farm. For the present purpose these data were adapted and the matrices reduced by retaining four labor constraints, four land constraints, and special restrictions on the amounts of three crops that could be grown: wheat, soybeans, and alfalfa.[24] The twenty-eight activities retained were production of seven crops—wheat, oats, corn, barley, alfalfa, milo, and

[23] An exploratory experiment was made by Letourneau [1966].

[24] Wheat and soybeans restrictions resulted from government control programs. The alfalfa restriction was introduced after preliminary results indicated that it would furnish more realistic solutions; it is a quota imposed on the basis of either previous alfalfa production or total cropland.

soybeans—each subclassified according to four qualities of land to be used in production.

The severing of these crop-producing activities from the larger set of activities, including milk production and marketing, required the development of some imputed net revenues in cases where the crops were really used by the farm itself. Sometimes imputed elements of the b vector also had to be derived. These modifications were made in order to reduce the size of the problem.

In the case where a farm produced none of a certain crop, the elements of the missing activity column had to be imputed. For example, if the farm had no Class B land it produced no wheat on Class B land. This imputation was made by computing for the missing columns average data from other farms in the same or neighboring size-region category.[25]

Wherever zero elements occurred in the b vector for a farm, a relatively small number (.1) was substituted for the zero, so that normalized cost coefficients could be computed.

After the normalized cost coefficients were computed, it was discovered that on all forty-nine farms the four labor constraint rows and the eight activity columns pertaining to oats and barley were redundant. Redundancy of a row may be defined as domination of the row by a convex combination of other rows—i.e., every normalized cost coefficient in the redundant row is less than or equal to the corresponding, or "parallel" coefficient in the row of the combination. A redundant row is associated with an ineffective constraint. A redundant column may be defined as a column that is dominated by a convex combination of other columns—i.e., every normalized cost coefficient in the column is larger than the corresponding coefficient of the combination. The activity associated with a redundant column is operated at zero level. After elimination of these redundant rows and columns, the cost matrix for each farm was reduced to size 7 by 20, and it also happened that the resulting coefficients (before normalization) were identical for all farms and were either unity or zero.[26] The pattern of these coefficients is shown in Table A16, and the b and c vectors for each farm are shown in Fisher and Kelley [1968, Table A2 and A3].

[25] The way the missing columns are filled out makes no difference in the micro-programming solution for the individual farm, since the zero (or near-zero) entry in the b vector makes the normalized cost coefficient in the artificial column in that row very large in any case, which is sufficient to cause that activity to be used at zero level. The procedure does matter, however, for the macro-programming solutions.

[26] The reduction in the size of the problem accomplished by this technique is striking (the reduced problem gives an A matrix of simpler form, having less than half the number of elements in the former A matrix) and indicates that examination for redundancy is worth the cost of computing normalized coefficients.

The linear programming problem of operating at maximum profit was solved for each of the forty-nine individual farms. The sum of these profits divided by forty-nine is the micro-programming solution on a per-farm basis. The farms were then stratified by three different methods—by the method of cost coefficients, the method of cost reciprocals, and by a conventional size-region classification that was used by Abou-el-Dahab in his study [1965]. These strata are defined in Table A15. In each method the number of strata used was nine.[27] For the method of cost coefficients and the method of cost reciprocals the progressive merger computer routine was used, starting the procedure off with the 49 by 49 symmetric matrix $P'P$, where P is a matrix of size 140 by 49, containing the normalized $a^*_{ij(k)}$, or their reciprocals.[28] Then, for each stratification method representative farms were constructed for each stratum by weighted averaging using the b_i and c_j as weights—i.e., using formula (4.29)—and the linear programming problem solved for each representative farm.

Results and Conclusions

The over-all average profit per farm, when computed as a weighted average of the profits of the nine representative farms for one of the methods of stratification, may be regarded as a macro-programming solution and may be compared with the micro-programming solution, or "true" profit per farm. The macro-solution less the micro-solution is the bias. One may also compute the bias for each representative farm, neglect the algebraic sign, and take a weighted average. This is referred to as the absolute bias. For all weighted averages just mentioned, the weights are the relative frequencies of farms per stratum. These summary results, for each of the three methods of stratification, are shown in Table 12. More detailed results for each method, giving the identification numbers of the individual farms that were assigned to each stratum, the programmed

TABLE 12.   EFFECT OF STRATIFICATION METHOD ON OVER-ALL PROFIT

	Profit per farm[a]		Profit bias per farm[a]	
Stratification method	Via strata	True	Algebraic	Absolute
Cost coefficients	$5,933	$6,028	$− 95	$339
Cost reciprocals	5,956	6,028	− 72	100
Size-region	5,891	6,028	−137	174

[a] Weighted average of strata figures with strata frequencies as weights. True profit is unweighted average of individual micro-programmed farms.

[27] The profits of the individual farms as micro-programmed and their size-region classification are shown in Table A14.

[28] Acknowledgment is due Mr. E. V. Brown of the Department of Mathematics at Kansas State University for programming and other assistance.

profit of the representative farm, the true average profit of the individual
farms, and the bias caused by the macro-programming, are shown in
Tables A11, A12, and A13.[29]

All of the methods gave a negative profit bias, but relatively small ones
percentage-wise—ranging from 1.2 per cent to 3.5 per cent of the true
profit figure. The average absolute biases are higher because there is no
opportunity for the algebraic signs to cancel each other. The method of
cost reciprocals performed the best, as judged by both algebraic and absolute bias. This is in accord with theoretical expectation, based on the previous discussion. The method of cost coefficients managed to come in
second best on the basis of algebraic bias, but the large value of the average absolute bias (the largest for the three methods) suggests that the
cancellation of signs might have been lucky, and that in another test, this
performance might not be repeated. It is not possible to assert that the
evidence of this example indicates any superiority of the method of cost
coefficients over the conventional size-region method. There does seem
to be some evidence to support the superiority of the method of cost
reciprocals.

As can be seen from Table A12, and as was expected, the method of
cost reciprocals segregates more finely the large farms. Of the four largest
farms of the forty-nine in terms of profit three are placed each in a separate stratum of its own. At the other end of the scale, fourteen of the
smaller farms are grouped together. The dispersion in farm numbers per
stratum is less for the other stratification methods, in neither of which are
any farms allotted singly to a stratum.

The representative-firm method has been found by previous investigators to be a feasible method of reducing the computational cost involved
in large programming studies while entailing reasonably small biases in
the solutions. This general finding is confirmed here, where only small
biases result from various methods of choosing nine representative firms
from an original population of forty-nine firms.

Our empirical findings of negative biases are at variance with most previous findings of positive ones. However, most previous investigators
studied response variations in only one commodity, while general profit
response was studied here; nor did we attempt to study changes in price
levels. Further research is needed to clarify the differences in results on
this point.

The way of looking at the representative-firm problem pursued here
leads to another question. If the final objective is a simplified analysis
with smaller matrices and lower computation costs, what about other

---

[29] The results for the size-region strata were obtained by Letourneau [1966].

ways of reducing the industry coefficient matrix besides aggregation over firms? For example, what about aggregation over activities or constraints, possibly within the same firm? The elimination of redundancy is another way. Given the size of the desired reduced matrix, these other ways may attain this size with lower biases than the representative-firm method.

3. CONVENTIONAL OPTIMA

With this title we include economic decision problems where the optimal detailed decisions can be obtained by use of the calculus—that is, where the objective functions are differentiable and have a domain sufficiently large to avoid the occurrence of corner solutions, and also sufficiently small to avoid maximum-maximorum problems. The conventional allocation problems with "smooth" utility contours or production functions are in this class.

Most of these problems could be handled to a satisfactory degree of approximation with linear programming models by using linear functions "piece-wise" as surrogates for the true nonlinear functions. Because, however, these techniques are sometimes cumbersome, and because the smooth quadratic functions are also very simple and beautiful, I have succumbed to the extent of including a brief discussion of them.

The Quadratic Decision Problem

It is now assumed that a decision-proper problem has been reduced to the following form: choose a vector of variables x such that the quadratic criterion function

$$(4.30) \qquad\qquad w = x'a - \tfrac{1}{2}x'Ax$$

is a maximum, where a is a given vector and A is a given symmetric positive semi-definite matrix. This form is assumed to have been derived from an original problem involving an economic model, an objective function, and decision variables in the sense of Chapter 1. The elements of x are, moreover, assumed to be unconstrained variables. If in the original problem there were constraints on the variables, it is assumed that these have now been removed, either by substitution or by the method of Lagrange multipliers. If Lagrange multipliers have been introduced, these are included as elements of x.

This formulation thus embraces the case of an original quadratic utility or objective function, subject to linear constraints, of which there has been much discussion in the literature.[30] The quadratic and linear func-

---

[30] See, for example, Theil [1958] and W. D. Fisher [1962a].

tions postulated must in most cases be regarded as approximations to other functions. In some rather specialized operations research applications, for example, the true functions may be known to be more complex. In more general economic policy-making this is unlikely; if anything, a general quadratic function is probably too complex.

The well-known example of consumer allocation under a quadratic utility function and a linear budget constraint may be placed in this framework in the following way. Let the utility function be represented by

$$(4.31) \qquad\qquad u = q'c - \tfrac{1}{2}q'Dq \; ,$$

where q is the vector of quantities of goods purchased, c is a known vector, and D is a known positive semi-definite Hessian matrix. The consumer is to choose q so as to maximize u subject to the budget constraint

$$(4.32) \qquad\qquad q'p = m \; ,$$

where p is the vector of prices and m is income—both known. Then, after introducing a Lagrange multiplier λ and converting the problem into an unconstrained maximization problem, we have (4.30) with

$$(4.33a)\;\; x = \begin{pmatrix} q \\ \lambda \end{pmatrix}, \qquad (4.33b)\;\; a = \begin{pmatrix} c \\ m \end{pmatrix}, \qquad (4.33c)\;\; A = \begin{pmatrix} D & p \\ p' & 0 \end{pmatrix}.$$

Consider next the example of pricing policy of a seller who is a monopolist in each of a number of markets that may be related in demand. Assume that unlimited quantities of each good may be obtained at zero marginal cost, so that the problem is one of pricing and allocating sales to bring maximum profit.[31] Assume that the set of demand curves facing the monopolist is linear, and given by

$$(4.34) \qquad\qquad q = a - Bp \; ,$$

where p is the vector of prices, q the vector of quantities, and B the matrix of demand slopes of quantity on price. The profit then is maximized if, and only if, prices are fixed so as to maximize the total revenue

$$(4.35) \qquad\qquad r = p'q = p'a - p'Bp \; ,$$

which is of the form of (4.30) when

$$(4.36a)\;\; x = p \; , \qquad\qquad\qquad (4.36b)\;\; A = 2\bar{B} \; ,$$

where $\bar{B}$ is a symmetric version of B obtained by averaging B and its

---

[31] This would be the case if a large surplus of some agricultural commodity were already on hand.

transpose. It is assumed that $\bar{B}$ is positive semi-definite, so the maximum exists.[32]

Consider now the situation where there are additive random disturbances with zero means and known covariance matrix attached to both a quadratic utility function and a set of linear constraints. Then we shall specify that expected utility is to be maximized, and without making the mathematical demonstration we assert that the problem can again be brought into the form of (4.30) after certain additive constants are neglected.[33]

We shall now examine the effects of the decision-maker assuming that the matrix A takes on some simplified form $\tilde{A}$—the precise form to be specified later—while degree of detail is held constant. The relevant cost of simplification then consists of the differential risk as given by (1.15) expressing the difference in risks resulting from the optimal detailed decision d^* and from the simplified decision $\tilde{d}$. In the present context we may say that a detailed optimal decision is

$$(4.37) \qquad d^* = x^* \ ,$$

where x^* is a value of x that maximizes w in (4.30)—it may not be unique because of the possible singularity of A—and that a simplified decision is

$$(4.38) \qquad \tilde{d} = \tilde{x} \ ,$$

where $\tilde{x}$ is a value of x that maximizes w in (4.30) when $\tilde{A}$ is substituted for A. Then from (1.15) simplification cost is

$$(4.39) \qquad c = r(\tilde{d}) - r(d^*) = w(x^*) - w(\tilde{x}) \ .$$

This is the same as (1.16) because cost of detail is held constant. We are now saying that the detailed batch of data X of Chapter 1 is A and the simplified batch of data $\tilde{X}$ is $\tilde{A}$.[34]

By differentiating (4.30) with respect to the vector x and setting the vector derivative equal to the zero vector, we have as a necessary condition on x^* for maximum w

$$(4.40) \qquad Ax^* = a \ ,$$

where A may be singular.

---

[32] If the Slutsky income effect of the "typical" consumer of this market were negligible, then classical utility theory would prescribe a symmetric and positive semi-definite B.

[33] When the expectation operator is applied to w, terms that are linear in the disturbances vanish and terms that are quadratic become functions of the covariance matrix, which is assumed constant and known.

[34] There are some difficulties in implementing this interpretation when A and $\tilde{A}$ have to be estimated in turn from more "original" data. See pages 97–98.

A generalization of a theorem of Theil can handle this case of singular A.

THEOREM 3. When the decision problem is to maximize w in (4.30) an optimal detailed decision x^* and a simplified decision $\tilde{x}$ are given by

(4.41a) $\quad x^* = A^g a$,   (4.41b) $\quad \tilde{x} = \tilde{A}^g a$,

and the cost is given by

(4.42) $\qquad\qquad\qquad c = \frac{1}{2}(x^* - \tilde{x})'A(x^* - \tilde{x})$,

where A^g and $\tilde{A}^g$ are the generalized inverses of A and $\tilde{A}$, respectively.[35]

Simplified Symmetric Matrices

Two general types of simplified matrices $\tilde{A}$ will now be considered. As in previous chapters we shall restrict consideration to simplification functions implying an aggregation-disaggregation sequence, where the disaggregation is partitioned.

As with the input-output matrices, the A matrix of this section is square with row and column indices corresponding. In addition, it is symmetric. It seems reasonable to require corresponding symmetry of the simplification operators by row and by column. So we shall first define a simplified matrix $\tilde{A}$ as was done for the input-output problem and in addition require that S and T be the same matrix. We may as well specify it to be of size J by H, but at this point will not require it to be of the unitary form. So we have

(4.43) $\qquad\qquad\qquad \tilde{A} = T'\bar{A}T$,

where $\bar{A}$ is some matrix of size J by J to be determined. This $\tilde{A}$ is seen to be of *block-homogeneous* form according to Definition 4 on page 29.[36]

To obtain the $\bar{A}$ in (4.43) that is optimal, conditional on a partition, we

---

[35] Proof: In (2.24) of Chapter 2 set $c = k - w$, $Y = x$, $2SCPMT' = a$, $2\bar{C} = A$, $\bar{M} = I$. Then (2.24) is equivalent to (4.30), and the problem of choosing a Y so that c in (2.24) is a minimum when $\bar{C}$ is possibly singular is equivalent to choosing an x so that w in (4.30) is a maximum when A is possibly singular. But the solution to the former problem is given by (2.35); hence in the new symbols (2.35) becomes (4.41a). Likewise, by putting a $\sim$ on A and associating Y^* in (2.35) with $\tilde{x}$, we obtain (4.41b). Then, by substituting (4.30) into (4.39) twice—once for x^* and once for $\tilde{x}$, and using also (4.40), (4.42) is obtained. In Theil's Theorem 3 of [1958] (and its later versions) a nonsingular matrix of the quadratic form of the welfare or preference function is assumed.

[36] Any two rows belonging to the same subset of the row-wise partition are proportional, as are also any two columns belonging to the same subset of the column-wise partition. Hence each block is of rank one.

need a formula analogous to the $\bar{P}$ of Theorem 2 that is given by formula (2.19). This formula is[37]

(4.44) $\bar{A} = TAT'$,

and the value of the associated cost is

(4.45) $c = \frac{1}{2}(x^{*\prime}Ax^* - \bar{x}'\bar{A}\bar{x})$,

where

(4.46) $\bar{x} = \bar{A}^gTAx^*$.

The one-way progressive merger procedure can be used to find an optimal partition over the rows and columns of A, and hence over the columns of x^*. The computational routine is similar to the proportional final demands case run on the Morgenstern matrix in Chapter 3.

Now let us examine the results from (4.44), (4.45), and (4.46) in terms of the decision problem of this section (forgetting about the analogy with the prediction problem that was used in footnote 37 to derive these formulas). We postulated a decision-maker who has control over the variables x, who is faced by the detailed state of the world (a, A), and who desires to maximize the criterion w. In the interest of making simpler decisions he mis-specifies the state of the world as $(a, \tilde{A})$, relative to some optimal partition of A, found by a suggested procedure, and comes out with an aggregated decision $\bar{x}$ (which could be disaggregated to $\hat{x} = T'\bar{x}$).

It is interesting that precisely the same results would be obtained if the decision-maker were to restrict his decisions directly by placing a linear restriction, conditional on a partition, on the decision space of the x, rather than mis-specifying the state of the world. Then the $\bar{A}$ would come out as a by-product. Further research on the aggregation-simplification

[37] To obtain (4.44) note first the correspondence in mathematical structure between the following equations from the prediction problem of Chapters 2 and 3 and certain equations derived in the present section:

(3.15a) $y = Pz$ $\rightarrow$ (4.41a) $x^* = A^g a$

(2.6) $\bar{y} = \bar{P}z$ $\rightarrow$ (4.41b) $\bar{x} = \tilde{A}^g a$

(2.1) $L = (y - \bar{y})'C(y - \bar{y})$ $\rightarrow$ (4.42) $c = \frac{1}{2}(x^* - \bar{x})'A(x^* - \bar{x})$.

If we forget the original economic context momentarily and imagine that our decision variables x are a kind of endogenous variables y, and that A^g is the coefficient matrix P of a kind of reduced form, while the vector a is a vector of *fixed and known* predetermined variables z, we can use the results of the proportional final demands case from Chapter 3. There is an additional peculiarity of the present situation: The A matrix is the matrix of the loss function—the analogue of the C matrix of the prediction model—and this matrix also happens to be the generalized inverse of the coefficient matrix of the reduced form (which is not necessarily the case in the prediction problem).

So the matrix we are looking for, $\bar{A}$, is given by the formula analogous to (3.1a) for $\bar{C}$, namely (4.44), while the analogues of (3.17) and (3.15b) become (4.45) and (4.46).

problem in a decision-theoretic framework may determine the set of correspondences between various types of simplifications on the space of actions, and those on the states of the world for which solutions are invariant, or at least give the same optimal cost. To this investigator it is not obvious that such simple correspondences as that above will always exist.

The second general type of simplified matrices are those in *block-diagonal* form. The simplification function for this class is defined as follows: with respect to some common partition of the rows and columns of the given matrix A, let each block (submatrix) on the main diagonal of A be unrestricted, and require that each off-diagonal block have all zero elements.

This condition may be imposed on the entire matrix A, or on some principal submatrix. For example, in (4.33c) where A is a bordered utility Hessian, block-diagonality could be imposed on the Hessian D alone.

This specification is of interest because it has been used in a number of recent discussions of economic models in the literature. For example, the additivity requirements for exact aggregation of factors of production stated by Nataf [1948] and Solow [1956] are equivalent to a requirement that the Hessian matrix of the production function be block-diagonal, where a subset of the partition of factors is associated with "capital," "labor," etc., and the elements of a subset are different "firms" or "vintages" within these classes.[38] The "two-level CES" production function advanced by Sato [1967] and used in empirical work by Parks [1967] also has this structure. In consumer-demand theory the "utility tree" hypothesis of Strotz [1957, 1959] and Gorman [1959a] postulates that a relevant utility function has a block-diagonal Hessian, which enables the consumer to allocate his expenditure in a two-stage maximization procedure. This postulate is made in the empirical work on demand by Barten [1964], Barten and Turnovsky [1966], and Theil [1967, Ch. 7].[39] The dynamic multi-sectoral model of Simon and Ando [1961] uses an "almost block-diagonal" matrix.

How does one describe the "degree of detail" of a block-diagonal matrix? The number of subsets of the partition seems to measure the *severity* of the restriction, rather than the degree of detail allowed. The specification of only one subset amounts to no restriction at all: the one "diagonal block" is the entire matrix; while at the other extreme the speci-

---

[38] These rather stringent aggregation conditions have been weakened by F. M. Fisher [1965] and Stigum [1967] by imposing marginal equilibrium conditions on some of the factors.

[39] The work of Frisch [1959] and Houthakker [1960] is based on the postulate that the utility Hessian is pure-diagonal.

fication of H subsets over row and column indices (i.e., element-wise partitions) requires a diagonal matrix. This behavior is inverse to that of the block-homogeneous matrix, where the numbers of subsets is associated with degrees of freedom from restrictions. Moreover, for a given number of subsets of the block-diagonal matrix, sets of equal size involve a more severe restriction—in terms of number of elements specified to be zero—than sets of unequal size.[40]

The block-diagonal form, broadly speaking, is an idealization of the notion of independence between sectors. The sectors themselves can be extremely large and complex and require further decomposition or simplification. The block-homogeneous form, on the other hand, is an idealization of the notion of simplicity or homogeneity of sectors and of the relationships between sectors.

Relation to Separability Concepts

It seems worth while to make a short digression to point out the relationships between the simplified symmetric matrices suggested here and the various definitions of separable function that have appeared in the literature. Proofs of the assertions to be made are given in Appendix E.

Let z be a twice-differentiable function of H variables x_1 to x_H. This may be thought of as a utility function, or a production function. Let z_i denote $\partial z/\partial x_i$. Say that the variables x_i and x_j are *neutral with*[41] the variable x_k if the marginal rate of substitution between x_i and x_j does not depend on x_k, that is if

$$(4.47) \qquad \frac{\partial(z_i/z_j)}{\partial x_k} = 0 \ .$$

Now partition the H variables into J subsets, where J is at least three. Following Strotz [1959] and Goldman and Uzawa [1964], we shall say that the function z is *weakly separable* with respect to the partition if every pair of variables within the same subset is neutral with any variable not in that subset.[42] It turns out that the Hessian matrix of a weakly separable function may be expressed as the sum of a block-homogeneous matrix and a block-diagonal matrix. A schematic drawing of such a matrix is shown in panel A of Figure 11. If, moreover, the function z is quadratic,

[40] While this trait does not seem to be possessed by the block-homogeneous matrix, we have not made a careful investigation of this question. The relevant description of "degree of detail" will depend on an investigation of the ways that costs vary with respect to alternative descriptions.

[41] This term is suggested by the "neutral want association" of Pearce [1964].

[42] It has been shown by Goldman and Uzawa [1964] that this definition is equivalent to "separable" as used by Leontief [1947a, 1947b] and Sono [1961]. Recently a more general notion of separability has been suggested by Gorman [1967b].

FIGURE 11. HESSIAN MATRICES FOR SEPARABLE FUNCTIONS

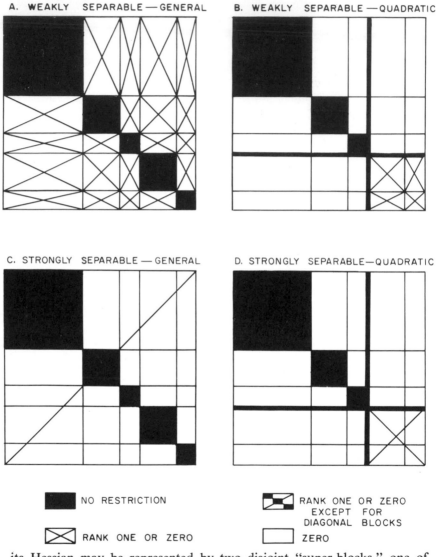

A. WEAKLY SEPARABLE — GENERAL

B. WEAKLY SEPARABLE — QUADRATIC

C. STRONGLY SEPARABLE — GENERAL

D. STRONGLY SEPARABLE — QUADRATIC

NO RESTRICTION

RANK ONE OR ZERO

RANK ONE OR ZERO
EXCEPT FOR
DIAGONAL BLOCKS

ZERO

its Hessian may be represented by two disjoint "super-blocks," one of which is block-diagonal and one of which is block-homogeneous. Either super-block may be null. An example of such a matrix, when one super-block contains three sets and the other two, is shown in panel B of Figure 11.

We shall say, following Strotz [1959, p. 482], that the function z is *strongly separable* with respect to the partition, if every pair of variables, whether members of the pair belong to the same subset or not, is neutral with any third variable belonging to still a different subset. It has been shown[43] that this definition is equivalent to requiring that z be in the form

(4.48) $$z = f [v^1(x_1) + v^2(x_2) + \ldots + v^J(x_J)] \; ,$$

where x_1 to x_J are vectors associated with subsets of the partition; that is, that after some monotonic transformation the function z be representable as an additive function of branch functions. It turns out that the Hessian of a strongly separable function is representable as the sum of a block-diagonal matrix and a matrix having rank one or zero. Such a matrix is shown in panel C of Figure 11. If, in addition, the function f is quadratic, its Hessian takes the form of panel D in Figure 11, where each super-block is either block-diagonal or of rank one or zero, and where either super-block may be null.

Following Pearce [1961a, 1964] and Goldman and Uzawa [1964], we define the function f as *Pearce-separable* with respect to the partition if any pair of variables within the same subset is neutral with any third variable, whether belonging to that subset or not.[44] It turns out that the Hessian in this case may be represented as the sum of a block-homogeneous matrix, and a purely diagonal matrix. Again, in the quadratic case, a division into two divisions, being either block-homogeneous or purely diagonal, takes place. This case would look like panels A and B of Figure 11 if the black squares represented only individual elements, the remainder of the blocks on the main diagonal being of rank one or zero. The empirical work of Pearce is based on this model without the quadratic restriction.

Problems of Implementation

I have not yet conducted empirical work on optimal simplification of models of the type discussed in this section that is on a scale sufficiently interesting to warrant inclusion in this book. Some problems must be overcome before such work can be accomplished.

It has been assumed that the input to the simplification problem is a matrix A, the "detailed data," and that such a matrix is in the hands of the investigator. But what is this matrix? In the case of consumer demand, for example, it is the complete Hessian, or bordered Hessian, of the utility function of some "typical" consumer, or some matrix approximating it. In the case of the monopolist it is a matrix giving all price and cross-price

[43] Gorman [1959], Strotz [1959], and Goldman and Uzawa [1964].

[44] Another way of expressing this definition is to require that the function be weakly separable with respect to the original partition, and also strongly separable with respect to the element-wise partition within each subset of the first partition.

elasticities of demand for a reasonably large number of goods. In the production function case the matrix is supposed to show all pair-wise rates of factor substitution. And so on. By assuming that such information is available we have side-stepped the question of how it is to be obtained.

In fact such parameters must be estimated by econometric means. And the truth is that in many practical situations there are not enough data to determine unique estimates of the many parameters postulated, a dilemma which has prompted comment by many researchers. Indeed, it is this dilemma that has led to the use of hypotheses such as block-diagonality of the Hessian as maintained hypotheses, which cut down on the number of parameters to be estimated. A question arising with such formulations is whether the investigator really has firm enough grounds to select one particular partition for his "maintained hypothesis," or whether he might not let the data help him decide on such a partition.

Suppose one wants to partition a set of thirty consumer goods, and has twenty degrees of freedom. In principle, one can still choose among partitions of the goods into five subsets according to the criterion of minimizing a cost function. One will find, however, that one is involved with a singular A matrix and its generalized inverse. While our formulas have been written to accommodate such matrices, our computational procedures have not attained this stage. The revision formulas for the progressive step-wise procedures use the assumption of nonsingular M and C matrices.[45]

This is admittedly a limitation of our work that must be overcome. When the matrices to be dealt with are very large, they will approach singularity, and even if they are technically nonsingular, they are essentially singular when probable errors are considered.[46]

There is still the possibility that by use of cross-section data with many degrees of freedom many of the difficulties referred to in the preceding paragraphs may be overcome. The studies of deJanvry [1966] and Kuznets, deJanvry, and Bieri [1967] on measurement of demand parameters by use of cross-section data are extremely interesting starts in this direction. They may even provide enough data to estimate separability partitions without the need to make arbitrary prior assumptions.

---

[45] See page 116.

[46] In Chapter 3 it will be recalled that we had to make an artificial change of one element in order to prevent a certain M matrix of size 18 by 18 from being singular. The impressive appearance of large input-output tables often gives a false impression of voluminous information. Given the techniques often used to estimate many cells of these tables—by ratios of other cells, etc.—the complete tables are closer to singularity than many researchers would care to admit.

5

□

A CLUSTERING METHOD

1. THE PROBLEM

The problem to be considered in this chapter may be crudely described
as that of finding an optimal or near-optimal partition, or system of
clustering a given set of points in a space of many dimensions, such that
a certain quadratic distance criterion is minimized. It has some relationships with "cluster analysis" as this term has come to be known in the
literature of a number of scientific fields. In some of the discussion in previous chapters this problem was referred to as the "second stage" in a
problem of optimal simplification, the first stage of which was to find
certain "condensed points" or "centers," for any given partition.

More specifically, let P, a matrix of size G by H, be given, and also two
symmetric positive definite matrices: C, of size G by G, and M, of size H
by H. Let S and T be two grouping matrices of the unitary type defined by
(1.5), but not necessarily of the same size nor associated with the same
partition. S is of size F by G, and T of size J by H where $F \leq G$ and $J \leq H$.
The general two-way problem is to choose the two partitions for S and T
so that the cost

(5.1) $$c = \operatorname{tr} CPMP' - \operatorname{tr} \bar{C}\bar{P}\bar{M}\bar{P}'$$

is a minimum, where

(5.2a) $\bar{C} = SCS'$,   (5.2b) $\bar{M} = TMT'$,

(5.3) $$\bar{P} = \bar{C}^{-1}SCPMT'\bar{M}^{-1} .$$

The integers F and J are given. There may be a series of them given.

The matrix P may be imagined to represent H points in G-dimensional
space. The M and C matrices may be regarded as weighting matrices,
with M defining a system of weighting the points and their interactions,

and C defining the distance metric in the G-space. The matrices with bars may be thought of as aggregated or reduced matrices.

To my knowledge, a computer routine for this general problem is not available. Routines for certain special cases will be described.

A special case of the above problem is the *one-way* problem, where either S or T is the identity matrix. Say that S is the identity matrix, and that C is also.[1] Then the original problem is specialized to the following one: choose a partition for T so that

$$(5.4) \qquad c = \operatorname{tr} PMP' - \operatorname{tr} \bar{P} \bar{M} \bar{P}'$$

is a minimum, where $\bar{M}$ is the same as before, and where now

$$(5.5) \qquad \bar{P} = PMT' \bar{M}^{-1} .$$

We may now speak of J "clusters" of points determined by the subsets of the partition, and also the columns of $\bar{P}$ as "condensed" points, with one condensed point associated with each cluster. However, the coordinates of the condensed points may depend on coordinates of points outside their own cluster, and may even lie outside of the convex hull of their own cluster. This is so because M may be a nondiagonal matrix.[2]

When, in addition to the assumptions already made, M is the identity matrix, the present problem becomes essentially equivalent to that de-scribed as *cluster analysis* in many disciplines other than economics, ex-cept that the criterion used for clustering may not be the same, and indeed varies widely among different investigators.[3] The condensed points repre-

---

[1] The handling of the problem would be completely the same, after transposition of the matrices with no change in the traces, if $T = I$ instead of S. The setting of $C = I$ is justified by the discussion on pages 36–37, in which it was shown that if C were not equal to I, a certain nonsingular transformation could be made leading to a new prob-lem in which $C = I$.

[2] An example of this occurrence is the following. Let

$$p = (p_1\, p_2\, p_3) \ , \qquad M = \begin{pmatrix} 1 & 0 & r \\ 0 & 1 & 0 \\ r & 0 & 1 \end{pmatrix} , \qquad T = \begin{pmatrix} 1 & 1 & 0 \\ 0 & 0 & 1 \end{pmatrix} , \qquad p_1 \neq p_2 \ , \qquad 0 < r < 1 \ .$$

Then

$$\bar{M} = \begin{pmatrix} 2 & r \\ r & 1 \end{pmatrix} , \qquad \bar{P} = (\bar{p}_{12}\, \bar{p}_3) = \left(\frac{p_1(1 - r^2) + p_2}{2 - r^2} \quad p_3 + \frac{r(p_1 - p_2)}{2 - r^2} \right) .$$

That is, the first condensed point $\bar{p}_{12}$ is a convex combination of the points of its cluster, p_1 and p_2, but the second condensed point $\bar{p}_3$ is not; it lies outside its "cluster," the original p_3.

[3] A comprehensive survey of these methods is given by Ball [1965]. In this case where $M = I$ our one-way procedure to be described below becomes equivalent to that of Ward [1963], except that Ward apparently runs only one chain. It is also very similar to the "Step-wise Clustering Method I" of King [1967], except that King's pair-wise correlation criterion is slightly different from ours. When P is a vector and M is block-

sented by $\bar{P}$ are now centers of gravity of their clusters, and cost is now the sum of moments of inertia around these centers of gravity.[4] We seek J clusters, such that this sum of moments is a minimum. The first numerical example of Chapter 1 illustrates this special case.

What we call the lockstep problem is the case where in (5.2) and (5.3) S and T involve the same partition—indeed are identical—and where P is square.

As stated, J may be a single integer or a series of integers. Typically, the investigator will want to try out a number of different J's and will specify a series.

Another basic distinction may be made in the original problem between two types: unrestricted and restricted. By *unrestricted* is meant that no restrictions or side conditions are imposed on the partitions allowed. By *restricted* is meant that such conditions are imposed a priori on the basis of previous knowledge, theory, or for convenience. The most convenient way of imposing such conditions is by means of specifying forbidden merger pairs—that is, listing pairs of points that are forbidden to be in the same subset of a partition.

2. SIMPLE CASES

For unrestricted problems where the points lie in only one or two dimensions and $M = I$, reasonably good solutions can be attained by plotting the points and determining the boundaries of the sets of the desired partition by visual inspection. The boundaries may be placed where the data are sparse. This method cannot be so readily applied where the distribution of the points is irregular, with sparse regions nonconformable to the pattern of boundaries required, but often tolerably good results are attainable. In some cases where the number of subsets J is not too large a method proposed by Dalenius [1950, 1957] may be used, which is based on the principle that for a continuous frequency distribution minimal sums of squares within sets is attained by placing points of division equidistant from the means of adjacent sets.[5]

---

diagonal, the present method appears to have a close resemblance to one described by Bottenberg and Christal [1961]. A method of splitting sets instead of merging them and using a squared error threshold concept has been used by Morgan and Sonquist [1963]. In many examples of cluster analysis the correlation matrix, or similarity matrix, used may be regarded as a normalized version of our symmetric $P'P$. A brief survey of studies in disciplines other than economics where cluster analysis is used is given in Chapter 6.

[4] For example, in footnote 2 set $r = 0$. Then $\bar{p}_{12}$ is the simple average of p_1 and p_2, and $\bar{p}_3 = p_3$.

[5] Dalenius has developed an iterative procedure for accomplishing this which will work in simple, well-behaved cases—e.g., where in the 2-set problem there is no extreme tri-modality of the frequency distribution. See W. D. Fisher [1958b, footnote 10].

Some small problems, restricted and unrestricted, are amenable to solution by complete enumeration of all possible partitions and computation of the c values. If the problems are small enough, this can be done by hand computation.[6]

One soon needs a computer, and even with a computer the task of obtaining a guaranteed optimal partition becomes infeasible with problems of realistic size. For the Lake Michigan problem, for example, it was possible, by exploiting the special restrictions of that problem, for a high-speed computer of the 1956 vintage to obtain the solution in 3 minutes, but had these restrictions not been present it is estimated that it would have required the same computer 280 years to compare, one by one, the 3 trillion or so possible partitions of the 96 elements into 4 subsets.[7] When one goes into a larger number of dimensions the numbers become greater yet. The number of possible partitions of n distinct elements into m subsets is given by Stirling's number of the second kind; for moderate to large n it can be approximated by $(m^{n-1} - 1)$.[8] To make further progress it seems that the requirement of obtaining a strictly optimal partition must be dropped and that one must settle for a near-optimal partition. This is the approach that has been taken here, as well as by others. The question of the proximity of the near-optimal solution to the optimal one is discussed in section 4.

3. PROGRESSIVE MERGER PROCEDURE

A procedure for finding a near-optimal partition in the one-way and lockstep cases when C and M are nonsingular will now be briefly described. Proofs of the lemmas used and more detailed outlines suitable for computer programming are given in Appendix G. The procedure is discussed and appraised in section 4.

The procedure is analogous to a step-wise multiple regression method where a large number of variables are used as regressors and then withdrawn one by one in such a manner that at each stage the increased residual variance of the dependent variable is least. Here condensed points are substituted for detailed points, merging two points at a time until a desired number of clusters or a desired level of cost is attained. As with the

---

[6] In [1953] I reported a numerical example of a one-dimensional problem where H was 19, J ranging from 1 to 4, which would have been beyond the scope of hand computation had not the large number of side conditions on permissible partitions reduced the number of partitions enumerated to 220.

[7] See W. D. Fisher [1958b, sec. 4]. The computer program mentioned could obtain an optimal partition for the case of $G = 1$, $H = 200$, $J = 10$, M diagonal in 14 minutes.

[8] See also the discussion in King [1967].

step-wise regression, it cannot be guaranteed that the terminal solution is the true optimal one; however, evidence will be offered that it comes close to it.

The One-way Case

The givens are P, M or M^{-1}, and the terminal number of subsets J. A partition of the columns of P into J subsets is desired and an associated $\bar{P}$ as defined by (5.5) so that cost c as given by (5.4) is a minimum. Consider first all possible partitions that involve putting two columns of P together and leaving all other columns single. The T matrix associated with such a partition is then the $H - 1$ by H matrix

$$(5.6) \qquad T_1 = \begin{pmatrix} 1 & 1 & 0 \\ 0 & 0 & I_{H-2} \end{pmatrix},$$

where the columns of P and the associated rows and columns of M have been permuted so that the rows and columns to be merged are the first two.

The cost is computed for each possible merged pair by means of formula (5.4). When we move from stage to stage the additional cost is called the *consequence* of the merger. It is shown in Appendix G that the consequence dc_{ij} of merging column p_i with p_j of P is given by

$$(5.7) \qquad dc_{ij} = \frac{d_{ij}}{m^{ii} + m^{jj} - 2m^{ij}} = \frac{\det M}{\det \bar{M}} d_{ij},$$

where

$$(5.8) \qquad d_{ij} = (p_i - p_j)'(p_i - p_j),$$

and where m^{ij} denotes an element of the inverse of M. A pair (i, j) is then chosen for which the consequence is as low as possible.

Then, with respect to the particular partition corresponding with the chosen pair, the $\bar{M}^{-1}$ and $\bar{P}$ matrices are computed. It is shown in Appendix G that these computations may be accomplished by the following additive revisions of the original P and M^{-1} matrices:

$$(5.9) \qquad \bar{p}_j = p_j - \frac{(m^{1j} - m^{2j})(p_1 - p_2)}{m^{11} + m^{22} - 2m^{12}} \text{ for } j = 2, \ldots, H,$$

$$(5.10) \qquad \overline{m}^{ij} = m^{ij} - \frac{(m^{i1} - m^{i2})(m^{1j} - m^{2j})}{m^{11} + m^{22} - 2m^{12}} \text{ for } i, j, = 2, \ldots, H,$$

where indices 1 and 2 denote the two points merged, and where the numbering of the revised points begins with 2. A record is kept of which points in terms of the original indices were merged and the resulting value of the cost c.

Now one acts as if the revised P and M^{-1} matrices were the original matrices of a new problem, with the new P of size G by $H-1$ and the M^{-1} of size $H-1$ by $H-1$. One repeats the procedure of merging two columns of the new P, thus reducing them to $H-2$ in number.

Denote by *stage K* the stage of the procedure when P has K columns and M is a K by K matrix, and where K runs from H down to $J+1$. One does a merger for each stage, applying formulas (5.7), (5.9), and (5.10), where P and M denote those matrices at the beginning of the stage, and $\bar{P}$ and $\bar{M}$ denote the matrices after merger, and where the range of i and j is up to K. At the conclusion of the last stage the $\bar{P}$ matrix is size G by J and the $\bar{M}$ matrix is size J by J. The procedure has developed a sequence of partitions of the original points, each partition being a subpartition of the following one, and a sequence of c values, one c associated with each partition. Either of these two sequences (or the pair) will be called a *chain*. The last partition will be called a *chained partition of order J*.

It is known that a chained partition of order J may not be an optimal partition of order J. Experience indicates that for J's that seem to be relevant to practical problems, a chain defined as in the preceding paragraph will contain some chained partitions that are optimal and some that are not, but whose c values differ by a small percentage from the c values of the corresponding optimal partitions. Experience also indicates that if additional chains are computed, starting with a different pair of points than the pair used for the first chain, different partitions will be found for some J's.[9]

The procedure therefore continues as follows. At some stage specified in advance, called the *branch-off point*, start a new chain or *branch* with a new pair of points whose merger entails a cost equal to or only slightly greater than the first cost. Form this new chain according to the same rules as those given above. Continue to form new chains until either (1) some pre-assigned number of chains has been run, or (2) the first cost term in a new chain would exceed some preassigned threshold.

Then, over the set of chained partitions of order J that have been found, select one that has a minimum c value. This chained partition is deemed a satisfactory approximation to the desired optimal partition.[10]

This procedure was used on the Goldberger reduced-form example of Chapter 2 and on the proportional final demands case of the partitioning of the input-output example in Chapter 3.

When M is diagonal, formulas (5.7), (5.9), and (5.10) take on the simpler forms:

[9] See the discussion of section 4.
[10] The program was written by L. A. Cammack and Jeanne Sebaugh of the Department of Mathematics at Kansas State University.

$$(5.11) \qquad dc_{ij} = \frac{m_{ii}m_{jj}}{m_{ii} + m_{jj}} d_{ij} \ ,$$

$$(5.12a) \quad \bar{p}_2 = \frac{m_{11}p_1 + m_{22}p_2}{m_{11} + m_{22}} \ , \qquad\qquad (5.12b) \quad \bar{p}_j = p_j \text{ for } j \geq 3 \ ,$$

$$(5.13a) \quad \overline{m}^{22} = \frac{m^{11}m^{22}}{m^{11} + m^{22}} \ , \qquad\qquad (5.13b) \quad \overline{m}^{jj} = m^{jj} \text{ for } j \geq 3 \ .$$

Note that these relationships, along with $\overline{m}^{22} = 1/\overline{m}_{22}$, imply

$$(5.14) \qquad \overline{m}_{22} = m_{11} + m_{22} \ .$$

This is the familiar "weighted center of gravity" case, where the aggregation procedure within any cluster is independent of what goes on in other clusters, where all centers lie within the convex hull of their respective clusters at all stages, and where cost is a weighted sum of moments of inertia. One may, of course start out with $M = I$, which is a simple unweighted problem, but in the course of the progressive stages weights would build up by the clusters acquiring more points, and the diagonal elements of the M matrix would acquire larger positive values.

Symmetric Input

With a slight modification of the input arrangements the procedure described above can be used to handle cluster analysis problems where the original data are in the form of symmetric matrices representing "moments," "correlations," or "distances" between pairs of points or variables, rather than a matrix representing coordinates of these points in some space. Consider the matrix $P'P$. If momentarily we think of the rows of P as "observations" and the columns of P as "variables," this symmetric matrix is a matrix of second moments of the "variables" around zero. If each variable is normalized so that its observed mean is zero (by expressing original observations as deviations from the original observed mean) and scaled so that its sum of squares is unity, then it can be seen that $P'P$ is a matrix of correlation coefficients.[11] Going back now to our geometric concept of the columns of P as points, and the rows as dimensions, it is seen that the suggested normalization has placed each point at a distance of unity from the origin—that is, all normalized points lie on the unit hypersphere.[12] Then we may speak of the typical element of

[11] If the words "tests" and "individuals" are used to replace "points" and "dimensions" respectively, we have the correlation matrix that is usually used as the starting point for factor analysis in psychology.

[12] This last sentence would still be true if the columns of P had been scaled so that the sum of squares of all elements were unity *without* first taking deviations from means. Note that the requirement of means zero imposes a linear condition on the points so that they have to lie in a space of dimensionality $G - 1$ instead of G.

$P'P$—call it r_{ij}—as the correlation coefficient between point i and point j and also as the cosine of the angle at the origin θ_{ij} formed by the rays from the two points. This last conclusion follows from trigonometry and from the relation

$$(5.15) \qquad r_{ij} = \sum_{h=1}^{G} p_{hi}p_{hj} = \cos \theta_{ij} \ .$$

For a high pair-wise correlation the angle θ is small, and the distance between the two points is small. It is not difficult to show that our one-way optimal partitioning problem when $M = I$ is equivalent to that of placing the points into J subsets so that pair-wise correlations within subsets are *maximized* in the sense of maximizing the weighted sum

$$(5.16) \qquad \bar{r} = \sum_{g=1}^{J} \bar{r}_g/n_g \ ,$$

where

$$(5.17) \qquad \bar{r}_g = \sum_{i,j \in g} r_{ij} \ ,$$

and where n_g is the number of points in the gth subset.[13] So, in a sense, we are trying to permute rows and columns of the correlation matrix to form blocks, so that the correlation coefficients in the blocks on the main diagonal will be large and the others small. In this sense we are trying to make the matrix as nearly block-diagonal as possible. This is apparently quite close to the "cascading" technique of Coleman and MacRae [1960] in a sociometric study to be mentioned in Chapter 6.[14]

In some problems the investigator has in hand a symmetric matrix representing distances, or squared distances (either Euclidean or generalized) between pairs of points.[15] The Euclidean distance between points i and j is given by d_{ij} in formula (5.8). A generalized distance using positive definite matrix C is

---

[13] PROOF: Since the first term of (5.4) does not depend on the partition, the optimal partitioning problem may be expressed as that of choosing the partition so that the second term of (5.4) is maximized. When $M = I$ this second term is

$$\text{tr}\bar{P}\bar{M}\bar{P}' = \text{tr}PT'(TT')^{-1}TP' = \text{tr}(TT')^{-1}TP'PT' \ .$$

TT' is a diagonal matrix of order J whose diagonal elements are n_g. $P'P$ is the correlation matrix $[r_{ij}]$. Hence $TP'PT'$ is another diagonal matrix of order J whose diagonal elements are $\bar{r}_g$ as defined in (5.17). Hence the last trace written above is precisely $\bar{r}$ as defined in (5.16), and the optimal partition is that which maximizes this quantity.

[14] The "mutual choice" coefficient used by these authors is not the ordinary Pearson product moment correlation defined above.

[15] The word "distance," as used in this chapter, or in Appendix G may refer either to what is ordinarily thought of as distance, or its square.

(5.18) $$d_{ij(C)} = (p_i - p_j)'C(p_i - p_j) \ .$$

Let

(5.19) $$B = P'CP \ .$$

Then the distances, generalized or Euclidean, may be also found from B as

(5.20) $$d_{ij} = b_{ii} + b_{jj} - 2b_{ij} \ ,$$

as may be verified by multiplying out (5.8) and using (5.19). This last relationship holds whether or not $C = I$ or whether or not the P matrix is normalized—that is, whether B represents a raw second-moment matrix or a correlation matrix. In the latter case, where the points all lie on a hypersphere, the distances measure lengths of chords of this sphere; otherwise the distances are taken wherever the points are located. A good partition is one that makes distances small within subsets.

From the above relationships it is not difficult to modify the one-way progressive merger procedure, now including the case where M is not the identity matrix, to accommodate the situation where either the B matrix, or the D matrix (containing the d_{ij}) are submitted as input in place of the P matrix. The d_{ij} are used anyway in the consequence formula (5.7) and are therefore needed at each stage. If an initial D matrix is available, the computer does not need to compute it from (5.18) or (5.20) but stores it directly. A recursive rule for revising the D matrix from stage to stage (rather than the P matrix) is obtained in Lemma G5 of Appendix G. The elements of M^{-1} appear in this rule, as before. Accordingly, the computer can compute consequences and optimal partitions at each stage, as before.

If an initial B matrix is available, rather than a D matrix, the computer computes the initial D matrix from the B matrix by means of (5.20) as a preliminary operation, and then applies the progressive merger procedure by using the D and M^{-1} matrices, as described in the preceding paragraph.

The procedure applied to the D matrix is illustrated by an example from Overall [1963] using his data on generalized distances between thirteen psychiatric "diagnostic types." Sixteen dimensions ("symptoms") were used to define the distances. Overall grouped the thirteen diagnostic types into five clusters based on a criterion of small distances within clusters. We checked his results using our procedure and obtained precisely the same clusters as his.[16] The distance matrix and the clusters, outlined by heavy lines, are shown in Table 13.

An initial B matrix was used in the representative-firm problem of Chapter 4. In this problem the P matrix was 140 by 49, so substantial computer storage space as well as time was saved by computing the 49 by

---

[16] I did not completely understand all of the steps of Overall's procedure.

TABLE 13. DISTANCES BETWEEN DIAGNOSTIC TYPES IN PSYCHIATRIC STUDY AND PARTITION INTO FIVE SUBSETS

Types	1	2	3	5	4	6	7	8	9	10	11	12	13
1	0	2.58	6.18	54.77	26.21	40.58	28.44	18.93	22.87	23.76	55.79	60.98	25.72
2		0	2.17	42.50	13.52	28.33	20.50	11.45	13.69	11.46	38.57	45.14	21.18
3			0	40.12	10.66	22.91	22.27	14.55	12.54	13.55	43.51	52.08	27.20
5				0	17.64	13.84	19.27	24.73	16.82	24.75	30.44	33.57	49.06
4					0	7.81	10.84	7.86	3.58	3.46	18.92	27.08	31.67
6						0	9.24	13.14	5.18	18.11	39.94	49.39	34.98
7							0	2.03	2.39	12.97	27.34	31.77	35.18
8								0	2.39	6.69	22.07	26.90	28.12
9									0	7.60	24.96	16.80	31.18
10										0	10.57		27.72
11											0	1.36	62.42
12												0	72.06
13													0

Source: Overall [1963, Table 4].

108

49 B matrix as a preliminary operation before starting the progressive merger procedure. This will be the case with other problems where G, the number of rows of P, greatly exceeds H, the number of columns.[17]

The Lockstep Case

Modifications in the procedures previously described are needed to deal with the lockstep case. Broadly stated, the situation now considered is this. Whenever two columns of P are merged, we will now be committed to merge also the two corresponding rows (making also the necessary adjustments in C and M). P is square, and either C or M or both of them may be nondiagonal. The consequence of the merger is then the sum of the separate consequences of the column-wise and the row-wise mergers. Let us then imagine that a stage, using the previous terminology, is divided up into two steps: a column step and a row step. After the column step, P will have one less column than row; M will have both one less column and one less row; and C will be unchanged. After the row step, P will be square again with one less column and one less row than originally; M and C will also have one less of each.

In our original geometrical framework, where the columns of P denote points, we are now merging both points and coordinate axes. The same conclusion would apply if we were to regard the rows of P as points, and the columns as coordinate axes. By "merging coordinate axes" is meant that the coordinates of all points on two or more original axes are projected on some third axis in the vector space; thus some information on each point is suppressed, and the points can be represented in a space of smaller dimensions than originally. Moreover, we must maintain a correspondence between points and axes; each point has its "favorite" axis, so that if we merge points 1 and 2, we must also merge axes 1 and 2. It must be admitted that this geometric interpretation becomes somewhat strained and that a considerable departure from the simple "cluster analysis" interpretation has been made. For some purposes it is useful to change the point of view when we change from the column step to the row step, so that we may speak of "merging points" in each case.

In the computer program developed for this case it has proved convenient to use a procedure analogous to the symmetric input variation of the one-way progressive merger procedure. Two "distance" matrices are

[17] When this is so, no more than H dimensions are really needed to describe the points; these are not the original dimensions but linear transforms of them, and it would often require some trouble to obtain the transforms. It is probable that in many cases substantially fewer than H dimensions would be needed to "essentially" describe the points. To obtain such a reduced set of dimensions would constitute a transposed factor analysis or cluster analysis problem, where the reduction desired is over the rows of P rather than over the columns.

computed at an initial stage of the program. One of these, called "$D(\text{col})$" contains as elements the distances between every pair of "points," when the columns of P denote "points"; these elements are generalized distances, using the metric of C; the formula is given by (5.18). The elements of the other, "$D(\text{row})$," denote generalized distances in the metric of M between "points" that would be represented by the rows of P. These two distance matrices, as well as the P, C^{-1}, and M^{-1} matrices, are all carried from stage to stage during the computer routine, and all five matrices are revised at each stage. These five revision formulas are given and derived in section G.3 of Appendix G. They involve computing revisions for both the column and row steps, and adding the two together.

The routine operates in a fashion very much like the one-way procedure, with the differences just noted. An augmented consequence formula is used that is the sum of the row-step and column-step consequences. This formula is (G.34) of Appendix G. The computer is instructed to choose the pair of indices such that consequence as measured by this formula is a minimum. After these indices are determined, they and the associated cost value are recorded. Then the five working matrices are revised for the next stage. A more detailed outline of the routine is contained in section G.4 of Appendix G.

The method of handling additional chains and the branch-off point is the same as for the one-way routine.

A question may occur to the reader that occurred to me as I was working on this program. Is it really necessary to develop a separate routine for this problem, and could not a correspondence be made between the P matrix of this lockstep problem and either the C or M matrices of the one-way problem? In the one-way procedure rows and columns of the C and M matrices *are* dealt with correspondingly.

This question received attention, and the answer seems to be that the problems are not the same, and that the one-way procedure is not rich enough in degrees of freedom to handle all the lockstep cases that are sometimes desired. In the input-output case with random final demands, for example, we seem to need both a square but nonsymmetric coefficient matrix and a square symmetric moment matrix, and possibly also a matrix of a loss function, and there is a row-column correspondence specified for all three.

The lockstep computer routine was used by Rubin [1968] for the input-output examples presented in Chapter 3.[18] It could be used effectively for problems of much larger size.

---

[18] The program was written by E. V. Brown of the Department of Mathematics at Kansas State University.

Forbidden Mergers

With both the one-way and the lockstep progressive merger programs, provision has been made for specifying forbidden merger pairs—that is, pairs of columns or rows of the matrix P that are not allowed to be members of a common subset of the partition. This provision makes it possible for the investigator to introduce prior ideas on the structure he is otherwise allowing the numerical data to determine for him, or to experiment with different restrictions on the structure. Examples of this type of restriction were presented in previous chapters.[19]

In the computer programs a special sub-routine is employed at the point where the computer is computing the consequences of alternative pairs. Every pair is checked to see whether it is on the forbidden list, and if so, it is not merged. This scanning is made at every stage. Thus, the restrictions are enforced, and in general the costs are higher than with unrestricted mergers.

4. DISCUSSION AND APPRAISAL

The clustering method, or set of methods, that forms the subject of this chapter has been described in some detail because it is believed to be useful in solving aggregation problems that arise in econometrics. This belief is based partly on the use it has had. But beyond this, what can be said for it—or against it? In an attempt to answer this question we shall first mention some strong points and then discuss some problems that could be limitations.

Strong Points

As methods of cluster analysis go—and reference is made to Ball's survey [1965]—this method is quite simple and relatively inexpensive.[20] With our bias toward simplification of problems and models this is a strong point. While a definitive comparison of computation costs is not submitted here, the assertion of relative economy is made without hesitation on three grounds: (1) the method of step-wise scanning and merging of pairs of points without reconsideration of mergers once made is relatively cheap; (2) the criterion function used is simpler than most alternatives; (3) the assumption of fixed weights is greatly simplifying. Of these three points the first and third are undoubtedly of greater importance.

Reconsideration of merged pairs employs computer time; a routine of

---

[19] Primarily in the input-output examples of Chapter 3. The restrictions of the Lake Michigan problem of Chapter 1 could be formulated, if desired, as a list of forbidden merger pairs—the list would be fairly long.

[20] A brief discussion of other clustering methods is included in Chapter 6, section 2.

starting with one large set and splitting sets, rather than merging them, does also.[21] When weights are unknown, the computational task is expanded tremendously.[22] The trace that is used in our criterion function is a simpler function than others sometimes suggested—in particular, functions requiring calculation of determinants.

Offsetting these claims to some extent is the inclusion in our formulation of the C and M matrices, which, when compared with typical cluster analysis problems, is a complicating and alien intrusion—at least when either C or M is nondiagonal. The lockstep requirement is an additional complication when introduced. These features are admittedly in the direction of increasing computation cost, but probably only to a small extent when compared with the considerations adduced in the preceding paragraph.[23] These features were introduced, moreover, in the course of derivations of loss or cost functions which appear to be reasonable in reference to the economic problems originally considered; therefore their inclusion seems to be a positive advantage when compared with competitive formulations that do not have such origins.

The argument can be advanced another step. It is a strong point of our approach that the clustering problem derives from an economic problem with a specifically formulated utility or loss function. With many clustering criteria used this is not the case, and the criteria used seem arbitrary. Of course, if the economic utility or loss function is arbitrary, our specific clustering criteria lack defensibility also, and we must admit that this is sometimes the case. We would still argue that the approach is right.

Proximity to Optimum

It has been recognized that the progressive merger procedure—largely because of the cost-saving features just described—cannot guarantee the selection of an optimal partition. This is the reason for the provision for more than one chain of mergers—to give the computer a chance to come out with a better chained partition at the end. It is a slight compromise in the direction of reconsideration of mergers effected, at least for purposes of testing the validity of the first chained partition.

[21] The routine of Morgan and Sonquist [1963] is of this general type. The first split is not costly, but the number of alternative splits increases rapidly in later stages, and it can be shown that the total number of possibilities to be examined by such a procedure greatly exceeds those required by the progressive merger routine.

[22] See Chapter 2 above and W. D. Fisher [1962b, sec. 5].

[23] Nondiagonal C or M are essentially elaborations on the quadratic function used—including cross-product terms in addition to squares—and do not increase computational costs by an order of magnitude of some positive power of the dimension of the matrix, as do some more complex iterative searching methods. Likewise with the lockstep requirement; it seems to double or slightly less than double the one-way cost.

In an interesting article King [1967] tested the validity of a step-wise procedure very similar to ours by running certain problems down to two subsets, and then comparing the two-set partitions obtained with the true optima, obtained by complete enumeration. In one series of forty-five problems, which in our notation would be symmetric input with $H = 10$ and $J = 2$, the step-wise procedure captured the true optimal partition twenty-two times; and in the remaining twenty-three problems the discrepancies between the chained partitions and the true optima were apparently quite small.[24] In another test, one where $H = 19$, $J = 13$, King found that his step-wise procedure gave identically the same partition as one obtained by a more expensive clustering method suggested by Fortier and Solomon [1966], although it was not claimed that this was the true optimum. Other comparisons were also made. This work provides support to a hypothesis that the step-wise short-cut gives results which are quite close to the true optima. Admittedly the case of two subsets is rather special and would constitute a drastic simplification of most real problems.

By comparing the chained partitions reached by our procedure for alternative chains of the same problem, a suggestive although inconclusive indication is obtained of the reliability to be attached to any one such partition. In fact the number of chains that give results that are discrepant from the least-cost chain is itself suggestive.[25] If a number of different partitions with large differences in simplification cost are found, especially when the partition at the end of the first chain is not low, this would suggest lack of confidence in our procedure. Conversely, if a number of chains give consistently the same final partition, or partitions with small differences in cost, it suggests confidence (but not a definite conclusion: they could all be wrong).

In the numerical examples presented in Chapters 3 and 4 from two to four chains were run per problem. The numbers of times that the chains gave different results, and the average difference of these results in terms of simplification cost, are shown in Table 14. The first, second, third, and fifth columns of numbers come from the input-output problems of Chapter 3 (including the 31 by 31 problems reported by Rubin [1968], but not in-

[24] In 15 of the last group of 23 problems there were only 4 or fewer partitions (out of a possible 511) that had lower cost than the chained partition. The cost criterion used was "intercluster correlation," which could be negative; it differs from our cost criterion in that it is not weighted to represent numbers of original elements in the clusters.

[25] The conclusions that may be drawn from such comparisons must be qualified by consideration of where the branch-off point is, and probably also the length of the chain. E.g., to put the branch-off point at the next-to-last stage would insure that the chained partitions were all different and that the first one was lower-cost than the others; while in our experience putting the branch-off point at the very beginning makes it unlikely that any variety of chained partition will be secured. We have placed the point usually between half and three-quarters of the "way down" the chain.

TABLE 14. DIFFERENCES IN SIMPLIFICATION COST DUE TO DIFFERENT CHAINS OF THE PROGRESSIVE MERGER PROCEDURE

	Lockstep		One-way		
	Unre-stricted	Re-stricted[a]	Unre-stricted	Unre-stricted[b]	Re-stricted[c]
Number of problems	7	9	3	2	5
Chains per problem	2	2	2–4	3	2–4
Ratio of discrepant[d] to total problems	.14	.44	0	1.00	.20
Average ratio of discrepant[e] to least cost	.015	.058	—	.041	.052

[a] Number of forbidden merger pairs ranges from 4 to 48.
[b] The 49 farm problem. Branch-off stage was 19, final stage was 9.
[c] Number of forbidden merger pairs ranges from 1 to 4.
[d] A "discrepant problem" is one that produces two or more distinct final partitions.
[e] "Discrepant cost" is the absolute difference in cost at final stage between the least cost partition and another partition.
Source: Rubin [1968], including 31 by 31 problems not reported in Ch. 3, and representative-firm data of Ch. 4.

cluded in Chapter 3); the fourth column comes from the representative-firm problem of Chapter 4. The original number of points, the branch-off stage, and the final number of subsets for these problems are the following:

	Input-output		Representative-firm
Original points	18	31	49
Branch-off stage	12	23	19
Final subsets	8	15	9

It is seen from Table 14 that the problems showing discrepant results amounted to between 14 and 44 per cent of problems run for the input-output problems; in the two representative-firm problems the three chains run were all different each time. But the differences in cost among these discrepant chains are quite small, when expressed as a per cent of the lowest cost found—less than six per cent (average per problem). The differences are lower for the unrestricted problems.

For the McGuire problem of Chapter 1 and the Goldberger problem of Chapter 2 alternative chains were also run, but the branch-off point was taken at the beginning of the chain each time.[26] For the McGuire problem five chains were run, and gave the same final partition each time. For the various Goldberger cases twenty-four chains were run; discrepancies oc-

[26] Because the computer routine, providing for a general preselected branch-off point was not available when this problem was run.

curred twice. Thus, not much variation occurs, but it is believed that these results are caused largely by the fact that chains were started in each case at the first stage.

All in all, our results tend to confirm those of King and lead us to believe that the solutions provided by the progressive mergers, although not identically the optima, come very close to them. It seems that the investment of appreciable computational outlay in order to close the small differences remaining would not be worth while.

Invariance Matters

It must be admitted that in situations where the investigator does not know what the appropriate weights are, the use of fixed weights in the aggregation or disaggregation process is arbitrary, and that our use of fixed weights in these situations is a limitation on the generality of our method. Our use of fixed weights is reflected in the use of preselected S and T matrices in the optimal simplification problem. More elaborate computational procedures can optimize the choice of weights. Some procedures developed by Friedman and Rubin [1967] are of this type.

It seems that further investigation is required to determine the instances where it will be worth while to incur the heavier computation cost in order to secure the advantages of these procedures.

The specification of the matrix T as in (1.5), having all of its nonzero elements unity, is for convenience and not so restrictive as it may appear. If one wished to define T more generally as having any positive numbers in place of unity (allowing for unequally weighted sums in the formulas for $\bar{M}$ and $\bar{P}$ in place of equally weighted sums), one can proceed as follows. Let Z be a known nonsingular diagonal matrix of order H. Substitute TZ for T, PZ for P, and $Z^{-1}MZ'^{-1}$ for M. Then it is seen that $\bar{M}$ as given by (5.2b) and $\bar{P}$ as given by (5.5) are both invariant with respect to these substitutions. Moreover, PMP', $\bar{P}\bar{M}\bar{P}'$, and c as given by (5.4) are also invariant. Therefore, if one originally desired to define a problem with the more general definition of T, one could get back to the specification of equation (1.5) by postmultiplying such a T by Z^{-1} and making other substitutions inverse to those stated above. In other words, the problem with the more general T can always be brought back into our framework by a rescaling of the data. Similarly for S.

Yet, the investigator must decide on the relevant relationship between his scales and his rule of consolidation. In other words, he must decide on the relevant scaling of his variables when our simple T, containing 1's, is to be used. There seems to be no escape from this need in our frame of reference.

Singularity of C or M

The difficulties encountered by having to assume nonsingularity of the C and M matrices have already been noted.[27] We have succeeded in deriving cost formulas that will accommodate the case of singular C and M by use of generalized inverses (e.g., Theorem 2). But we have not succeeded in developing appropriate recursive formulas so that the progressive merger procedure may be applied to the singular case, although the matter has been given considerable attention. A certain relation that is needed in the proof of a number of the lemmas of Appendix G depends on the assumption of nonsingular M or C and does not hold for singular M or C, except in special cases.[28]

Pending a solution of this problem the following suggestion is made to handle singular matrices: perturb them slightly into nonsingular matrices. If the perturbation is not excessive, the resulting nonsingular matrices may well lie within the bounds of observation error and provide relevant solutions in many economic problems.

So we persist in our belief that the clustering method described is useful. The extent of its usefulness will be ascertained and its limitations better understood as it is applied in further concrete economic problems.

[27] Chapter 4, section 3.
[28] In Lemma G.1, for example, this relation is (G.6a).

6

RELATED MATTERS

1. FIELDS OUTSIDE ECONOMICS[1]

Clustering and aggregation is important throughout the range of scientific endeavor. In many fields it is a fundamental necessity to have an over-all summary of a vast quantity of data which our minds can comprehend. Only then are we able to study a particular group of observations intensively and at the same time know how our work fits into the over-all picture.

In showing how we observe the universe Gerard [1957] describes some fundamental types of aggregates.

> Man thus types his observed concrete entities into sets and, as a second abstraction (the first being entity from ground), draws sharp boundaries about them. . . . A mere collection of seemingly unrelated entities is first given meaning or pattern in terms of perceived similarities; only later is it possible to look more closely at the individuals and to reintroduce differences, but now ordered differences with significance to the larger whole. Moreover, once the initial integration (or induction) has been achieved, progressive differentiations (and deductions) can be meaningful, and subclasses can be conceived and identified, later to become graded subpopulations.[2]

While we are concerned primarily with Economics, it is worth while to take a brief look abroad and turn to some examples of clustering and aggregation in other disciplines: first, in the social sciences and then in the natural sciences.

Social Sciences

The social science that is often defined as the study of the forms, functions, and history of human groups is Sociology.

[1] This section was written by Marjorie Fisher.
[2] Gerard [1957, p. 429].

R. C. Tryon [1955] worked on "identification of social areas by cluster analysis." Census of 1940 data were used to divide the San Francisco Bay region into "social areas." From 243 census tracts he used 222 tracts which were "homogeneous," or which had a recognizable pattern of characteristics. He took 33 "demographic variables from the U.S. Census (1940)."[3] "For each of 33 variables its pattern or profile of correlations with the other 32 measures is inspected. Variables of like pattern are put in the same composite, called a *cluster of variables*."[4] He found seven clusters—disjoint and exhaustive. He chose three which were most nearly independent as "social dimensions" for grouping the original 243 census tracts into eight "relatively homogeneous" social areas. A few residual tracts were left over.

Note that this is an example of what we have called "two-way aggregation."

In the branch of Sociology called Sociometry groups are defined on the basis of mutual preferences of individuals for each other. "One of the major problems in analyzing the structure of social groups of 50 or more persons is to identify subgroups of individuals who associate with each other."[5] For example, Coleman and MacRae study the mutual choices of 198 boys in a four-year high school. However, they are troubled by "chains" of choices and do not get satisfactory groups. In a concurrent study MacRae gets eleven subgroups out of data giving sociometric choices in a group of sixty-seven men.[6]

Alexander [1963] defines a clique in terms of mutual choice relationships. Then, using data on "1,411 cases who made over 4,300 choices"[7] he obtains 38 cliques. The number of isolates is not mentioned. However, under his definition of a clique[8] it is probable that there were many.

Using "clique" defined as containing at least three members, each of which has a mutual choice relationship with all other members, Chabot [1960] studied clique structure in a group of twenty-five clerks typing customer bills. He was interested in whether there was a relationship between production rate and clique membership. He gets a negative corre-

---

[3] R. C. Tryon [1955, p. 8].
[4] *Ibid.*, p. 13.
[5] Coleman and MacRae [1960, p. 722].
[6] MacRae [1960].
[7] Alexander [1963, p. 269].
[8] "A clique is defined as a group of four or more members, each of whom either has (a) three reciprocal relationships with the others, or has (b) two reciprocal relationships, both of which are with members who have three; between any two clique members there must be at least two connecting paths which do not contain the same reciprocal choice. A path is defined as a connection between two members via a series of reciprocal choices." *Ibid.*, p. 269.

lation of − .56, which he feels is reasonable if one thinks that individuals with a high production rate tend to be isolated socially.

In Psychology when a considerable amount of data is available about individuals—usually in the form of scores on many tests—it has been customary to try to group the individuals, or the tests, into clusters. A matrix of correlation coefficients between each pair of individuals on all test scores is used. Clusters are built up by examining the matrix and listing "linkages" (a linkage is an "r" greater than an arbitrary number).

R. C. Tryon [1939] clustered together individuals. An example of the use of correlation profiles for clustering traits of adolescents is given by C. M. Tryon [1943]. Clusters of traits are found in this study for each of four age-sex groups. These clusters involve some overlapping and they are not exhaustive—some traits are left out.

In the analysis of psychiatric diagnostic concepts that was used as a numerical illustration in Chapter 5, Overall [1963] uses sixteen symptom areas and asks a group of experts to characterize (on a scale of seven from "not present" to "extremely severe") thirteen diagnostic types in terms of the symptom areas. He uses cluster analysis of generalized distances to obtain clusters of diagnostic types. (Two were isolates.)

The field of Linguistics could be included in the social sciences and in recent years has been making increased use of classification theory and cluster analysis. Suggestions have been made of indices that might be used for grouping languages. Two illustrations are given.

Pierce [1962] uses one measure, "consonant phonemes per word"[9] (where a phoneme is regarded as one sound) for the purpose of grouping fourteen languages into types. He uses from 1,600 to 3,000 words (divided into 100-word samples) from each language to show that the fourteen languages differ and can be grouped into types on the consonancy index alone.

Dyen [1962] is interested in grouping Malayopolynesian languages. He hopes to show which are more closely related and in this way throw some light on possible patterns of historical migration. "For the purpose of comparing the Malayopolynesian languages a list of 196 basic meanings was employed."[10] He used 371 lists. Some of the lists were not Malayopolynesian and for some languages he had more than one list—from different sources. "We can estimate that the number of languages dealt with here is about 275 of the posited approximately 500 Malayopolynesian languages."[11] A word could not be found for each meaning for every list— however, all the lists included had at least 150 items. "For each pair of

---

[9] Pierce [1962, p. 216].
[10] Dyen [1962, p. 39].
[11] *Ibid.*, p. 40.

languages we are interested in the percentage of homosemantic cognates[12] shown on their lists, for this is regarded as a measure of their similarity. Since 371 lists imply 68,635 pairs of lists and since in each pair of lists there are at least one hundred pairs of entries, calculation of the percentages of cognates of each list with each other list is based on more than 7,000,000 pairs of words."[13] Each pair was examined beforehand to decide whether or not they were cognate. Then languages were grouped according to high percentage of cognates. Some of his groupings are the same as previous classifications and some are not.

The problem of grouping voters is important in Political Science. How can legislators be grouped so as to predict their behavior on issues? Rice [1928] wrote of the difficulty of this problem: "Numerous lines of cleavage run through a legislative body. It is quite impossible to take account by classification (the method here adopted) of all of these simultaneously."[14]

A few studies using cluster analysis have been made of legislative roll call votes. After roll call selection the next step has been to calculate an index of agreement between every pair of legislators. Of course, the number of indices to be calculated increases very rapidly with the size of the legislative body studied. It is probably for this reason that only a few studies of this sort have been made.[15] Rice [1928] did the pioneering study on "bloc indentification in small political bodies" for the 1914 New Jersey Senate. Beyle [1931] made a study of blocs in the 1927 Session of the Minnesota State Senate. Truman [1959] made a cluster-bloc analysis of the U.S. Senate during the 81st Congress and showed blocs of different sizes and degrees of cohesion. Lijphart [1963] made a study of "bloc voting in the General Assembly" of the United Nations. Computers facilitate this sort of study.

A number of studies of legislative districting have followed the U.S. Supreme Court decision on state legislative apportionment. Harris [1964] uses equal population and "compactness"—minimum difference between length and width of a district—as criteria for dividing a state into districts. He presents a solution for Colorado. Thoreson and Littschwager [1967] work out districting suggestions for Iowa.[16] They obtain some districts

---

[12] Homosemantic cognates are words which are believed to have developed from the same root word in the past.

[13] *Ibid.*, p. 40.

[14] Rice [1928, p. 219, footnote 6].

[15] See Anderson, Watts, and Wilcox [1966, pp. 59–60].

[16] They take an arbitrary reference county. Then start with the county furthest from it and add closest contiguous counties as long as total population is less than population for a district. Then add the county that will make population closest to the average for a district. Continue until the state is complete. Iterate by taking each county as a reference county. Then see which solution is "best" in terms of population and contiguousness. Some counties will have more than one representative. They also do it in terms of townships.

with smaller population deviations from the average than when usual political boundaries are used. Hess, Weaver, Siegfeldt, Whelan, and Zitlau [1965] made a redistricting study for Delaware using minimum moment of inertia for units of population and "integer linear programming." Weaver and Hess [1963] made districting proposals for Connecticut.

An example from the field of public administration is provided by Weiss and Jacobson [1955], who analyzed the structure of a government bureau, used a questionnaire to determine "work contacts," and obtained responses from 196 employees who reported 2,400 "work relationships." They used only the reciprocated ones for they felt that these tend to be the strongest. They set up a matrix in the order given by the organization chart and got many work groups immediately. They divided the large matrix by inspection into segments. Then eliminated "liaison members" and their "contacts." Then eliminated supposed isolates. Then reordered rows and columns. When groups were established they put in the liaison members again and made a graph of the structure of the organization. When they looked at "non-reciprocated" reports of contacts, only one isolate remained. He was an "observer on leave from another organization."[17]

In this book, while considering questions of grouping and clustering, we have not dealt directly with the obvious sequel: matters of hierarchy and organization structure. Social science, of course, does become involved in these questions, and increasingly so in recent years.

Theories of departmentalization go back to the time of Aristotle, who considered the distribution of offices, their number and tenure, and how variation would have to occur in states of different size and constitution.

> For example, should one person keep order in the market, and another in some other place, or should the same person be responsible everywhere? Again, should offices be divided according to the persons with whom they deal: I mean to say, should one person see to good order in general, or one look after the boys, another after the women, and so on?[18]

A rather general problem of organization may be stated from a decision-theoretic viewpoint: to group tasks into man-jobs, jobs into administrative units and hierarchy.[19] An assignment problem can be stated as follows: Given any possible set S of elemental activities and the time $t(S)$ required for a person to perform the set, to partition the set of activities into *tasks*, each task having some maximum t (say eight hours), so as to minimize the number of tasks.[20]

[17] Weiss and Jacobson [1955, p. 666, footnote 13].
[18] Jowett [1885, p. 138].
[19] See March and Simon [1958, p. 22].
[20] *Ibid.*, pp. 23–24.

Many questions remain. Why not specify *components* of each elemental task? Or specify components as individual units with certain *task indivisibilities* as side conditions? Coordination is needed. We need to recognize *contingent* activity—i.e., contingent on demand, capacity, etc. Program development needs to be considered. March and Simon outline a revised assignment (organization) problem. Given: (1) a roster of activities that *may* be performed; (2) conditional statements specifying conditions when they will be performed, these possibly depending on the assignment of other activities, and on communications network and cost; the problem is to determine the administrative units, hierarchy, and signaling and coordination system. Critical variables are: degree of *self-containment* of a unit (often related to the degree of purpose-organization) versus degree of *skill-specialization*. Dynamic program development[21] still needs to be added to this formulation.

The work on information and organizational theory conducted by J. Marschak and Radner should of course also be mentioned and is closely related to the problem just stated.[22]

From the brief survey that has just been made it is evident that empirical work on the subject of grouping in the social sciences has not been oriented toward such an ambitious formulation of the decision problem. It will probably be some time before optimal organization systems in the sense defined in this chapter can be determined or estimated from empirical data. The goal is nevertheless there to see.

Natural Sciences

Bertalanffy [1950] points out that many times in the natural sciences gross concepts are substituted for detailed reactions.

Already in chemistry, gross formulas—for example, those for photosynthesis or oxidation—indicate the net result of long chains of many partly unknown reaction steps. The same procedure is applied on a higher level in physiology when total metabolism is measured by O_2 consumption and CO_2 and calorie production, and bulk expressions, like Rubner's surface rule, are formulated; or when in clinical routine the diagnosis of, say, hyperthyroidism is based upon determination of basal metabolism.[23]

Thus in very many fields we have need for aggregate formulations.

[21] See March and Simon [1958, pp. 26–29].
[22] Marschak [1964], Marschak and Miyasawa [1968], and Marschak and Radner [1968].
[23] Bertalanffy [1950, p. 28].

Recently there has been a great deal of interest in clustering techniques in certain fields of Biology. A number of workers have felt that with the advent of the electronic computer it is possible to take many measurements on organisms or note the presence or absence of many qualitative characteristics and to combine this multitude of data into "indices of similarity."

Many problems are involved in this approach, which its adherents have named "numerical taxonomy." In the first place, it is necessary to decide what group of organisms to study for the purpose of clustering them into subgroups. Then, one must decide which of their characteristics to study and tabulate. One answer is: as many as possible so long as they are not "logical consequences of each other" or different ways of measuring the same thing. "We cannot use both hemoglobin and redness of blood if the latter is defined as possession of hemoglobin."[24] The included characters can be microscopic data on cells as well as measurements on the shape and size of the organisms (morphological characters); also, behavioral, ecological, and distributional characters.[25]

Often all these characters are weighted equally,[26] with no regard for differences in variance or for intercorrelations. Over the question of weighting there is controversy. Traditionally, biologists have tried to classify according to "important" characteristics of organisms. Of course, there is not always agreement as to which characteristics are "important" or "fundamental." Since the time of Darwin biological classifications have been interpreted as indicating the course of evolution. Often, biologists have chosen characters which they think indicate common ancestry as a basis for their classification.[27] Other characters which are believed to have arisen in quite different species as a result of adaptation to environment ("convergence") are omitted. Numerical taxonomists have claimed that if a sufficient number of characters is included in the study, convergence in a few will not affect the index of similarity. It would certainly seem true that equal weighting of characters is not the ideal system. However, in view of the fact that relative importance of characters is speculative and their variances and intercorrelations are unknown, equal weighting is a possible working hypothesis and one that has been used especially in bacteriology and entomology.

[24] Sokal and Sneath [1963, p. 66].

[25] *Ibid.*, p. 93.

[26] "Numerical taxonomy gives each feature equal weight when creating taxonomic groups." *Ibid.*, p. 118.

[27] "Of Darwin's *a priori* proposition that those characters least likely to be modified in the course of evolution will be the most important taxonomically, all one can say is that no doubt in general it is right, but without a good fossil record, who can say which they are in any given group?" Cain [1959, p. 239].

An example by Sneath [1957] in Microbiology deals with clustering of 45 strains of bacteria on the basis of 105 observed features. Some features have to do with shape and size, others with resistance to heat and certain chemicals; others relate to growth rates in particular environments. All features are coded into presence, absence or "no comparison." Measured data are divided into categories and then each strain of bacteria is coded as to the presence or absence of its data in each category. For each pair of strains a similarity index is calculated by counting the number of features which both strains have present and dividing by this same number plus the number of features which one strain of bacteria has and the other lacks. Then Sneath clusters, according to highest indices of similarity, gradually lowering the criterion and admitting new strains when their index with one strain in the cluster is sufficiently high.[28] He obtains two large groups, two pairs and three isolates.

In Entomology Michener and Sokal [1957] worked with a "group of four genera of bees. One hundred and twenty-two characters were studied for 97 species of this group."[29] They state that "almost all of the characters used in our study are morphological or color features of the adult insects."[30] Each character had from two to eight states. No attempt was made to normalize the data.[31] All ninety-seven species were correlated two by two. Then clustering was performed. Michener and Sokal obtain elaborate groupings which they display in the form of branching diagrams, one for each of the four genera of bees. On the whole, the resulting groupings were similar to those from previous work.

In Botany, Rogers and Tanimoto [1960] have done similar work in a study of cassava, yucca, and manioc plants. In a later study of twenty-eight species and subspecies of marine algae Rogers and Fleming [1964] obtained clusters and isolates.

In Plant Ecology some work has been done on grouping quadrats (plots of vegetation chosen for intensive study) on whether or not they contain the same species of vegetation. Some studies have used weights to indicate the quantity of each species present. As would seem obvious, classification of quadrats into groups works best when the total area studied is large enough to include diverse parts; for example, hilltop and ravine, or swampy and dry areas. Also, the size and placing of the quadrats affect the results.[32]

---

[28] This is the same grouping method that McQuitty [1957] has suggested as "elementary linkage analysis" for use in psychology.

[29] Michener and Sokal [1957, p. 162].

[30] *Ibid.*, p. 132.

[31] *Ibid.*, p. 142.

[32] See Grieg-Smith [1964, Ch. 7].

In Soil Science, Bidwell and Hole [1964] have calculated indices of similarity based on thirty soil characteristics of twenty-nine Kansas soils. On the basis of this they have constructed a hierarchical grouping of the soils.

A few studies have used cluster analysis in Geology. For example, Imbrie and Purdy [1962] have studied the classification of carbonate sediments in the Great Bahama Bank. They do a factor analysis using twelve measures on forty samples. Then they locate five clusters by inspecting the plot of sample vectors in four-factor space (two dimensions at a time).

Chave and Mackenzie [1961] take the studies that have been made of muds on the ocean floor and for each study they correlate the chemical elements that were found by analysis. These chemicals are reported as percentages; usually one element predominates. They also take partial correlation coefficients holding the predominant element constant. Then they find clusters of elements that occur together. This same technique is used in Psychology. Elements belong to a cluster if their correlation coefficient is greater than a certain arbitrary number. They get a number of isolates—as also occurs in Psychology.

Harbaugh [1964] uses "factor analysis in recognizing facies boundaries" in a study of "27 localities along a 250-mile-long outcrop belt in Kansas and Oklahoma."[33] At each locality fourteen different constituents were measured. Factor analysis reduced the problem to two factors and then it was possible to mark boundaries between four different "facies."

The universality of hierarchy in science is described by Gerard in the following terms.

We can find organizations or aggregates at all levels: the atom

> . . . is built of subordinate differentiated and interacting units, . . . and [it] is built into a superordinate molecule. The individual molecule, in turn, with like or unlike fellows becomes a crystal or a colloid or some other material aggregate; the colloids form particulates; these, cells, tissues and organs; these, organisms; and organisms, species and larger taxonomic categories, or, in another way, groups, communities and larger eco-systems.[34]

We need to see the over-all organization as well as our particular specialties.

2. RELATED METHODS

In section 1 we have attempted to provide some perspective in viewing grouping problems in economics by surveying similar problems in other

[33] Harbaugh [1964, p. 529].
[34] Gerard [1957, p. 430].

substantive fields. In the present section the objective is to deepen further this perspective by describing briefly some relationships between the method used in this book to solve the grouping problem and other closely related methods. It is not possible to be exhaustive; three methods have been selected for this discussion: cluster analysis, factor analysis,[35] and entropy (or information) measurement.

Cluster Analysis

From one viewpoint the method described in Chapter 5 is a generalization of cluster analysis, as this term has come to be known.[36] The accommodation of three matrices, P, M, and C, as input in our method constitutes a more general and flexible formulation than a single matrix of coordinates, or of similarity coefficients, which was the specification in all of the studies surveyed in section 1.[37]

Likewise, the lockstep method, providing for corresponding row and column partitions, is an innovation in traditional cluster analysis. It may even be an unwelcome one to analysts who find that it puts a strain on the notion of clustering "points."[38] The same could be said about a two-way partitioning of the P matrix where row and column partitions are not linked.

From other viewpoints, which were mentioned in section 4 of Chapter 5, our method is a special case of more general or flexible clustering methods. Our progressive merger procedure may be regarded as "one iteration" in a more general program that would provide many iterations— possibly breaking up clusters already formed. The clustering procedures described by Rogers and Fleming [1964] and by Friedman and Rubin [1967], for example, iterate a number of times. Our prior specification of weights, as also mentioned in Chapter 5, is a specialization, which is also generalized by Friedman and Rubin [1967].

Judging by the survey of other fields in section 1 of this chapter, it seems that many, if not a majority, of clustering studies are based on measures of similarity that originate in non-numerical attributes. The elemental

---

[35] Including component analysis.

[36] The development of clustering methods in diverse fields is growing so rapidly— along with the literature describing them—that it is difficult to make any firm assertion regarding the scope and definition of "cluster analysis." A large majority of the literature is dated in the 1960's. See, for example, Ball [1965], Friedman and Rubin [1967], King [1967], Johnson [1967], and other work surveyed in Ball [1965]. A general computational approach that includes the problem of finding an optimal partition is outlined in Reiter and Sherman [1965].

[37] The data in the C, M, and P matrices could be rearranged in one matrix; but then unusually complicated side conditions on grouping would have to be imposed.

[38] See the previous discussion in section 3 of Ch. 5.

scoring is 0–1, and the measures of similarity are built up on percentages of ones, and contingency tables. To the writer, it does not seem a fundamental distinction whether the measures of association are built up this way, or are computed from original numerical data like the Pearson correlation coefficient. Similar scaling problems and similar clustering problems arise in each case, although some of the mathematical details are different.[39] Some attention, of course, must be given, in formulating a measure of association or similarity, to whether one wants to allow negative values of this measure.

A more fundamental matter is whether a partition into subsets is really what one wants, or whether one wants, or should want, a different structure. The sociometrists are not finding a "clique" easy to define.[40] At least one, Luce [1950], has proposed that a concept of "generalized clique," or "chain" be employed, where the sets are not necessarily disjoint. In another context it has been proposed that intersecting chains or "octopi" are appropriate.[41] Compared with such exotic possibilities, our insistence on disjoint subsets is humdrum indeed.

It may be that more attention to and study of cluster analysis in social science by economists may reveal interesting and relevant formulations of the aggregation problem in economics that have not yet been tried.

Factor Analysis

A brief comparison of our method with factor analysis seems desirable. We are using this term in the sense of a statistical technique, apart from any particular substantive field, but occasionally for concreteness we shall use the language of psychology. The objective of factor analysis, broadly described, is to express a number of observed variables in terms of a fewer number of "fundamental" variables or "factors," where each factor may be a linear function of the observed variables. In the psychological language, let us associate "variable" with "test" and "observation" with "individual (person)." Then we seek to explain the tests in terms of a fewer number of factors.[42]

To be more specific, and also to make a correspondence with the nota-

[39] So, also, with different formulations of the "distance."

[40] The definitions of Forsyth and Katz [1946], Coleman and MacRae [1960], MacRae [1960], Alexander [1963], Luce and Perry [1949], and Luce [1950], for example, seem to be all different from each other.

[41] "Examination of the mutual-choice sociograms of this group and others shows that in large measure they are composed of chains of choices and have an octopus-like configuration rather than a clear division into cliques." Coleman and MacRae [1960, p. 726].

[42] The problem of explaining "individuals" in terms of factors could, of course, also be formulated.

tion of Chapter 5, let there be G individuals and H tests, and a detailed "score matrix" X of size G by H, representing the performance of the individuals on the tests. We bypass the question of how these scores are normalized, if at all. The reduction of H tests to J factors is accomplished by a transformation matrix T of size J by H, and the detailed score matrix is reduced to an aggregate score matrix $\bar{X}$ by the transformation

$$(6.1) \qquad\qquad \bar{X} = XT' \, ,$$

where $\bar{X}$ is a G by J matrix. This matrix evidently shows the scoring of the G individuals in terms of the J factors. (The elements of T are sometimes called the "factor loadings" of the tests.)

In order to determine T, and hence $\bar{X}$, additional criteria are needed, and several variations of the problem have developed. In most of these formulations T need not be a partitioning operator, as we have defined the term in Definition 3 of Chapter 2. In general, it will be just some J by H matrix, so any one of the H tests may be involved in (have a non-zero loading on) any one of the factors.

A special specification of the T matrix that is well known in factor analysis is Thurstone's "simple structure." As originally formulated in his early work[43] (but in our notation), simple structure requires that each row of T have at least one zero in it—more, if possible, but at least one. We require that in every *column* of T there be only one non-zero element (see [1.5]). This is a more severe restriction. Our requirement that T be a partitioning operator is thus seen to be a special case of simple structure—an especially "simple" simple structure.[44]

In geometric language, let the tests be considered to be H points in G space (coordinates given by X), and let the factors be considered to be J points defining new coordinate axes in the same space. We want to represent the old points by the new ones. With simple structure we can accomplish an excellent representation if the old points lie on coordinate hyperplanes defined by the new axes. With partitioning form we want the old points to coincide with the new axes themselves. Figure 12 is intended to represent 15 points in 3-space (in perspective). On the left diagram the three black dots represent the best reduction to 3 factors that can be made with partitioning form; on the right the three black dots represent the

---

[43] Thurstone [1935, p. 151]. More recent techniques of factor analysis, such as the varimax method, come closer to partitioning. The present discussion also ignores the "communality problem." For a complete treatment of factor analysis, see Harman [1967].

[44] We originally defined T as a disaggregation operator, and it became an aggregation operator via THEOREM 2. Since the form of $\bar{X}$ in our formulation depends on M as well as on T (see, e.g., equation [2.38] in Ch. 2) our formulation will reach (6.1) only if M is diagonal. In the following discussion this assumption is made.

FIGURE 12. ALTERNATIVE REDUCTIONS OF 15 POINTS IN 3-SPACE

PARTITIONING   SIMPLE STRUCTURE

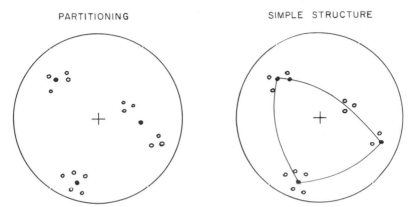

best three factors under simple structure. The curved lines represent hyperplanes. It can be seen that the simple structure does quite well (no dot is very far off a hyperplane). Partitioning form does not do so well; two clusters are reasonably tight, but the third is not.

To summarize: in factor analysis, as in the present simplification problem, a reduction in the number of categories of reference is sought. Our partitioning requirement—and cluster analysis also—is an additional requirement; formally it could be considered a special case of factor analysis. In both problems some sort of optimal simplification is sought.

Entropy and Information Measurement

As is well known, there is a parallel between such concepts as distance, scatter, and variance, on the one hand, and entropy and information content on the other. These analogies have been applied in economic contexts. Skolka [1964] used these concepts to analyze the aggregation problem in input-output analysis, and in fact used a progressive merger procedure similar to ours, but with an information measure as a criterion, to obtain optimal partitions. He applied his procedure to a Japanese input-output table for 1954 of size 8 by 8 and to a larger Israeli table for 1960 of size 30 by 30. Theil and his associates have expounded on, and used the information measures in, input-output analysis, consumer demand theory, and other areas. A comprehensive treatment of this work is provided in Theil's book [1967]. Theil's studies of the input-output application have included consideration of the effects of aggregating these matrices.

Because of the use of these measures in the evaluation of aggregation effects, it is desirable to describe the relationship between them and the measures we use in this book. Because of the closeness of Skolka's work to some of our own we find it useful to use much of his terminology.

The information measures apply to a matrix X which is assumed to be of size n by n, non-negative and elements summing to unity.[45] Such a matrix may be called a *share matrix*. The vectors of marginal totals

$$(6.2a) \quad v = Xj \ , \qquad\qquad\qquad (6.2b) \quad w' = j'X \ ,$$

where j is a column of n unit elements, may be called *share vectors*. These also sum to unity.

Then the *entropy* of a share matrix is defined as

$$(6.3) \qquad\qquad H(X) = -\sum_{i,\,j=1}^{n} x_{ij}\log x_{ij} \ .$$

This may be considered a measure of the degree of sameness, or homogeneity of the elements of the matrix X.

The *marginal entropy* of a share matrix X may be defined as

$$(6.4) \qquad\qquad H^m(X) = -\sum_{i,\,j=1}^{n} v_i w_j \log(v_i w_j) \ ,$$

which is Skolka's "entropy of a table with marginal information." It is the same as the sum of the entropies of the two marginal share vectors, and the same as the entropy of a matrix of rank 1 where $X = vw'$. Then the *information content* of a share matrix is the difference between its marginal entropy and its entropy:

$$(6.5) \qquad\qquad I(X) = H^m(X) - H(X) \ .$$

Theil [1967, Ch. 9, formula (4.10)] expresses this formula as

$$(6.6) \qquad\qquad I(X) = \sum_{i,\,j=1}^{n} x_{ij}\log \frac{x_{ij}}{v_i w_j} \ ,$$

after converting his notation to ours.[46]

Now consider an aggregated share matrix X^*, whose elements x_{IJ} have been obtained by partitioning the rows and columns of X into subsets ("large" sectors) and then summing both ways within the blocks so formed. That is, if S and T are of size m by n and of the form of (1.5) of Chapter 1,

$$(6.7) \qquad\qquad X^* = SXT' \ .$$

---

[45] They could also be used for non-square matrices.

[46] The equivalence can be proved by substituting (6.3) and (6.4) into (6.5) after factoring (6.4) into separate sums and using the fact that certain x_{ij} sum to unity; then doing something similar for Theil's formula. The expressions eventually become the same.

Consider also a simplified n by n matrix $\tilde{X}$ constructed from the aggregated matrix X^* in the following fashion: each block $\tilde{X}_{IJ}$ is a share matrix of rank 1 multiplied by the scalar share x_{IJ}; that is,

$$(6.8) \qquad \tilde{X}_{IJ} = x_{IJ}\tilde{v}_I\tilde{w}'_J \ ,$$

where $\tilde{v}_I$ and $\tilde{w}'_J$ are share vectors. Thus, $\tilde{X}_{IJ}/x_{IJ}$ is a share matrix, and $\tilde{X}$ is also a share matrix. Crudely speaking, $\tilde{X}$ is an arbitrarily reallocated, or disaggregated, version of the original X, where the reallocation is made independently for rows and columns within each block.

The reallocation may or may not be made proportional to the original marginal totals of corresponding blocks of X. In the case that it is, then corresponding marginal totals of X and $\tilde{X}$ are equal.[47] Then it will follow that the marginal entropies of the two matrices are also equal. But if the reallocation is made in a different manner from the original proportions of the row and column totals of X, then this will not follow. In the case of equal margins we shall denote $\tilde{X}$ by the symbol $\tilde{X}_{vw}$.

A useful Lemma that is used by Skolka and Theil is the following one:

LEMMA 1. The entropy of any share matrix X that is partitioned into blocks X_{IJ}, with block shares by simple summation x_{IJ} forming the aggregate share matrix X^*, may be expressed as[48]

$$(6.9) \qquad H(X) = H(X^*) + \sum_{I,\,J=1}^{m} x_{IJ}H[(X_{IJ})/(x_{IJ})] \ .$$

Essentially the Lemma states that total entropy may be decomposed into an "entropy between" large sectors and a weighted sum of "entropies within" each large sector, the weights being the large sector shares. The analogy with the analysis of variance sum of squares identity is striking.

The *information loss from simplification* is defined as

$$(6.10) \qquad dI = I(X) - I(\tilde{X}) \ .$$

[47] PROOF: Let $\tilde{v}_i$ be a marginal total of a row of $\tilde{X}$—i.e.,

$$\tilde{v}_i = \sum_{j=1}^{n} \tilde{x}_{ij}$$

and let $\tilde{v}_i = k_I v_i$ where k_I is some constant for set I and v_i is the marginal total of row i of X. Then, because $\tilde{X}$ and X each have the same block totals x_{IJ} and hence the same marginal block totals, say x_I, it is true that

$$\sum_{i \in I} \tilde{v}_i = x_I = \sum_{i \in I} v_i \ .$$

That is, $\tilde{v}_i$ and v_i are proportional and also have the same sum, and hence must be equal. The same method of proof will establish that $\tilde{w}_j = w_j$.

[48] Proof of this Lemma is given in Appendix B.

This is analogous to Skolka's and Theil's "information loss from aggregation," only here the simplified matrix $\tilde{X}$ is used instead of the aggregated matrix X^*.[49] Using (6.5) we get immediately

(6.11) $dI = [H(\tilde{X}) - H(X)] - [H^m(\tilde{X}) - H^m(X)]$,

i.e., the information loss is equal to the difference in entropies minus the difference in marginal entropies. Now, because of the structure of $\tilde{X}$, the following Lemmas can be proved.

LEMMA 2: For any simplified matrix $\tilde{X}$ constructed from a given aggregated matrix X^* according to rule (6.8), the information content of the simplified matrix is equal to that of the aggregated matrix:

(6.12) $I(\tilde{X}) = I(X^*)$.

LEMMA 3: The information loss from simplification as given by formula (6.10) is precisely equal to the information loss from aggregation:

(6.13) $dI = I(X) - I(X^*)$.

LEMMA 4: The information loss from simplification may also be expressed in the form:

(6.14) $$dI = \sum_{i,\,j=1}^{n} x_{ij}\left(\log \frac{x_{ij}}{\tilde{x}_{ij}} - \log \frac{v_i w_j}{\tilde{v}_i \tilde{w}_j}\right) .$$

LEMMA 5: In the special case where the marginal share vectors of X are equal to those of $\tilde{X}$ (i.e., $v = \tilde{v}$ and $w = \tilde{w}$), we have

(6.15) $$d(I) = I(X) - I(\tilde{X}_{vw}) = \sum_{i,\,j=1}^{n} x_{ij}\log \frac{x_{ij}}{\tilde{x}_{ij}} .$$

Proofs of Lemmas 2 and 4 are given in Appendix B. The proof of Lemma 3 is immediate by substituting (6.12) into (6.10). This formula (6.13) is the same as Skolka's (116) and also Theil's [1967, p. 337]. The proof of Lemma 5 is immediate by substituting $v = \tilde{v}$ and $w = \tilde{w}$ into (6.14).[50]

Quadratic Approximation to the Information Measures. In his discussion Theil, [1967, pp. 38–39, 350–52] uses a power series approximation of the logarithm to derive an approximation to the information content of a

[49] The information losses will be proved equal in Lemma 3.
[50] In this special case we also have $dI = H(\tilde{X}_{vw}) - H(X)$, i.e., the information loss equals the entropy gain. This follows from the fact that in this case the last square bracket of (6.11) is zero (because the blocks have the same marginal share vectors), so dI equals the total entropy gain within blocks which in turn equals the total entropy gain (from [6.9]).

share matrix, which is a weighted sum of squared deviations. Applying this approximation to (6.15) we obtain

$$(6.16) \qquad dI = I(X) - I(\tilde{X}_{vw}) \approx \tfrac{1}{2} \sum_{i,\,j=1}^{n} \frac{(x_{ij} - \tilde{x}_{ij})^2}{x_{ij}}$$

$$\approx \tfrac{1}{2} \sum_{i,\,j=1}^{n} \frac{(x_{ij} - \tilde{x}_{ij})^2}{\tilde{x}_{ij}} \ .$$

The approximation is valid if the absolute differences $|x_{ij} - \tilde{x}_{ij}|$ are not large as compared with x_{ij} or $\tilde{x}_{ij}$. If (6.14) is used, rather than (6.15), the expression would contain two additional weighted sums of squares, one involving $(v_i - \tilde{v}_i)^2$ and one involving $(w_j - \tilde{w}_j)^2$, which would be subtracted from dI, as given by (6.16).

If one is content to use total entropy gain, $H(\tilde{X}) - H(X)$, as a measure of information loss, rather than dI, one could use (6.16), even in those cases where the simplified share matrix $\tilde{X}$ has different marginal share vectors than those of the original share matrix X. There seems to be no inherent logical reason why one should use dI rather than the entropy gain—in fact the latter formula is simpler.

Application to Input-Output Analysis. To go from the share matrix X to the flow matrix of input-output analysis involves only multiplication by a scalar denoting grand total production, say x. Although the measures from information theory all are presumed to apply to a share matrix (sometimes referred to as a stochastic matrix or matrix of probabilities), all of the formulas for entropy, information content, and information loss need only be multiplied by a scalar x to apply to the flow matrix. For this reason the symbol X will now be used for both, to save notation.

Now let's write another expression for the quadratic approximation to dI. From (6.13) we have, using also (6.4),

$$(6.17) \qquad dI = \sum_{i,\,j=1}^{n} x_{ij}\log\frac{x_{ij}}{v_i w_j} - \sum_{I,\,J=1}^{m} x_{IJ}\log\frac{x_{IJ}}{x_I x_J} \ .$$

From the quadratic approximation formula, applied twice, we have

$$(6.18) \qquad dI \approx \tfrac{1}{2}\left[\sum_{i,\,j=1}^{n} \frac{(x_{ij} - v_i w_j)^2}{v_i w_j} - \sum_{I,\,J=1}^{m} \frac{(x_{IJ} - x_I x_J)^2}{x_I x_J} \right] .$$

By expanding the squares, dividing through by the denominators, performing the summations, and noting that certain sums of shares equal unity, we obtain

$$(6.19) \qquad dI \approx \tfrac{1}{2}\left[\sum_{i,\,j=1}^{n}\frac{x_{ij}^{2}}{v_{i}w_{j}} - \sum_{I,\,J=1}^{m}\frac{x_{IJ}^{2}}{x_{I}x_{J}}\right].$$

It is interesting to note that in this application the approximation amounts to multiplying the right side of (6.17) by one-half and forgetting about the logarithm symbols.

Now look back at the conventional consolidation of section 2 of Chapter 3. Let the V and W diagonal matrices of that section be assumed to contain the elements v_{i} and w_{j} of the present section. Then the $\overline{W}$ of (3.19b) is a diagonal matrix containing the x_{J} of the present section as diagonal elements, and the diagonal matrix $\overline{V}$ defined as

$$(6.20) \qquad\qquad\qquad \overline{V} = TVT'$$

contains the x_{I} as diagonal elements. Then (6.19) says

$$(6.21) \qquad dI \approx \tfrac{1}{2}(\operatorname{tr} V^{-1}XW^{-1}X' - \operatorname{tr}\overline{V}^{-1}X^{*}\overline{W}^{-1}X^{*\prime})\ .$$

Since the V, W, $\overline{V}$, $\overline{W}$ matrices and their inverses are all diagonal, the traces are weighted sums of squares. Moreover, when we make the substitutions of (3.18), (3.19), (3.20), and (3.21), the parenthesis of (6.21) is found to be precisely the simplification cost c, as given by (2.21) of Chapter 2. So (6.21) says

$$(6.22) \qquad\qquad\qquad dI \approx \tfrac{1}{2}c\ .$$

So it turns out that when the quadratic approximation to the information loss is used, the loss in information due to aggregation given by the information theory is equivalent (except for a factor of one-half) to the simplification cost that is incurred in a prediction problem using an input-output model, where the coefficient matrix being simplified is the technical coefficient matrix A and the moment matrix of the predetermined variables is, or at least is proportional to, the diagonal matrix W. (See (3.21).) Note that the same difficulties with the assumption of the diagonal matrix that were noted in section 2 of Chapter 3 apply here too.

Theil [1967, Ch. 9] has proposed that one particular component of the information content—what he calls "input heterogeneity"—be used as a criterion for measuring aggregation effects rather than the complete information content. He shows a relationship between this component and the aggregation bias in a macro sense.[51] Skolka in his measurements of aggregation effect uses the complete information content.

Finally, we mention that in the cluster analysis programs of Rogers and Tanimoto [1960] and Rogers and Fleming [1964] a measure of distance based on entropy is used.

[51] See especially Theil [1967, pp. 352–53] where explicit algebraic comparisons are made.

7

CONCLUSION

1. SUMMARY

A need was felt for solutions to clustering and aggregation problems that arise in economics. Moreover, it was felt that the solutions should be specific and of a form that could be applied to concrete, numerical problems. From my own research experience and from my own reading I have observed that although in the present age voluminous data are available, reduction of the data to a smaller scale is most desirable for easier management and comprehension.

A problem, labeled the "optimal simplification problem," was formalized. It is a decision problem having either determinate or random data, having an objective expressing loss or utility resulting from alternative decisions, and involving the assumption that detailed data incur higher costs than coarse data. The decision to be made is the manner of reducing the detailed elements of the problem to a smaller number. This formalization is a fairly new variety of "the aggregation problem" in economics.

Two types of decision problem were distinguished: "prediction" and "decision-proper." Of the first type we considered two examples: a reduced form of simultaneous equations and an input-output model. Of "decision-proper" (meaning a problem whose objective function was truly economic-inspired) we discussed linear programming and conventional economic allocation problems. Of these four kinds of economic problems we conducted experiments on the first three, using data from the real world.

When some additional assumptions were made, containing some admittedly arbitrary features, the decision-theoretic structure described above led us to a method of aggregation called "progressive merger procedure."

This method, with the help of computers, enabled us to find specific groups—or clusters—for the economic problems. We believe these clusters are useful in understanding such problems, and that they represent near-optimal clusters in the sense of the decision theory. In each of the problems considered, we believe that they are an improvement over previously suggested simplified models.

The computational method used was described and embraces two sub-methods: "one-way," where the columns alone of a given matrix are partitioned, and "lockstep," where both rows and columns of a square matrix are partitioned correspondingly. The "one-way" case has strong similarities with "cluster analysis," as this term has come to be known in a number of scientific fields. While our experiments were on a fairly small scale, as realistic economic models run—the largest being a reduction of a 49 by 49 matrix to a 9 by 9—the methods used can be applied to larger problems.

When compared with other clustering methods, our method appears to be simpler and cheaper than the average, but dependent upon stronger than usual assumptions regarding weighting and the relevant distance metric. It is similar to methods using entropy and information measures.

The need for clustering and aggregation seems to be felt in a number of fields of social science—particularly in Sociology, Psychology, Political Science, and Linguistics—as well as in Biological Taxonomy, and Geology.

2. MAIN THEMES

Practically all of the partitions arrived at as solutions to the various problems are, in a sense, *skew*. There are practically always a few "single-tons"—industries with very high final demands, or farms with very large acreages, and so on, that are placed in a group all by themselves. At the other end of the scale, there are relatively large "bunches" of units, each of which has a relatively small measure.

This result should not be surprising to an economist who is accustomed to deal with such things as extremely skew distributions of such things as income, wealth, size of firm, development of nations, and so on. Nor should it surprise a statistician familiar with the problems of designing strata for sampling surveys of human populations; there are usually certain units of the population so large and important—and small in numbers—that a 100 per cent sample is taken of them. A partition that is skew, in the sense that we are now using the word, is usually optimal from the viewpoint of minimizing sampling variance of some central estimate.

In some cases, however, the skewness may suggest a redefinition of original units. After seeing the results from an input-output problem, one may ask oneself whether "Trade" or "Miscellaneous" should not be subdivided before an optimal partition is sought. The answer depends on the purpose of the analysis. If one is interested in predicting the production of the rubber industry alone, one would expect some asymmetry of aggregation.

Another main theme running through our work is the distinction between *homogeneity* and *independence*. Most of the simplification procedures assumed in this book are based on an assumption that homogeneity is desirable, in the sense of equality or proportionality of elements within sets. Yet we have recognized and occasionally discussed the property of independence; a leading example is block-diagonality of matrix structure; the implied reason for interest in this structure is that one can solve one problem independently of others, and so use simpler decision procedures over-all. Yet, if one stage (or one block) is unduly large or complicated, not much benefit has been accomplished by the independent, or block-diagonal, structure. One wants to reduce the large block further, or simplify it in some way. The answer to the question as to whether, in some specific problem, one really wants homogeneity, or independence, or some combination of the two, probably depends upon an adequately specific formulation of the decision problem involved, including a properly specified cost function.

3. LIMITS AND PROSPECTS

At various points in our discussion the limitations of the specializing assumptions made have been recognized. Sometimes, however, the solution of an aggregation problem depends—and rightly so—on special assumptions. For example, if there is no very obvious clustering, the weights assumed will determine the solution, and an alternative set of weights would change it. If one really does not know which system of weights should be adopted, one therefore has no means of solving the problem. In other problems—say, when clusters are well structured—the system of weights will not matter. This reasoning suggests that perhaps an arbitrary assignment of weights is not so serious as may be thought—if it is not clearly a wrong assignment. We do not wish to press this point too far. It is clearly beneficial that more research be done with more general assumptions.

It would also be desirable to learn more about possibilities for solving the simplification problem *before* the detailed problem is solved. We feel somewhat embarrassed, in outlining the computer programs for the progressive merger procedure, to request the inverse of the detailed M matrix as a preliminary operation. To be sure, we can plead that we have investigated approximations to this inverse, and that these have proved promising, but more research needs to be accomplished in this area.

With reference to homogeneity, an interesting field for future research would be an investigation of the class of problems for which homogeneity is *not* desirable. We know that the science of gerrymandering voting districts is based on a search for a partition of a population into subsets that are *heterogeneous*. What characteristics of decision problems lead to this result?

Another generalization of the present inquiry could be in the direction of multi-person games. Some interesting observations of Nyblen [1951] have not been pursued.

This study is limited also, obviously, by its small scope in relation to a more general theory of organization, and of hierarchy. The formulation of an optimal organization problem reported on pages 121–22 should provide stimulus and challenge for ambitious researchers.

While we claim that our suggested methods are useful, we surely cannot claim that others may not be more useful. Let the search continue.

REFERENCES

Abou-el-Dahab, M. G. 1965. An aggregation procedure for deriving representative firms in estimating supply functions. Ph.D. dissertation, Kansas State University.

Alexander, C. N., Jr. 1963. A method for processing sociometric data. *Sociometry* 26 (June): 268–69.

Anderson, L. F., M. W. Watts, Jr. and A. R. Wilcox. 1966. *Legislative roll-call analysis*. Evanston, Illinois: Northwestern University Press.

Anderson, T. W. 1958. *Introduction to multivariate statistical analysis*. New York: Wiley.

Ando, A. and F. M. Fisher. 1963. Near-decomposability, partition and aggregation, and the relevance of stability discussions. *International Economic Review* 4 (January): 53–67.

Ara, K. 1959. The aggregation problem in input-output analysis. *Econometrica* 27 (April): 257–62.

Arrow, K. J. 1948. Summarizing a population of behavior patterns (abstract). *Econometrica* 16 (April): 203.

Arrow, K. J. 1951. *Social choice and individual values*. New York: Wiley.

Arrow, K. J. and M. Hoffenberg. 1959. *A time series analysis of interindustry demands*. Amsterdam, North Holland.

Balderston, J. B. and T. M. Whitin. 1954. Aggregation in the input-output model. In *Economic activity analysis*, O. Morgenstern, ed., pp. 79–128. New York: Wiley.

Ball, G. H. 1965. Data analysis in the social sciences: What about the details? *Proceedings of the Fall Joint Computer Conference*, pp. 533–59.

Banerjee, K. S. 1961. A unified statistical approach to the index number problem. *Econometrica* 29 (October): 591–601.

Banerjee, K. S. 1963. Best linear unbiased index numbers and index numbers obtained through a factorial approach. *Econometrica* 31 (October): 712–18.

Barna, T. 1954. Classification and aggregation in input-output analysis. Chapter 7, in *The structural interdependence of the economy*, T. Barna, ed., pp. 173–85. New York: Wiley.

Barten, A. P. 1964. Consumer demand functions under conditions of almost additive preferences. *Econometrica* 32 (January–April): 1–38.

Barten, A. P. 1967. Evidence on the Slutsky conditions for demand equations. *Review of Economics and Statistics* 49 (February): 77–84.

Barten, A. P. and S. J. Turnovsky. 1966. Some aspects of the aggregation problem for composite demand equations. *International Economic Review* 7 (September): 231–59.

Bellman, R. 1960. *Introduction to matrix analysis*. New York: McGraw-Hill.

Bertalanffy, L. von. 1950. The theory of open systems in physics and biology. *Science* 111 (January): 23–29.

Beyle, H. C. 1931. *Identification and analysis of attribute-cluster-blocs.* Chicago: The University of Chicago Press.

Bidwell, O. W. and F. D. Hole. 1964. An experiment in the numerical classification of some Kansas soils. *Proceedings of the Soil Science Society of America* 28 (March–April): 263–68.

Boot, J. C. G. and G. M. de Wit. 1960. Investment demand: an empirical contribution to the aggregation problem. *International Economic Review* 1 (January): 1–30.

Bottenberg, R. A. and R. E. Christal. 1961. An iterative technique for clustering criteria which retains optimum predictive efficiency. Lackland Air Force Base, Texas: Personnel Laboratory, Wright Air Development Division, March 1961. (Technical Note WADD–TN–61–30.)

Bowker, A. H. 1947. On the norm of a matrix. *Annals of Mathematical Statistics* 18 (June): 285–88.

Cain, A. J. 1959. The post-Linnaean development of taxonomy. *Proceedings of the Linnean Society of London* 170 (April): 234–44.

Chabot, J. 1960. A simplified example of the use of matrix multiplication for the analysis of sociometric data. *Sociometry* 13 (May): 131–40.

Chave, K. E. and F. T. Mackenzie. 1961. A statistical technique applied to the geochemistry of pelagic muds. *Journal of Geology* 69 (September): 572–82.

Chipman, J. S. 1964. On least squares with insufficient observations. *Journal of the American Statistical Association* 59 (December): 1078–1111.

Chipman, J. S. and M. M. Rao. 1964. The treatment of linear restrictions in regression analysis. *Econometrica* 32 (January–April): 198–209.

Coleman, J. S. and D. MacRae, Jr. 1960. Electronic processing of sociometric data for groups up to 1,000 in size. *American Sociological Review* 25 (October): 722–26.

Dalenius, T. 1950. The problem of optimum stratification. *Skandinavisk Aktuarietidskrift* 33: 203–13.

Dalenius, T. 1957. *Sampling in Sweden.* Stockholm: Almqvist and Wiksell.

Dalenius, T. and M. Gurney. 1951. The problem of optimum stratification, II. *Skandinavisk Aktuarietidskrift* 34: 133–48.

Dantzig, G. B. and P. Wolfe. 1960. Decomposition principle for linear programs. *Operations Research* 8 (January–February): 101–11.

Dantzig, G. B. and P. Wolfe. 1961. The decomposition algorithm for linear programs. *Econometrica* 29 (October): 767–78.

Day, R. H. 1963. On aggregating linear programming models of production. *Journal of Farm Economics* 45 (November): 797–813.

de Janvry, A. 1966. Measurement of demand parameters under separability. Ph.D. dissertation, University of California, Berkeley.

Dorfman, R. 1951. *Application of linear programming to the theory of the firm.* Berkeley: University of California Press.

Dyen, I. 1962. The lexicostatistical classification of the Malayopolynesian languages. *Language* 38 (January–March): 38–46.

Fei, J. C. H. 1956. A fundamental theorem for the aggregation problem of input-output analysis. *Econometrica* 24 (October): 400–12.

Fisher, F. M. 1965. Embodied technical change and the existence of an aggregate capital stock. *Review of Economic Studies* 32 (October): 263–88.

Fisher, I. 1922. *The making of index numbers.* Boston and New York: Houghton Mifflin.

Fisher, W. D. 1951. California fresh tomatoes—marketing channels and gross margins from farm to consumer. Giannini Foundation, Mimeographed Report No. 113, University of California (June).

Fisher, W. D. 1953. On a pooling problem from the statistical decision viewpoint. *Econometrica* 21 (October): 567–85.

Fisher, W. D. 1958a. Criteria for aggregation in input-output analysis. *Review of Economics and Statistics* 40 (August): 250–60.

Fisher, W. D. 1958b. On grouping for maximum homogeneity. *Journal of the American Statistical Association* 53 (December): 789–98.

Fisher, W. D. 1962a. Estimation in the linear decision model. *International Economic Review* 3 (January): 1–29.

Fisher, W. D. 1962b. Optimal aggregation in multi-equation prediction models. *Econometrica* 30 (October): 744–69.

Fisher, W. D. 1966. Simplification of economic models. *Econometrica* 34 (July): 563–84.

Fisher, W. D. and P. L. Kelley. 1968. *Selecting representative firms in linear programming.* Kansas Agricultural Experiment Station Technical Bulletin No. 159, Manhattan, Kansas.

Forsyth, E. and L. Katz. 1946. A matrix approach to the analysis of sociometric data: preliminary report. *Sociometry* 9 (November): 340–47.

Fortier, J. J. and H. Solomon. 1966. Clustering procedures. In *Multivariate analysis*, P. R. Krishnaiah, ed., pp. 493–506. New York: Academic Press.

Frick, G. E. and R. A. Andrews. 1965. Aggregation bias and four methods of summing farm supply functions. *Journal of Farm Economics* 47 (August): 696–700.

Friedman, H. P. and J. Rubin. 1967. On some invariant criteria for grouping data. *Journal of the American Statistical Association* 62 (December): 1159–78.

Frisch, R. 1936. Annual survey of general economic theory: the problem of index numbers. *Econometrica* 4 (January): 1–38.

Frisch, R. 1950. L'emploi des modèles pour l'élaboration d'une politique économique rationclle. *Revue d'Économie Politique* 60 (septembre–octobre): 474–98; (novembre–décembre): 601–34.

Frisch, R. 1959. A complete scheme for computing all direct and cross demand elasticities in a model with many sectors. *Econometrica* 27 (April): 177–96.

Gale, D. 1960. *The theory of linear economic models.* New York: McGraw-Hill.

Gerard, R. W. 1957. Units and concepts of biology. *Science* 125 (March): 429–33.

Ghosh. A. 1960. Input-output analysis with substantially independent groups of industries. *Econometrica* 28 (January): 88–96.

Goldberger, A. S. 1959. *Impact multipliers and dynamic properties of the Klein-Goldberger model.* Amsterdam, North Holland.

Goldman, S. M. and H. Uzawa. 1964. A note on separability in demand analysis. *Econometrica* 32 (July): 387–98.

Gorman, W. M. 1953. Community preference fields. *Econometrica* 21 (January): 63–80.

Gorman, W. M. 1959a. Separable utility and aggregation. *Econometrica* 27 (July): 469.

Gorman, W. M. 1959b. The empirical implications of a utility tree: a further comment. *Econometrica* 27 (July): 489.

Gorman, W. M. 1967a. Measuring the quantities of fixed factors. Technical Report No. 150, Stanford University (July).

Gorman, W. M. 1967b. The structure of utility functions. Technical Report No. 151, Stanford University (August).

Green, H. A. J. 1964. *Aggregation in economic analysis, an introductory survey.* Princeton, N. J.: Princeton University Press.

Grieg-Smith, P. 1964. *Quantitative plant ecology*, 2nd ed. Washington: Butterworths.

Grunfeld, Y. and Z. Griliches. 1960. Is aggregation necessarily bad? *Review of Economics and Statistics* 42 (February): 1–13.

Hagood, M. J. and E. H. Bernert. 1945. Component indexes as a basis for stratification in sampling. *Journal of the American Statistical Association* 40 (September): 330–41.

Harbaugh, J. W. 1964. Use of factor analysis in recognizing facies boundaries (abstract). *Bulletin of the American Association of Petroleum Geologists* 48 (April): 529.

Harman, H. H. 1967. *Modern factor analysis*, 2nd ed. Chicago: The University of Chicago Press.

Harris, C. C., Jr. 1964. A scientific method of districting. *Behavioral Science* 9 (July): 219–25.

Hartley, H. O. 1962. Total supply functions estimated from farm surveys. Paper presented before the North Central Farm Management Research Committee (March).

Hatanaka, M. 1952. Note on consolidation within a Leontief system. *Econometrica* 20 (April): 301–3.

Hess, S. W., J. B. Weaver, H. J. Siegfeldt, J. N. Whelan, and P. A. Zitlau. 1965. Nonpartisan political redistricting by computer. *Operations Research* 13 (November–December): 998–1006.

Holzman, M. 1953. Problems of classification and aggregation. In *Studies in the structure of the American economy*, W. Leontief, ed., pp. 326–59. New York: Oxford University Press.

Hooper, J. W. and A. Zellner. 1961. The error of forecast for multivariate regression models. *Econometrica* 29 (October): 544–55.

Houthakker, H. S. 1960. Additive preferences. *Econometrica* 28 (April): 244–57.

Hurwicz, L. 1952. Aggregation in macroeconomic models (abstract). *Econometrica* 20 (July): 489–90.

Imbrie, J. and E. G. Purdy. 1962. Classification of modern Bahamian carbonate sediments. *Memoir I classification of carbonate rocks*. Tulsa, Oklahoma: The American Association of Petroleum Geologists (November): 253–72.

Johnson, S. C. 1967. Hierarchical clustering schemes. *Psychometrika* 32 (September): 241–54.

Jowett, B. 1885. *The politics of Aristotle*, vol. 1. Oxford: Clarendon Press.

Kelley, P. L. and D. A. Knight. 1965. Short-run elasticities of supply for milk. *Journal of Farm Economics* 47 (February): 93–104.

Kemeny, J. G., O. Morgenstern, and G. L. Thompson. 1956. A generalization of the von Neumann model of an expanding economy. *Econometrica* 24 (April) 115–35.

Kendall, M. G. 1957. *A course in multivariate analysis*. London: Griffin.

King, B. F. 1966. Market and industry factors in stock price behavior. *Journal of Business* 39 (January): 139–90.

King, B. F. 1967. Step-wise clustering procedures. *Journal of the American Statistical Association* 62 (March): 86–101.

Klein, L. R. 1946a. Macroeconomics and the theory of rational behavior. *Econometrica* 14 (April): 93–108.

Klein, L. R. 1946b. Remarks on the theory of aggregation. *Econometrica* 14 (October): 303–12.

Klein, L. R. 1953. *A textbook of econometrics.* Evanston: Row Peterson.

Klein, L. R. 1960. The efficiency of estimation in econometric models. In *Essays in Economics and Econometrics*, R. W. Pfouts, ed., pp. 216–32. Chapel Hill: University of North Carolina Press.

Kloek, T. and L. B. M. Mennes. 1960. Simultaneous equations estimation based on principal components of predetermined variables. *Econometrica* 28 (January): 45–61.

Koopmans, T. C., H. Rubin, and R. B. Leipnik. 1950. Measuring the equation systems of dynamic economics. In *Statistical inference in dynamic economic models*, T. C. Koopmans, ed., pp. 53–237. New York: Wiley.

Kuznets, G. M., A. de Janvry, and J. Bieri. 1967. Measurement of demand parameters under a dynamic quadratic preference function. Paper read to Econometric Society, Washington, D.C. (December).

Lave, L. B. 1964. Technological change in U.S. agriculture: the aggregation problem. *Journal of Farm Economics* 46 (February): 200–17.

Lee, J. E., Jr. 1966. Exact aggregation—a discussion of Miller's theorem. *Agricultural Economic Research* 18 (April): 58–61.

Leontief, W. 1947a. Introduction to a theory of the internal structure of functional relationships. *Econometrica* 15 (October): 361–73.

Leontief, W. 1947b. A note on the interrelation of subsets of independent variables of a continuous function with continuous first derivatives. *Bulletin of the American Mathematical Society* 53 (April): 343–50.

Leontief, W. 1951. *The structure of American economy, 1919–1939.* New York: Oxford University Press.

Leontief, W. 1953. *Studies in the structure of the American economy.* New York: Oxford University Press.

Letourneau, J. L. 1966. Testing methods of aggregating linear programming problems. Master's Report, Kansas State University.

Lijphart, A. 1963. The analysis of bloc voting in the General Assembly: a critique and a proposal. *American Political Science Review* 54 (December): 902–17.

Luce, R. D. 1950. Connectivity and generalized cliques in sociometric group structure. *Psychometrika* 15 (June): 169–90.

Luce, R. D. and A. D. Perry. 1949. A method of matrix analysis of group structure. *Psychometrika* 14 (March): 95–116.

MacRae, D., Jr. 1960. Direct factor analysis of sociometric data. *Sociometry* 23 (December): 360–71.

Mahalanobis, P. C. 1936. On the generalized distance in statistics. *Proceedings of the National Institute of Sciences of India* 2: 49–55.

Malinvaud, E. 1954. Aggregation problems in input-output models. In *The structural interdependence of the economy*, T. Barna, ed., pp. 187–202. New York: Wiley.

Malinvaud, E. 1956. L'agrégation dans les modèles économiques. In *Cahiers du Séminaire d'Économétrie No. 4*, pp. 69–146. Paris: Centre National de la Recherche Scientifique.

Malinvaud, E. 1966. *Statistical methods of econometrics*. Chicago: Rand McNally.

March, J. G. and H. A. Simon. 1958. *Organizations*. New York: Wiley.

Marschak, J. 1951. Optimal aggregation of inventories under certainty, (hectographed). Cowles Commission Discussion Paper, Economics no. 2015 (March).

Marschak, J. 1964. Problems in information economics. In *Management controls: new directions in basic research*, C. P. Bonini, R. K. Jaedicke, and H. M. Wagner, eds., pp. 38–74. New York: McGraw-Hill.

Marschak, J. and K. Miyasawa. 1968. Comparability of Information Systems. *International Economic Review* 9 (June): 137–74.

Marschak, J. and R. Radner. 1968. *Economic Theory of Teams*. New York: Wiley.

May, K. 1946. The aggregation problem for a one-industry model. *Econometrica* 14 (October): 285–98.

May, K. 1947. Technological change and aggregation. *Econometrics* 15 (January): 51–63.

May, K. 1954. Transitivity, utility and aggregation in preference patterns. *Econometrica* 22 (January): 1–13.

McCarthy, John. 1956. Aggregation in the Leontief model. Paper presented at Joint Allied Social Science Association meeting in Cleveland, Ohio (December 27).

McGuire, C. B. 1960. An illustrative application of economic analysis. In *The economics of defense in the nuclear age*, C. J. Hitch and R. N. McKean, pp. 133–58. Cambridge: Harvard University Press.

McManus, M. 1956a. General consistent aggregation in Leontief models. *Yorkshire Bulletin of Economic and Social Research* 8 (June): 28–48.

McManus, M. 1956b. On Hatanaka's note on consolidation. *Econometrica* 24 (October): 482–87.

McQuitty, L. L. 1957. Elementary linkage analysis for isolating orthogonal and oblique types and typal relevancies. *Educational and Psychological Measurement* 17 (Summer): 207–29.

Michener, C. D. and R. R. Sokal. 1957. A quantitative approach to a problem in classification. *Evolution* 11 (June): 130–62.

Miller, T. A. 1966. Sufficient conditions for exact aggregation in linear programming models. *Agricultural Economics Research* 18 (April): 52–57.

Miller, T. A. 1967. Aggregation error in representative farm linear programming supply estimates. Ph.D. dissertation, Iowa State University.

Morgan, J. N. and J. A. Sonquist. 1963. Problems in the analysis of survey data. *Journal of the American Statistical Association* 58 (June): 415–34.

Morgenstern, O., ed. 1954. *Economic activity analysis*. New York: Wiley.

Morishima, M. and F. Seton. 1961. Aggregation in Leontief matrices and the labor theory of value. *Econometrica* 29 (April): 203–20.

Mundlak, Y. 1961. Aggregation over time in distributed lag models. *International Economic Review* 2 (May): 154–63.

Nataf, A. 1948. Sur la possibilité de construction de certains macromodèles. *Econometrica* 16 (July): 232–44.

Nataf, A. 1953a. Possibilité d'agrégation dans le cadre de la théorie des choix. *Metroeconomica* V, fasc 1 (Avril): 22–30.

Nataf, A. 1953b. Sur des questions d'agrégation en économétrie, Thèses présentées a la Faculté des Sciences de l'Université de Paris. Paris: Imprimerie J & R Sennac, 1954.

Nataf. A. 1958. Forme réduite d'agrégats de consommation dans le cadre de la théorie des choix. *Publications de l'Institut de statistique de Paris*, vol. 7, no. 1.

Nataf, A. 1960. Résultats et directions de recherche dans la théorie de l'agrégation. In *Logic, methodology and philosophy of science—Proceedings of the 1960 International Congress*, E. Nagel, P. Suppes, and A. Tarski, eds., pp. 484–93. Stanford, California: Stanford University Press, 1962.

Neudecker, H. 1968. Aggregation in input-output analysis. University of Birmingham, Faculty of Commerce and Social Science Discussion Paper A93 (February).

Nyblen, G. 1951. *The problem of summation in economic science*. Lund: C. W. K. Gleerup.

Overall, J. E. 1963. A configural analysis of psychiatric diagnostic stereotypes. *Behavioral Science* 8 (July): 211–19.

Parks, R. W. 1966. An econometric model of Swedish economic growth. Doctoral dissertation, University of California, Berkeley.

Parks, R. W. 1967. Estimation of a two level CES production function and tests of alternative specifications. Paper read to Econometric Society, Washington, D.C. (December).

Pearce, I. F. 1961a. An exact method of consumer demand analysis. *Econometrica* 29 (October): 499–516.

Pearce, I. F. 1961b. A method of consumer demand analysis illustrated. *Economica* 28 (November): 371–94.

Pearce, I. F. 1964. *A contribution to demand analysis*. New York: Oxford University Press.

Penrose, R. 1955. A generalized inverse for matrices. *Proceedings of the Cambridge Philosophical Society* 51 (July): 406–13.

Peston, M. H. 1959. A view of the aggregation problem. *The Review of Economic Studies* 27 (October): 58–64.

Pierce, J. E. 1962. Possible electronic computation of typological indices for linguistic structures. *International Journal of American Linguistics* 28 (October): 215 26.

Plaxico, J. S. 1955. Problems of factor-product aggregation in Cobb-Douglas value productivity analysis. *Journal of Farm Economics* 37 (November): 664–75.

Prais, S. J. and J. Aitchison. 1954. The grouping of observations in regression analysis. *Revue de l'Institut International de Statistique* 22: 1–22.

Radner, R. 1961. The evaluation of information in organizations. Management Science Research Grant Technical Report No. 2, Berkeley (June).

Radner, R. 1962. Team decision problems. *Annals of Mathematical Statistics* 33 (September): 857–81.

Rajaoja, V. 1958. *A study in the theory of demand functions and price indexes*. Helsinki: Societas Scientiarum Fennica.

Reiter, S. 1957. Surrogates for uncertain decision problems: minimal information for decision-making. *Econometrica* 25 (April): 339–45.

Reiter, S. and G. R. Sherman. 1965. Discrete optimizing. *Journal of the Society for Industrial and Applied Mathematics* 13 (September): 864–89.

Rice, S. A. 1928. *Quantitative methods in politics*. New York: Knopf.

Rogers, D. J. and H. Fleming. 1964. A computer program for classifying plants. II A numerical handling of non-numerical data, *Bioscience* 14 (September): 15–28.

Rogers, D. J. and T. T. Tanimoto. 1960. A computer program for classifying plants. *Science* 132 (October): 1115–18.

Rubin, R. M. 1968. Aggregation criteria in input-output analysis. Ph.D. dissertation, Kansas State University.

Samuelson, P. A. 1947. *Foundations of economic analysis.* Cambridge: Harvard University Press.

Sargan, J. D. 1958. The estimation of economic relationships using instrumental variables. *Econometrica* 26 (July): 393–415.

Sato, K. 1967. A two-level constant elasticity of substitution production function. *Review of Economic Studies* 34 (April): 201–18.

Savage, L. J. 1954. *The foundations of statistics.* New York: John Wiley.

Schneeweiss, H. 1965. Das Aggregationsproblem. *Statistische Hefte,* vol. 6, no. 1, pp. 1–26. Frankfurt am Main: Vittorio Klostermann.

Sheehy, S. J. 1964. Selection of representative benchmark farms in synthetic supply estimation. Ph.D. dissertation, Pennsylvania State University.

Sheehy, S. J. and R. H. McAlexander. 1965. Selection of representative benchmark farms for supply estimation. *Journal of Farm Economics* 47 (August): 681–95.

Shou Shan Pu. 1946. A note on macroeconomics. *Econometrica* 14 (October): 299–302.

Simon, H. A. and A. Ando. 1961. Aggregation of variables in dynamic systems. *Econometrica* 29 (April): 111–38.

Skolka, J. 1964. *Agregace v Bilanci Meziodvětvových Vztahů* [The aggregation problem in input-output analysis], Praha, Nakladatelství Československé Akademie Věd [Czechoslovakian Academy of Sciences].

Sneath, P. H. A. 1957. The application of computers to taxonomy. *Journal of General Microbiology* 17 (August): 201–26.

Sokal, R. R. and P. H. A. Sneath. 1963. *Principles of numerical taxonomy.* San Francisco and London: W. H. Freeman.

Solow, R. M. 1956. The production function and the theory of capital. *Review of Economic Studies* 23 (1955–56): 101–18.

Sono, M. 1961. The effect of price changes on the demand and supply of separable goods. *International Economic Review* 2 (September): 239–71.

Stigum, B. P. 1967. On certain problems of aggregation. *International Economic Review* 8 (October): 349–67.

Strotz, R. H. 1956. The role of stereotypes in welfare economics. *Metroeconomica* 8 (December): 199–202.

Strotz, R. H. 1957. The empirical implications of a utility tree. *Econometrica* 25 (April): 269–80.

Strotz, R. H. 1959. The utility tree—a correction and further appraisal. *Econometrica* 27 (July): 482–89.

Theil, H. 1954. *Linear aggregation of economic relations.* Amsterdam, North Holland.

Theil, H. 1957. Linear aggregation in input-output analysis. *Econometrica* 25 (January): 111–22.

Theil, H. 1958. *Economic forecasts and policy.* Amsterdam, North Holland (2nd edition, 1961).

Theil, H. 1959. The aggregation implications of identifiable structural macro-relations. *Econometrica* 27 (January): 14–29.

Theil, H. 1960. Best linear index numbers of prices and quantities. *Econometrica* 28 (April): 464–80.

Theil, H. 1962. Alternative approaches to the aggregation problem. In *Logic, methodology and philosophy of science—Proceedings of the 1960 International Congress*, E. Nagel, P. Suppes, and A. Tarski, eds., pp. 507–27. Stanford, California: Stanford University Press.

Theil, H. 1967. *Economics and information theory*. Chicago: Rand McNally.

Thoreson, J. D. and J. M. Littschwager. 1967. Legislative districting by computer simulation. *Behavioral Science* 12 (May): 237–47.

Thurstone, L. L. 1935. *The vectors of mind*. Chicago: University of Chicago Press.

Tilanus, C. B. 1964. Thirteen aggregated input-output tables, The Netherlands, 1948–1960. Report 6423 of the Econometric Institute of The Netherlands School of Economics, Rotterdam.

Tilanus, C. B. and H. Theil. 1965. The information approach to the evaluation of input-output forecasts. *Econometrica* 32 (October): 847–61.

Tinbergen, J. 1952. *On the theory of economic policy*. Amsterdam: North Holland.

Tinbergen, J. 1956. *Economic policy: principles and design*. Amsterdam: North Holland.

Truman, D. 1959. *The congressional party*. New York: Wiley.

Tryon, C. M. 1943. Evaluation of adolescent personality by adolescents. In *Child behaviour and development*, R. G. Barker, J. S. Kounin, and H. F. Wright, eds., pp. 545–66. New York and London: McGraw-Hill.

Tryon, R. C. 1939. *Cluster analysis: correlation profile and orthometric analysis for the isolation of unities in mind and personality*. Ann Arbor, Michigan: Edward Brothers.

Tryon, R. C. 1955. Identification of social areas by cluster analysis. *University of California Publications in Psychology*, vol. 8 (August), pp. 1–100.

Wald, A. 1950. *Statistical decision functions*. New York: John Wiley.

Wallis, W. A. and H. V. Roberts. 1956. *Statistics: a new approach*. Glencoe, Illinois: The Free Press.

Ward, J. H., Jr. 1963. Hierarchical grouping to optimize an objective function. *Journal of the American Statistical Association* 58 (March): 237–44.

Waugh, F. V. 1950. Inversion of the Leontief matrix by power series. *Econometrica* 18 (April): 142–54.

Waugh, F. V. 1951. The minimum-cost dairy feed. *Journal of Farm Economics* 33 (August): 299–310.

Weaver, J. B. and S. W. Hess. 1963. A procedure for non-partisan districting: development of computer techniques. *Yale Law Journal* 73 (December): 288–308.

Weil, R. L., Jr. 1968. The decomposition of economic production systems. *Econometrica* 36 (April): 260–78.

Weiss, R. S. and E. Jacobson. 1955. A method for the analysis of the structure of complex organizations. *American Sociological Review* 20 (December): 661–68.

APPENDIXES

APPENDIX A. SUPPLEMENTARY TABLES

TABLE A1. ORIGINAL P AND M MATRICES FOR REDUCED-FORM EXAMPLE

P

	1	2	3	4	5	6	7	8	9	10	11	12	13	14
C	−.777	.398	.378	.364	.363	.415	.114	.415	.101	.054	−.056	.414	.116	−.254
D	−.032	.058	−.026	.015	.015	.087	.005	.087	.004	.015	.087	.087	.005	−.080
W_1	−.183	.333	−.147	.087	.087	.525	.268	.525	.024	.046	−.030	.525	.268	−.246
Q	−.764	1.386	.386	.360	.360	1.187	.115	1.187	.010	.192	−.127	1.186	.116	−1.025

M

	1	2	3	4	5	6	7	8	9	10	11	12	13	14
1	33.77	53.46	6.34	15.92	46.82	9.26	38.56	−1.20	8.31	6.77	61.22	25.65	12.92	20.87
2		203.97	52.76	55.63	88.13	19.90	119.68	19.02	−27.01	33.89	194.31	113.78	6.49	65.44
3			30.89	10.20	−15.42	6.48	20.94	1.96	−4.15	35.48	15.28	29.89	6.91	19.98
4				52.38	73.92	13.06	46.77	−1.94	−29.06	−28.11	116.16	25.05	2.77	12.38
5					278.57	19.16	166.40	20.66	−27.51	−68.76	257.37	134.20	−15.33	17.50
6						12.64	24.63	−5.98	−16.20	−1.42	42.78	15.19	6.57	9.95
7							180.48	27.85	−55.85	−13.65	225.56	152.10	−15.18	42.56
8								22.55	−17.98	−14.49	23.49	29.21	−19.48	5.28
9									158.63	79.89	−195.44	−43.75	45.26	−11.09
10										128.83	−114.49	28.32	36.63	16.94
11											657.82	166.58	−38.49	54.71
12												177.29	−17.81	38.00
13													34.93	5.09
14														26.56

Note: For names of variable symbols and relevant units see Table 4.
Source: Goldberger [1959], P from Table 3.2. M computed from Table 4.1.

TABLE A2. RANDOM r_{ij} USED TO FORM ASSUMED MOMENT MATRIX FOR INPUT-OUTPUT EXAMPLE

	1	2	3	4	5	6	7	8	9	10	11	12	13	14	15	16	17	18
1	1	−.7	−.5	.9	.9	−.3	−.8	−.4	−.4	.6	0	−.6	−.2	.8	.4	−.6	.5	−.9
2		1	.7	−.3	−.4	.4	−.3	.5	−.8	−.1	−.6	−.7	−.3	−.4	.7	−.7	0	.2
3			1	−.8	0	.9	.3	.5	.1	−.9	.8	−.7	−.9	.5	.1	−.8	.6	−.4
4				1	−.3	−.6	−.8	.4	.4	−.1	0	−.4	−.9	0	−.8	0	.1	−.2
5					1	.8	−.3	.7	.3	−.9	0	−.7	.6	.7	−.6	−.6	−.5	−.7
6						1	.1	.8	.1	0	−.6	.5	.5	−.1	.2	−.5	.7	.7
7							1	−.2	.8	.4	−.2	0	.7	0	.7	.1	.9	−.8
8								1	.6	.4	−.1	0	−.6	−.7	.3	.5	.8	−.8
9									1	−.1	.2	−.8	.7	−.2	.7	0	.5	.6
10										1	1	−.4	.5	−.3	.5	.5	.4	−.5
11											1	−.5	.8	.1	.1	.7	−.5	−.2
12												1	0	0	.5	0	−.2	−.8
13													1	1	.7	.7	.7	.3
14														1	−.4	−.6	0	−.8
15															1	−.8	−.5	.3
16																1	.4	−.2
17																	1	0
18																		1

Note: For industry names see Table 6.
Source: Rubin [1968, Table 28].

	1	2	3	4	5	6	7	8	9
1	8.3	7.4	77.3	399.9	74.2	39.5	8.1	8.5	115.7
2		31.7	243.8	421.2	106.1	120.6	15.5	18.0	267.5
3			6,199.5	7,381.0	1,774.0	1,515.0	352.4	337.1	3,273.5
4				48,109.4	4,935.6	2,963.7	635.1	638.2	6,995.5
5					1,903.6	1,019.9	164.3	118.5	1,833.9
6						1,109.4	147.5	118.9	1,412.4
7							47.6	24.7	333.9
8								32.3	258.1
9									5,944.1
10									
11									
12									
13									
14									
15									
16									
17									
18									

	10	11	12	13	14	15	16	17	18
1	26.8	57.8	158.4	24.6	173.2	33.4	10.9	302.1	12.7
2	52.2	67.7	361.9	42.4	212.5	103.0	25.5	625.5	35.5
3	690.2	1,403.5	3,816.5	574.3	4,475.0	1,213.7	308.1	13,488.3	468.9
4	3,330.9	3,235.6	11,541.3	1,584.2	13,975.1	2,389.2	1,062.6	22,193.2	1,127.3
5	410.2	637.1	2,071.0	443.1	3,111.6	559.4	100.4	6,651.8	269.0
6	350.1	411.8	2,132.6	367.2	1,653.5	566.4	144.6	4,254.1	251.6
7	92.5	133.1	367.3	77.8	449.9	117.2	30.6	850.2	44.6
8	59.9	93.1	323.7	41.4	263.4	96.9	26.9	865.4	40.5
9	856.5	1,447.2	4,570.8	888.4	3,602.0	1,285.9	351.1	11,044.2	473.2
10	546.5	347.0	1,396.3	233.6	934.7	369.9	107.2	1,812.3	121.2
11		766.5	1,299.6	246.5	1,843.0	384.7	129.8	3,663.0	167.6
12			13,167.9	1,023.5	3,308.7	1,671.8	553.6	11,305.4	914.2
13				296.1	828.5	258.2	62.9	1,509.1	119.2
14					11,264.1	1,293.5	357.0	14,787.2	528.8
15						798.4	124.1	3,435.2	194.8
16							68.4	779.0	47.3
17								45,230.9	1,304.2
18									144.3

Note: For industry names see Table 6. Figures are in units of 1939 dollars $\times$ 10^{16}.
Source: Rubin [1968, Table 30]. Decimals rounded.

TABLE A4. TECHNICAL COEFFICIENT MATRIX FOR INPUT-OUTPUT EXAMPLE

	1	2	3	4	5	6	7	8	9	10	11	12	13	14	15	16	17	18
1	.3056		.0019		.0624	.1003	.0145			.0008	.0072	.0025	.0008	.0587	.0091			.0174
2		.0171	.0043	.0002	.0254	.0026			.0001		.0001	.0485	.0030	.0004	.0042	.0011	.0016	.0165
3			.0760	.2660						.0351	.0208	.0130	.0008	.0166				.0071
4			.0515	.0811						.0094	.0008							.0164
5	.0010	.0137	.0151	.0038	.2144	.0008	.0030	.0069	.0081	.0014	.0108	.0085	.0051	.0419	.0101	.0041	.0001	.0741
6	.0095		.0347	.0163	.0794	.0839	.0017		.0092	.0080	.0071	.0013	.0212	.1281	.0499	.0058	.0095	.0859
7	.0280		.0004	.0012	.0152	.0252	.4481	.0015	.0038	.0187	.0006	.0001	.0034	.0143			.0003	.0131
8	.0075	.0043	.0011	.0073	.0091	.0073	.0020	.1024	.0004	.0255	.0057	.0002	.0191	.1389	.0017	.0001	.0001	.0078
9	.0689	.0256	.0376	.0089	.0100	.0284	.0247	.0475	.1890	.0395	.0228	.0115	.0178	.0122	.1001	.0370	.0037	.0845
10	.0093	.0265	.0286	.0071	.0044	.0107	.0034	.0080	.0021	.1682	.0135	.0271	.0123	.0431	.0020		.0018	.0336
11	.0003	.0043	.0075	.0138	.0046	.0073	.0020	.0168	.0003	.0138	.2420	.0047	.0064	.0902	.0012	.0145	.0684	.0644
12		.0496	.0052	.0023	.0137	.0009		.0007		.0026	.0094	.2592	.0763	.0002		.0004	.0014	.0186
13			.0002		.0017	.0027	.0003			.0002	.0011	.0097	.0047	.0016	.0039	.0030	.0181	.0165
14	.0105	.0034	.0274	.0037	.0031	.0047	.0027	.0066	.0608	.0040	.0047	.0018	.0030		.1089	.0109	.0115	
15	.0687	.0265	.0637	.0208	.0141	.0154	.0250	.1079	.1630	.0448	.0435	.0042			.0181	.0002		.0232
16	.0201	.2308	.1159	.2160	.1642	.1461	.0081	.1437	.1435	.1595	.1119	.2434	.2330					.1233
17	.0033	.0350	.0442	.0199	.0111	.0087	.0010	.0044	.0029	.0367	.0071	.0069	.0068	.0004	.0096	.0369	.0196	.1013
18	.1410	.1316	.0938	.0925	.1008	.2161	.1031	.2121	.1210	.1559	.1447	.1322	.2021		.0089	.2594	.1162	.0090

Note: For industry names see Table 6. Blank spaces in table above stand for zero.
Source: Balderston and Whitin [1954, Table I–c, p. 117].

154

TABLE A5. LEONTIEF INVERSE MATRIX $(I - A)^{-1}$ FOR INPUT-OUTPUT EXAMPLE

	1	2	3	4	5	6	7	8	9
1	1.47072	.02259	.03490	.03000	.15470	.18655	.05810	.03065	.03694
2	.00786	1.02511	.01200	.00943	.04112	.01217	.00628	.00947	.00815
3	.00836	.01226	1.10919	.32749	.00965	.00997	.00636	.00984	.00869
4	.00694	.00780	.06779	1.11295	.00753	.00870	.00563	.00816	.00617
5	.04215	.05343	.05475	.04902	1.31313	.04813	.03775	.05594	.05324
6	.06970	.04558	.09143	.08077	.15990	1.15020	.04343	.06207	.07754
7	.09125	.01546	.01921	.02011	.06258	.07688	1.82680	.02190	.02718
8	.02551	.01427	.01679	.02090	.02480	.02158	.01257	1.12714	.02358
9	.19716	.09962	.11912	.10082	.10410	.13159	.10945	.15235	1.31949
10	.03670	.05213	.05713	.04000	.03098	.03928	.02320	.03389	.02559
11	.04466	.05169	.05740	.07248	.05657	.06413	.03789	.07633	.05129
12	.01077	.07861	.01779	.01681	.03712	.01512	.00964	.01421	.01017
13	.00854	.00968	.00873	.00966	.01228	.01375	.00665	.01043	.00880
14	.04805	.02290	.05559	.03495	.02600	.02862	.02347	.04052	.11155
15	.15486	.06248	.11190	.08125	.06785	.07375	.08128	.16898	.23828
16	.13968	.34484	.25276	.37800	.33850	.27986	.09475	.27592	.26830
17	.05036	.08667	.09369	.08911	.06978	.06947	.03755	.06214	.05039
18	.32952	.30264	.26055	.31311	.34003	.41675	.27150	.39029	.29200

	10	11	12	13	14	15	16	17	18
1	.02975	.04129	.02804	.02665	.12790	.04369	.02365	.01516	.06894
2	.01001	.00861	.01317	.00971	.00709	.00751	.00877	.00573	.02564
3	.05925	.03994	.08833	.01413	.02835	.00529	.00799	.00666	.02445
4	.02283	.01029	.03199	.00965	.00619	.00231	.00715	.00411	.02476
5	.04691	.05782	.06047	.04398	.08088	.03278	.04315	.02183	.12629
6	.06829	.06298	.06045	.05826	.17860	.09084	.05207	.03642	.14417
7	.05892	.01948	.02025	.05942	.05205	.01495	.01567	.01035	.04827
8	.04581	.01954	.01190	.01437	.16638	.02485	.00921	.00667	.02154
9	.14287	.11172	.10540	.10210	.09007	.15753	.10072	.03875	.17798
10	1.22655	.04281	.06906	.04536	.07162	.01688	.01953	.01499	.06183
11	.07677	1.36555	.06504	.06954	.15261	.03116	.06291	.11512	.13259
12	.01722	.02856	1.36416	.02235	.01032	.00439	.01207	.00930	.03811
13	.01101	.01088	.02503	1.09290	.00780	.00762	.01206	.02458	.02755
14	.03331	.03011	.02462	.04272	1.02003	.12746	.02419	.01869	.02860
15	.10701	.09961	.05118	.36300	.06449	1.05777	.03439	.02036	.08297
16	.31600	.25826	.46090	.06724	.14299	.06971	1.09465	.06505	.27878
17	.10337	.06155	.07793	.39267	.03670	.02654	.08130	1.04494	.14861
18	.37097	.33909	.39158		.20043	.09742	.35029	.18646	1.23349

Note: For industry names see Table 6.
Source: Balderston and Whitin [1954, Table I–d, p. 118].

155

TABLE A6. AGGREGATION PARTITIONS OBTAINED ON 18 BY 18 MATRIX FOR $P = (I - A)^{-1}$

Aggregate sector	Detailed sectors included in aggregate sector[a]			
	No forbidden merger pairs	7 forbidden merger pairs	48 forbidden merger pairs	
			Branch 1	Branch 2 (least cost)
1	3	2	4	4
2	4	4	5	5
3	9	1,10	3,6,9,11,12	12
4	12	7,13	1,2,7,8,10,13	1,2,6,7,8,10,11,13
5	1,2,7,8,10,13	5,6,8,11,14,15	14	14
6	5,6,11,14,15	3,12,16	15	15
7	17	17	17	17
8	16,18	9,18	16,18	3,9,16,18

[a] For titles of detailed sectors see Table 6.
Source: Rubin [1968, Table 2].

TABLE A7. AGGREGATION PARTITIONS OBTAINED ON 18 BY 18 MATRIX FOR $P = (I + A)$

Aggregate sector	Detailed sectors included in aggregate sector[a]				
	No forbidden merger pairs		7 forbidden merger pairs		48 forbidden merger pairs
	Branch 1	Branch 2 (least cost)	Branch 1 (least cost)	Branch 2	
1	4	4	4	4	4
2	9	9	1,5,6	1,5,6	5
3	12	5,6,11	12	12	12
4	1,2,7,8,13	12	7,13	7,13	1,2,6,7,8,10,11,13
5	14	14	8,10,11,15	8,10,11,15	14
6	5,6,10,11,15	1,2,7,8,10,13,15	3,14,16	2,9,16	15
7	17	17	17	17	17
8	3,1,18	3,16,18	2,9,18	3,14,18	3,9,16,18

[a] For titles of detailed sectors see Table 6.
Source: Rubin [1968, Table 3].

TABLE A8. SEQUENCE OF COSTS FOR PARTITIONS OF 18 BY 18 MATRIX FOR $P = (I - A)^{-1}$

	Cost after merger (units of 1939 dollars $\times 10^{16}$)			
Number of sets in partition	No forbidden mergers	7 forbidden mergers	48 forbidden mergers	
17	62	107	62	
16	180	469	180	
15	356	1,044	356	
14	792	1,817	792	
13	1,368	2,954	1,424	
12	2,032	5,612	2,197	
			Branch 1	Branch 2
11	2,819	9,603	3,064	3,970
10	3,653	14,122	6,626	8,691
9	4,806	19,554	11,793	13,717
8	8,792	31,112	23,666	20,776

Source: Rubin [1968, Table 9].

TABLE A9. SEQUENCE OF COSTS FOR PARTITIONS OF THE 18 BY 18 MATRIX FOR $P = (I + A)$

	Cost after merger (units of 1939 dollars $\times 10^{16}$)				
Number of sets in partition	No forbidden mergers		7 forbidden mergers		48 forbidden mergers
17	35		98		35
16	102		422		102
15	210		931		210
14	378		1,567		378
13	854		2,471		854
12	1,331		3,703		1,421
	Branch 1	Branch 2	Branch 1	Branch 2	
11	1,841	2,045	5,412	5,568	2,132
10	2,667	2,742	7,328	8,185	4,255
9	3,946	3,857	12,205	12,977	6,603
8	6,310	6,213	17,555	18,404	11,035

Source: Rubin [1968, Table 10].

TABLE A10. LEAST COST AGGREGATED $\bar{P}$ MATRICES FOR RANDOM FINAL DEMANDS CASES FOR 18 BY 18 MATRIX

$\bar{P}$ MATRIX FOR $P = (I − A)^{-1}$ WITH NO FORBIDDEN MERGER PAIRS

1	1.10909	0.32950	0.00747	0.08573	0.03030	0.02139	0.00623	0.00774
2	0.06713	1.11316	0.00483	0.03195	0.01746	0.00616	0.00439	0.01687
3	0.11852	0.09810	1.31580	0.10666	0.15641	0.09802	0.04233	0.18972
4	0.01754	0.01652	0.01281	1.36557	0.01962	0.01663	0.00972	0.02206
5	0.02148	0.02307	0.01482	0.02754	0.21168	0.06502	0.01248	0.00475
6	0.07174	0.06580	0.10751	0.05156	0.04891	0.30166	0.04373	0.05205
7	0.09012	0.08831	0.04705	0.07982	0.09373	0.04495	1.04763	0.12136
8	0.24408	0.34133	0.28417	0.43611	0.36828	0.21832	0.13184	0.72503

$\bar{P}$ matrix for $P = (I − A)^{-1}$ with 7 forbidden merger pairs

1	1.03186	0.00915	0.00575	0.02512	0.01249	0.01250	0.00743	0.00726
2	0.06178	1.11307	0.00753	0.04552	0.00526	0.03860	0.01303	−0.00430
3	0.02634	0.03792	0.58247	0.06512	0.09228	0.04587	0.01437	0.02007
4	−0.07371	0.01298	0.03754	0.62739	0.03629	0.02442	0.01505	0.01846
5	−0.08309	0.05864	0.04106	0.03147	0.27070	0.04606	0.04048	0.08912
6	−0.21571	0.23767	0.16807	0.00606	0.07965	0.60065	−0.01200	0.14152
7	0.13823	0.08914	0.08689	0.10531	0.04580	0.08531	1.04913	0.04822
8	0.25567	0.20600	0.27157	0.26751	0.16894	0.23811	0.10456	0.81747

$\bar{P}$ matrix for $P = (I − A)^{-1}$ with 48 forbidden merger pairs

1	1.11367	−0.00817	0.02900	0.01266	0.00714	−0.00380	0.01101	0.03039
2	0.04880	1.31458	0.06238	0.04962	0.08191	0.03528	0.02180	0.05582
3	0.01687	0.03530	1.36493	0.01932	0.01126	0.00592	0.00898	0.01616
4	0.03496	0.06617	0.03695	0.19454	0.09754	0.02794	0.02947	0.03401
5	0.03454	0.04216	0.02355	0.02568	1.01685	0.12831	0.01416	0.08585
6	0.08132	0.09517	0.04782	0.07919	0.05713	1.06149	0.01085	0.17915
7	0.09064	0.05736	0.08009	0.07694	0.03653	0.03299	1.04957	0.06676
8	0.27977	0.21657	0.26138	0.20110	0.10932	0.08819	0.07068	0.45067

Note: For description of the aggregated sectors see Tables A6 and A7.
Source: Rubin [1968, Table 34].

TABLE A10 (cont.)

$\bar{P}$ matrix for $P = (I + A)$ with no forbidden merger pairs

	1	2	3	4	5	6	7	8
1	1.08101	-0.00164	-0.00067	0.01062	-0.00076	0.00149	0.00095	0.04805
2	0.00740	1.18418	0.01360	0.01284	0.01128	0.06679	0.00608	0.03928
3	0.01195	0.00742	0.40727	0.00501	0.09001	0.00850	0.02789	0.01619
4	0.00229	0.00130	0.00986	1.25988	0.00076	0.00189	0.00129	0.00537
5	0.00087	0.05440	-0.00524	-0.00075	0.99945	0.05225	0.01662	0.02325
6	0.00582	0.02287	0.02179	0.00653	0.03645	0.16389	0.00259	0.01389
7	0.02059	0.00095	0.01123	0.00916	-0.00053	0.01928	1.01938	0.04439
8	0.19396	0.09368	0.10835	0.14140	0.00240	0.06565	0.03334	0.42966

$\bar{P}$ matrix for $P = (I + A)$ with 7 forbidden merger pairs

	1	2	3	4	5	6	7	8
1	1.07831	-0.00925	0.01689	0.01453	0.01265	0.01393	0.00781	-0.00462
2	0.01008	0.44286	-0.00183	-0.00836	-0.00284	0.05911	-0.00389	0.00962
3	0.00197	0.00929	1.26022	-0.00160	0.00457	0.00290	0.00147	0.00279
4	0.00010	0.01182	0.00517	0.57840	0.00868	0.00829	0.00760	0.00091
5	0.01629	0.01366	0.00327	0.01282	0.28189	0.05658	0.01130	0.04390
6	0.15929	0.03919	0.10081	0.08863	0.05699	0.35495	0.01479	0.06079
7	0.01808	-0.00539	0.01497	0.01842	0.02893	0.01273	1.02493	0.00138
8	0.03306	0.04711	0.05127	0.08329	0.06191	0.01504	0.04622	0.43247

$\bar{P}$ matrix for $P = (I + A)$ with 48 forbidden merger pairs

	1	2	3	4	5	6	7	8
1	1.08154	-0.01305	0.01054	0.00257	0.00110	-0.00494	0.00578	0.02049
2	0.00364	1.21408	0.01050	0.00396	0.04321	0.01197	0.00027	0.01316
3	0.00219	0.01285	1.25991	0.00395	0.00104	0.00183	0.00130	0.00414
4	0.00565	0.02224	0.00602	0.15598	0.06088	0.00728	0.01346	0.00533
5	0.00326	0.01309	0.00060	0.00202	0.99826	0.10893	0.00841	0.04543
6	0.02106	-0.03425	0.00091	0.02364	-0.00524	1.02006	-0.00744	0.11760
7	0.02121	-0.00135	0.00912	0.01765	0.00103	0.01486	1.02364	0.01991
8	0.14560	0.08349	0.10875	0.08935	0.00280	0.03183	0.02647	0.34710

TABLE A11. STRATIFICATION BY THE METHOD OF COST COEFFICIENTS

Stratum			Profit—dollars per farm		
Identification numbers	Farm ident. numbers	Number of farms	Representative farm	True average	Bias
B1	12, 13, 14	3	$6,401	$5,956	$ 445
B2	2, 5, 7, 8, 9, 10	6	3,063	3,571	−508
B3	14, 19, 28, 29, 31	5	6,883	6,719	164
B4	18, 25, 26, 32	4	7,076	7,090	− 14
B5	3, 27, 42, 43, 46, 48	6	4,141	4,587	−446
B6	4, 6, 22, 40, 41, 44, 45, 47, 49	9	7,909	7,486	423
B7	11, 15, 17, 20, 21	5	5,267	5,682	−415
B8	16, 23, 30, 33, 34, 35	6	6,438	6,486	− 48
B9	1, 36, 37, 38, 39	5	5,885	6,384	−499

TABLE A12. STRATIFICATION BY THE METHOD OF COST RECIPROCALS

Stratum			Profit—dollars per farm		
Identification numbers	Farm ident. numbers	Number of farms	Representative farm	True average	Bias
C1	4, 11, 16, 21, 27, 29, 32, 40, 42, 44, 45, 46, 48, 49	14	$4,503	$4,631	$−128
C2	6, 17, 19, 20, 22, 23, 28, 30, 33, 34, 35, 43	12	7,077	7,199	−122
C3	3, 7, 8, 10, 15, 26, 31, 36, 38, 41	10	2,521	2,592	− 71
C4	2, 5, 9, 12, 13	5	5,471	5,493	− 22
C5	24, 37, 39	3	7,377	7,147	230
C6	14, 18	2	9,779	9,844	− 65
C7	1	1	10,701	10,701	0
C8	25	1	12,690	12,690	0
C9	47	1	26,250	26,250	0

TABLE A13. STRATIFICATION BY SIZE–REGION

Stratum			Profit—dollars per farm		
Identification number	Size-region class[a]	Number of farms	Representative farm	True average	Bias
D1	Small—NE	3	$4,593	$4,663	$− 70
D2	Small—SE	3	5,719	6,027	−308
D3	Small—W	4	2,672	2,621	51
D4	Medium—NE	11	5,031	4,999	32
D5	Medium—SE	6	5,574	5,691	−117
D6	Medium—W	8	5,271	5,644	−373
D7	Large—NE	5	11,011	11,329	−318
D8	Large—SE	4	6,770	7,078	−308
D9	Large—W	5	6,787	6,720	67

[a] See Table A15 for definitions.
Source: Unpublished data of P. L. Kelley, Kansas State University.

TABLE A14. SIZE–REGION CLASS AND PROFIT SOLUTION FOR FORTY-NINE KANSAS FARMS

Farm	Size–Region[a]	Profit	Farm	Size–Region[a]	Profit
1	Large—NE	$10,701	26	Medium—NE	$ 3,426
2	Large—SE	5,837	27	Medium—W	3,600
3	Medium—W	2,721	28	Small—SE	8,071
4	Medium—NE	5,612	29	Large—W	6,236
5	Large—NE	4,228	30	Small—NE	5,848
6	Small—NE	4,863	31	Medium—NE	2,153
7	Medium—W	1,490	32	Medium—SE	2,942
8	Small—W	952	33	Large—W	7,295
9	Medium—W	6,892	34	Medium—SE	6,021
10	Medium—NE	2,025	35	Large—W	8,103
11	Small—W	4,127	36	Small—SE	3,703
12	Medium—SE	6,342	37	Large—W	7,777
13	Medium—SE	4,167	38	Medium—NE	3,432
14	Large—NE	10,387	39	Small—SE	6,306
15	Large SE	2,428	40	Large—NE	5,077
16	Large—W	4,187	41	Medium—NE	3,584
17	Medium—SE	7,926	42	Small—W	3,291
18	Medium—NE	9,300	43	Medium—W	11,935
19	Medium—SE	6,747	44	Medium—NE	5,279
20	Medium—W	7,191	45	Medium—NE	8,498
21	Medium—NE	6,738	46	Medium—W	3,861
22	Medium—NE	4,927	47	Large—NE	26,250
23	Medium—W	7,462	48	Small—W	2,112
24	Large—SE	7,358	49	Small—NE	3,278
25	Large—SE	12,690			

[a] See Table A15 for definitions.
Source: Unpublished data of P. L. Kelley, Kansas State University.

TABLE A15. DEFINITIONS OF SIZE AND REGION CATEGORIES FOR KANSAS FARMS

Size of farm (Daily milk production)	
Large	500 lbs. or more
Medium	200–499 lbs.
Small	Less than 200 lbs.

Region (Counties in the State of Kansas)	
Northeast	Brown, Doniphan, Jackson, Atchison, Shawnee, Jefferson, Douglas, Leavenworth, Wyandotte.
Southeast	Osage, Franklin, Coffey, Linn, Anderson.
West	Clay, Riley, Dickinson, Geary, Morris, Marion, Chase, Greenwood, Lyon, Pottawatomie, Wabaunsee, Washington, Marshall.

Source: Unpublished data of P. L. Kelley, Kansas State University.

TABLE A16. Structure of Cost Coefficients for Each of Forty-nine Kansas Farms[a]

Constraint (Resource)	Wheat grown on land class[b]				Corn grown on land class[b]				Alfalfa grown on land class[b]				Milo grown on land class[b]				Soybeans grown on land class[b]			
	A	B,C	D	E,F	A	B,C	D	E,F	A	B,C	D	E,F	A	B,C	D	E,F	A	B,C	D	E,F
Wheat allotment	1	1	1	1																
Land class A	1				1								1							
Land class B, C		1				1				1				1				1		
Land class D			1				1				1				1				1	
Land class E, F				1				1				1				1				1
Soybean restriction																		1	1	1
Alfalfa restriction										1	1	1								

[a] After elimination of redundancy.
[b] The letters refer to different qualities of land. Classes A, B, and C are owned; classes D, E, and F are rented.
Source: Unpublished data of P. L. Kelley, Kansas State University.

APPENDIX B. GROUPING AND RESTRICTIONS

First, it will be shown that the simplified matrix $\tilde{P}$ that results from the specification (2.15) of Chapter 2 of the text is equivalent to placing certain linear homogeneous restrictions on the elements of $\tilde{P}$.

Let the S and T in (2.15) now be denoted by S_1 and T_1. These are now simply full-rank matrices of size F by G and J by H respectively, without further specification. Let S_2 and T_2 be the orthogonal complements of S_1 and T_1 respectively—that is S_2 and T_2 are matrices of size $(G - F)$ by G and $(H - J)$ by H respectively, such that

(B.1a) $S_1 S_2' = 0$;   (B.1b) $T_1 T_2' = 0$.

Let $\bar{P}$ be a full-rank F by J matrix. Then (2.15) is now written

(B.2) $P = S_1' \bar{P} T_1$,

where the tilde is omitted for the present purpose.

LEMMA B.1. A matrix P satisfies (B.2) if, and only if, it satisfies the following linear homogeneous restrictions:

(B.3a) $S_2 P = 0$;   (B.3b) $P T_2' = 0$.

PROOF. To show that (B.2) implies (B.3), premultiply (B.2) by S_2 and then postmultiply it by T_2'. The results are

(B.4a) $S_2 P = S_2 S_1' \bar{P} T_1$;   (B.4b) $P T_2' = S_1' \bar{P} T_1 T_2'$.

From (B.1) the right side of each of these equations is 0, which gives (B.3a) and (B.3b). To show that (B.3a) and (B.3b) imply (B.2), note first that by making suitable rearrangements in the order of the columns of S_2 and corresponding rows of P, and of the columns of P and corresponding rows of T_2', and by finding suitable nonsingular matrices K and L, equations (B.3a) and (B.3b) may be put in the form

(B.5a) $K(I_r M)\begin{pmatrix} P_{rs} & P_{rJ} \\ P_{Fs} & P_{FJ} \end{pmatrix} = (0 \ 0)$;

(B.5b) $\begin{pmatrix} P_{rs} & P_{rJ} \\ P_{Fs} & P_{FJ} \end{pmatrix}\begin{pmatrix} I_s \\ N \end{pmatrix} L = \begin{pmatrix} 0 \\ 0 \end{pmatrix}$;

where M is an r by F matrix, N is a J by s matrix, $r + F = G$, and $s + J = H$, and where P is partitioned into the four submatrices with subscripts indicating their order. By multiplying out (B.5a) and (B.5b), solving for P_{rs}, P_{rJ}, and P_{Fs} in terms of P_{FJ}, it is found that

$$\text{(B.6)} \qquad P = \begin{pmatrix} MP_{FJ}N & -MP_{FJ} \\ -P_{FJ}N & P_{FJ} \end{pmatrix} = \begin{pmatrix} M \\ -I_F \end{pmatrix} P_{FJ}(N : -I_J) \ ,$$

where there are no restrictions on P_{FJ}. Moreover, it is evident that

$$\text{(B.7)} \qquad S_2 \begin{pmatrix} M \\ -I_F \end{pmatrix} = K(I_r M) \begin{pmatrix} M \\ -I_F \end{pmatrix} = 0 \ ;$$

$$\text{(B.8)} \qquad (N : -I_J)T_2' = (N : -I_J)\begin{pmatrix} I_s \\ N \end{pmatrix} L = 0 \ .$$

Hence the matrices $\begin{pmatrix} M \\ -I_F \end{pmatrix}$ and $(N : -I_J)$ qualify for being labeled S_1' and T_1 respectively, since they satisfy conditions (B.1). Hence denoting P_{FJ} as $\bar{P}$ (B.6) becomes (B.2).[1]

We now consider the relationship between these matrices and the aggregated and simplified matrices dealt with in the last subsection of Chapter 6. Let

$$\text{(B.9)} \qquad\qquad\qquad \bar{P} = X^* \ ,$$

where X^* is defined by (6.7). Let S_1' and T_1 assume the special block-diagonal forms

$$\text{(B.10a)} \qquad\qquad S_1' = \begin{bmatrix} \ddots & & 0 \\ & \tilde{v}_I & \\ 0 & & \ddots \end{bmatrix} \ ;$$

----

[1] I am indebted to Professor Leonard Fuller of the Department of Mathematics of Kansas State University for assistance with this proof.

(B.10b)
$$T_1 = \begin{bmatrix} \cdot & & & 0 \\ & \cdot & & \\ & & \tilde{w}'_J & \\ & & & \cdot \\ 0 & & & \cdot \end{bmatrix} ;$$

where $\tilde{v}_I$ and $\tilde{w}'_J$ are the share vectors that appear in (6.8). That is, S'_1 and T_1 are partitioning operators according to Definition 3 of Chapter 2. Then (6.8) is equivalent to

(B.11)
$$\tilde{X} = S'_1 \bar{P} T_1 .$$

That is, $P = \tilde{X}$, from (B.2) and (B.11).

Proofs will now be given of three of the Lemmas of Chapter 6.

PROOF OF LEMMA 1 OF CHAPTER 6. From definition (6.3)

(B.12)
$$H(X) = -\sum_{i,\,j=1}^{n} x_{ij} \log x_{ij}$$

$$= -\sum_{i,\,j=1}^{n} x_{ij} \log \frac{x_{IJ} x_{ij}}{x_{IJ}}$$

$$= -\sum_{I,\,J=1}^{m} \left[\sum_{\substack{i \in I \\ j \in J}} x_{ij} \left(\log x_{IJ} + \log \frac{x_{ij}}{x_{IJ}} \right) \right]$$

$$= -\sum_{I,\,J=1}^{m} x_{IJ} \left[\log x_{IJ} + \sum_{\substack{i \in I \\ j \in J}} \frac{x_{ij}}{x_{IJ}} \log \frac{x_{ij}}{x_{IJ}} \right] .$$

Since x_{IJ} is an element of the share matrix X^* and x_{ij}/x_{IJ} is an element of the share submatrix X_{IJ}/x_{IJ}, the application of the entropy definition (6.3) to these matrices brings this last form of (B.12) into equivalence with (6.9), which establishes the Lemma.

PROOF OF LEMMA 2 OF CHAPTER 6. From (6.6), applied to $\tilde{X}$,

(B.13)
$$I(\tilde{X}) = \sum_{i,\,j=1}^{n} \tilde{x}_{ij} \log \frac{\tilde{x}_{ij}}{\tilde{v}_i \tilde{w}_j} = \sum_{i,\,j=1}^{n} \tilde{x}_{ij} \log \frac{x_{IJ} \tilde{x}_{ij}/x_{IJ}}{x_I(\tilde{v}_i/x_I) x_J(\tilde{w}_j/x_J)} .$$

But from (6.8)

(B.14)
$$\frac{\tilde{x}_{ij}/x_{IJ}}{(\tilde{v}_i/x_I)(\tilde{v}_j/x_J)} = 1 \ .$$

Hence (B.13) becomes

(B.15)
$$I(\tilde{X}) = \sum_{i,\,j=1}^{n} \tilde{x}_{ij} \log \frac{x_{IJ}}{x_I x_J} = \sum_{I,\,J=1}^{m} x_{IJ} \log \frac{x_{IJ}}{x_I x_J} \ .$$

The last term is precisely $I(X^*)$, which establishes (6.12).

PROOF OF LEMMA 4 OF CHAPTER 6. Since the block total of the elements of both $\tilde{X}_{IJ}$ and X_{IJ} is the same scalar, x_{IJ}, (B.15) may also be written

(B.16)
$$I(\tilde{X}) = \sum_{i,\,j=1}^{n} x_{ij} \log \frac{x_{IJ}}{x_I x_J} = \sum_{i,\,j=1}^{n} x_{ij} \log \frac{\tilde{x}_{ij}}{\tilde{v}_i \tilde{w}_j},$$

the last term being obtained by working backwards via (B.14) and (B.13). Then, from (6.10) and (6.6) and (B.16),

(B.17)
$$dI = I(X) - I(\tilde{X}) = \sum_{i,\,j=1}^{n} x_{ij} \left(\log \frac{x_{ij}}{v_i v_j} - \log \frac{\tilde{x}_{ij}}{\tilde{v}_i \tilde{v}_j} \right) \ .$$

By recombining the logarithms in the parentheses and subtracting again in a different manner (6.14) results.

We now prove a Lemma relating to minimal distance projections, which is essentially a "one-way" special case of Theorem 2.

LEMMA B.2. Let P be a given G by H matrix representing H points in G space. Let S be a given F by G matrix of rank F whose rows represent the basis of an F-dimensional subspace within the G space. Let C be a given G by G symmetric positive semi-definite matrix that defines distances between any two points p_1 and p_2 in the G space as

(B.18)
$$d(p_1, p_2) = \sqrt{(p_1 - p_2)' C (p_1 - p_2)} \ .$$

Then a set of H points X, which (1) lies in the subspace defined by S, and (2) is such that the sum of the squared distances $d^2(x, p)$ of each member point x from its corresponding point p in P is a minimum, is given by the following projection of P on the subspace:

(B.19)
$$\tilde{X} = [S'(SCS')^g SC] P \ ,$$

where superscript g defines generalized inverse.

PROOF. The condition that a point x lie in the subspace whose basis is S may be expressed by

(B.20)
$$x = S'y \ ,$$

where y is an arbitrary F vector. The condition that all H points of the set X lie in this subspace may be expressed by

(B.21) $X = S'Y$,

where Y is an arbitrary F by H matrix. The desired sum of squared distances to be minimized is

(B.22) $s = \text{tr}(X - P)'C(X - P)$.

This is precisely the problem of Theorem 2 with the correspondences

(B.23) $\tilde{P} = \tilde{X}$, $\bar{P} = Y$, $T = M = I$,

with P, S, and C carrying over to the present problem. Then (2.19), along with (2.15) and (2.20a), give (B.19), which defines a projection because the matrix in square brackets is idempotent.

APPENDIX C. RANK RESTRICTIONS AND SIMPLIFICATION

The simplification functions used in the text have employed partitioning operators with given weights. For example, in the simplification expressed by (2.15) the operators S and T are assumed given a priori. It is shown in Appendix B that this specification is equivalent to the imposition of linear restrictions on the simplified matrix $\tilde{P}$. But suppose that the assumption that S and T are partitioning operators is dropped. In fact, assume that S and T are completely unknown to start with, except for their order. Then condition (2.15) simply specifies that $\tilde{P}$ must be of rank no greater than F or J, whichever is lower. The optimal simplification problem then is one of minimization subject to rank conditions. We could formulate the problem as that of finding the simplified matrix $\tilde{P}$ that minimizes the quadratic simplification cost as given by (2.7) when $\tilde{P}$ can be of rank no greater than some specified integer.

For this problem the following Lemma will prove helpful.

LEMMA C.1. Given a matrix A of order G by H and rank G, the matrix $\tilde{X}$, of rank F, where $F \leq G$, that minimizes

(C.1) $s = \text{tr}(X - A)'(X - A)$

is

(C.2) $\tilde{X} = R'_F R_F A$,

where R_F is the F by G matrix whose rows are the normalized characteristic vectors associated with the F largest characteristic roots of the matrix AA'.

PROOF. Let A denote a set of H points in G space. Then AA'/H is the matrix of second-order moments (regarded as statistical observations) about the origin, and X is required to be a set of H points restricted to a subspace of dimension F passing through the origin. Moreover from (C.1) s is seen to be the sum of squared Euclidean distances of each point in X from its corresponding point in A.

Consider now the extended set of points $(A : -A)$ containing both the original set and the reflection of each original point through the origin. It is easily verified that the centroid of this extended set is the origin and that its covariance matrix is AA'/H. Moreover the desired set X satisfies the specified requirements if, and only if, each point of an extended set $(X : -X)$ lies on the same subspace of dimension F, and if the sum of the square Euclidean distances of these points from the corresponding points in $(A : -A)$ be a minimum. It is known that under these conditions each point of the required set X is the orthogonal projection of its corresponding point in set A onto the subspace having as a basis the first F characteristic vectors of AA'—i.e., the subspace containing the F largest principal axes of the ellipsoid $x'(AA')^{-1}x = 1$, where x is a G vector. (See, for example, Kendall [1957, pp. 13–17].) A basis of this subspace is then given by the rows of R_F.

Then Lemma B.2 is applicable to the present problem with

$$(C.3) \qquad P = A , \qquad S = R_F , \qquad C = I .$$

From the fact that the normalized characteristic vectors are orthogonal to each other, and each of length unity, we have

$$(C.4) \qquad R_F R_F' = I .$$

Then by substituting (C.3) and (C.4) into (B.19), the projecting matrix is found to be $R_F' R_F$, and (B.19) itself becomes (C.2), which was to be proved. A different proof of this proposition for the case where A is square was developed by McCarthy [1956]. The present proof comes from W. D. Fisher [1962b].

Then the following proposition follows.

LEMMA C.2. The simplified matrix $\tilde{P}$, of rank F, that minimizes the quadratic simplification cost as given by (2.7), when C and M are nonsingular is

$$(C.5) \qquad \tilde{P} = D^{-1} R_F' R_F D P$$

when P is of rank G, and

$$(C.6) \qquad \tilde{P} = P N Q_F' Q_F N^{-1}$$

when P is of rank H, where R_F is the F by G matrix whose rows are the normalized characteristic vectors associated with the F largest characteristic roots of the matrix $DPNN'P'D$, Q_F is the F by H matrix whose rows are the normalized characteristic vectors associated with the F largest roots of the matrix $N'P'D'DPN$, D is a nonsingular matrix such that $D'D = C$, and N is a nonsingular matrix such that $NN' = M$.

PROOF. Let

(C.7a) $X = D\tilde{P}N$,   (C.7b) $A = DPN$.

Then (2.7) becomes

(C.8) $c = \text{tr}(X - A)'(X - A)$,

which is in the form of s in (C.1). When P is assumed to be of rank G, A is also of rank G. Moreover, X is of rank F if and only if $\tilde{P}$ is of rank F. So the given problem is equivalent to that of Lemma C.1. By using Lemma C.1 and transforming back into the original variables (C.5) is obtained. When P is of rank H, Lemma C.1 is applied to A' and X', which yields (C.6). In the statement of this Lemma in W. D. Fisher [1962b, p. 763] it was erroneously assumed that the matrices Q_F and R_F were identical. While the relevant characteristic roots are the same, the characteristic vectors are not. The author is obliged to Schneeweiss [1965, p. 18] for the correction of this error.

It may also be remarked that the matrix D is obtainable by elementary congruent operations on the identity matrix, the operations being those that diagonalize the symmetric matrix C. Similarly for N and M.

Lemma C.2 may also be used when $J < F$, in which case the letter J is substituted for F throughout the proof.

APPENDIX D. THE GENERALIZED INVERSE OF A MATRIX

In this Appendix some elementary properties of generalized inverses as defined by Penrose [1955] are derived. A more general treatment of the subject is available in Chipman [1964]. We have specialized Penrose's definitions to the case of a matrix with real elements, and sometimes, for brevity, abbreviate "generalized inverse" to "ginverse."

DEFINITION D.1 (Penrose [1955, p. 406]). A given matrix A has the generalized inverse A^g when the following four conditions are satisfied:

(i) $AA^gA = A$;   (iii) AA^g is symmetric ;

(ii) $A^gAA^g = A^g$;   (iv) A^gA is symmetric .

Penrose demonstrates that any matrix, whether nonsingular, singular, or nonsquare, has a unique generalized inverse, and that when A is nonsingular the generalized inverse is the ordinary inverse. Among the lemmas that he proves concerning the ginverse are the following [1955, p. 408]:

(P1.1) $(A^g)^g = A$;

(P1.2) $(A')^g = (A^g)'$;

(P1.5) $(A'A)^g = A^g A'^g$;

(P1.9) $\text{rank}(A) = \text{rank}(A^g) = \text{rank}(AA^g) = \text{tr}(AA^g)$.

Note also that AA^g is idempotent, from condition (i), as is also $A^g A$, from condition (ii).

LEMMA D.1. For any matrix A, the ginverse of A is given by

(D.1) $A^g = A'(AA')^g$.

PROOF. $A^g = A^g A A^g$, by condition (ii),
              $\quad = (A^g A)' A^g$, by condition (iv),
              $\quad = A' A^{g'} A^g$, by regular transpose rule,
              $\quad = A' A'^g A^g$, by (P1.2),
              $\quad = A'(AA')^g$, by (P1.5).

DEFINITION D.2. A *full-rank matrix* is a matrix whose rank is the maximum for its order.

DEFINITION D.3. A *horizontal matrix* has fewer rows than columns. A *vertical matrix* has fewer columns than rows.

LEMMA D.2. The ginverse of a full-rank horizontal matrix A is

(D.2) $A^g = A'(AA')^{-1}$.

PROOF. Since A is horizontal and full-rank, A' is vertical and full-rank, and AA' is nonsingular and has a regular inverse, which is also the ginverse $(AA')^g$. Hence, by applying (D.1), (D.2) results.

LEMMA D.3. The ginverse of a full-rank vertical matrix A' is

(D.3) $A'^g = (AA')^{-1}A$.

PROOF. Immediate from (P1.2) and (D.2) and the symmetry of AA'.

LEMMA D.4. If M is a symmetric positive semi-definite matrix of order n by n and rank r, its ginverse may be written

(D.4) $M^g = A'(AA')^{-2}A$,

where A is a full-rank horizontal matrix of order r by n.

PROOF. Under the stated conditions on M in the premise there exists a matrix A of order r by n and full rank such that M may be written

(D.5) $M = A'A$.

Then the ginverse of M is

(D.6) $M^g = (A'A)^g = A^g A'^g$,

and substituting in (D.2) and (D.3) leads directly to (D.4). This result is used in the proof of Theorem 2 in Chapter 2.

APPENDIX E. SEPARABILITY AND HESSIAN MATRICES

Let z be a twice differentiable function of n variables denoted by the vector x. Consider a partition of the elements of x into m disjoint and exhaustive subsets, denoted by the vectors $x^1, \ldots, x^m$. The Hessian matrix of interest here is that of the second derivatives

(E.1) $H(x) = [z_{ij}] = [\partial^2 z / \partial x^i \partial x^j]$.

The definitions of *block-homogeneous* and *block-diagonal* matrices are those given on pages 92 and 94.

E.1. Weakly Separable Functions

It has been shown by Goldman and Uzawa [1964, Theorem 2] that the definition of *weakly separable* given in the text is equivalent to the following one proposed by Strotz [1957, 1959]:

DEFINITION E.1. The function z is *weakly separable* with respect to the partition if it can be expressed in the form

(E.2) $z(x) = f[v^1(x^1), \ldots, v^m(x^m)]$,

where f and v^r are twice differentiable functions. (The set of functions v^r are sometimes referred to as a vector, v, of m elements.)

LEMMA E.1. The Hessian matrix of a weakly separable function with respect to a partition may be expressed as the sum of a block-homogeneous matrix and a block-diagonal matrix.

PROOF. Let z_i denote the partial derivative $\partial z / \partial x^i$. Then, from the form of (E.2), this derivative may be expressed as

(E.3) $z_i(x) = f_r(v) v_i^r(x^r)$,

where

(E.4a) $f_r(v) = \partial f / \partial v^r$;   (E.4b) $v_i^r(x^r) = \partial v^r / \partial x^i$;

and where r is the subset of the partition containing variable x^i.

When x^i and x^j belong to the same subset, say subset r, the second order derivative z_{ij} is found from (E.3) to be

(E.5) $z_{ij}(x) = f_{rr}(v)v_i^r(x^r)v_j^r(x^r) + f_r(v^r)v_{ij}^r(x^r)$, $i, j \epsilon r$;

where

(E.6a) $f_{rr}(v) = \partial^2 f/(\partial v^r)^2$;   (E.6b) $v_{ij}^r(x^r) = \partial^2 v^r/\partial x^i \partial x^j$.

When x^i and x^j belong to different subsets, say r and s, the derivative of $v_i^r(x^r)$ in (E.3) with respect to x^j vanishes, so that the second order derivative z_{ij} is then found to be

(E.7) $z_{ij}(x) = f_{rs}(v)v_i^r(x^r)v_j^s(x^s)$, $i \epsilon r, j \epsilon s, r \neq s$.

Now let v_r denote the column vector of first derivatives $[v_i^r]$ and V_r denote the Hessian matrix $[v_{ij}^r]$. Then, combining (E.5) and (E.7), we have

(E.8) $H(x) = \begin{bmatrix} f_{11}v_1v_1' & \cdots & f_{1m}v_1v_m' \\ & & \\ \cdot & & \cdot \\ & & \\ \cdot & & \cdot \\ & & \\ \cdot & & \cdot \\ & & \\ f_{m1}v_mv_1' & \cdots & f_{mm}v_mv_m' \end{bmatrix} + \begin{bmatrix} f_1V_1 & & 0 \\ & \cdot & \\ & \cdot & \\ & \cdot & \\ 0 & & f_mV_m \end{bmatrix}$.

The first matrix on the right of (E.8) is seen to be in the form

(4.43) $\tilde{A} = T'\bar{A}T$,

where T is the m by n partitioning operator

(E.9) $T = \begin{bmatrix} v_1' & & 0 \\ & \cdot & \\ & & \cdot \\ & & & \cdot \\ 0 & & v_m' \end{bmatrix}$

and $\bar{A}$ is the symmetric matrix of order m

(E.10) $\bar{A} = \begin{bmatrix} f_{11} & \cdots & f_{1m} \\ & & \\ \cdot & & \cdot \\ & & \\ \cdot & & \cdot \\ & & \\ f_{m1} & \cdots & f_{mm} \end{bmatrix}$, and so is block-homogeneous according to definition (4.43). The second matrix on the right of (E.8) is seen to be block-diagonal. Hence the Lemma is proved. This type of matrix is sketched in panel A of Figure 10 in Chapter 4.

DEFINITION E.2. A *super-block* of a matrix whose rows and columns are partitioned into disjoint subsets is a submatrix whose rows and columns comprise some set of sets of the partitions.

DEFINITION E.3. A *diagonal super-block* of a square symmetric matrix is a square super-block whose main diagonal is part of the main diagonal of the original matrix. An *off-diagonal super-block* is a super-block which is not a diagonal super-block.

LEMMA E.2. The Hessian matrix of a weakly separable function that is also quadratic in x is either block-homogeneous or block-diagonal, or may be partitioned so that there exist two diagonal super-blocks, one of which is block-diagonal and the other block-homogeneous, and two off-diagonal super-blocks, each with all zero elements.

PROOF. Since z is quadratic, its Hessian matrix is constant for all x. Call it A. Since z is weakly separable, a partition of the variables x into m subsets is implied with (E.8) holding. Assume that these m subsets have been ordered into two divisions (by permutation if necessary) so that the following is true: the diagonal blocks A_{rr} for which in (E.8)

$$(E.11) \qquad\qquad f_r V_r \neq 0$$

are together and first in order (call the set of subsets associated with these blocks the "first division"), and the diagonal blocks A_{ss} for which

$$(E.12) \qquad\qquad f_s V_s = 0$$

are together after the blocks of the first division (call the set of subsets associated with these blocks the "second division"). Then A may be represented by four super-blocks, thus

$$(E.13) \qquad A =$$

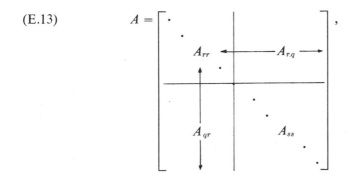

where the possibility exists that one division may be empty, but not both empty. Call the diagonal super-blocks associated with the two divisions, when they exist, super-block I and super-block II.

1. When the second division is not empty, super-block II is a block-homogeneous matrix. This follows immediately from the requirement (E.12) above, in which case super-block II coincides with a diagonal super-block of the first matrix on the right (E.8), which was shown in the proof of Lemma E.1 to be block-homogeneous.

2. There exist three cases: Case 1, first division empty; Case 2, second division empty; Case 3, neither division empty.

3. If the first division is empty, super-block II coincides with the entire Hessian A. Since, from Step 1 above, super-block II was shown to be block-homogeneous, it follows that in this case A is block-homogeneous. This proves the Lemma for this case.

4. If the first division is not empty, the Lemma is true if, and only if, the following proposition is true: for every diagonal block A_{rr} of super-block I, every off-diagonal block of the entire matrix A that has either the same rows as A_{rr}, say A_{rq}, or the same columns as A_{rr}, say A_{qr}, has all zero elements. In Case 2 this proposition would establish the block-diagonality of A; in Case 3 it would establish the block-diagonality of super-block I and all zero elements for the off-diagonal super-blocks; so the Lemma would be established for both Cases 2 and 3. (In the above notation and in (E.13) r refers to a subset of division I, and q refers to a subset that may be either in division I or in division II).

5. Assume the contrary to the proposition stated in the preceding step: i.e., assume that there exists an off-diagonal block A_{qr} that is not zero. From (E.8) this would imply that

$$\text{(E.14)} \qquad\qquad A_{qr} = f_{qr} v_q v'_r \neq 0 \ .$$

Moreover, from the condition (E.11) on super-block I, it follows that

$$\text{(E.15)} \qquad\qquad V_r \neq 0 \ .$$

6. But V_r is the matrix of derivatives of the elements of v'_r with respect to the elements of x^r. Condition (E.15) then implies that at least one of the elements of v'_r is a function of some $x^i (i \epsilon r)$, for otherwise V_r would be a zero matrix. But then (E.14) would imply that there exists an element of A_{qr} that is a function of some x^i. This would be a contradiction to the assumption that z is a quadratic function with its Hessian constant for all x (see first sentence of this proof). Hence, a contradiction has been found to the assumption of step 5, which establishes the proposition of step 4, which establishes the Lemma for Cases 2 and 3 and completes the proof. The typical Hessian characterized is sketched in panel B of Figure 10.

E.2. Strongly Separable Functions

It has been shown by Goldman and Uzawa [1964, Theorem 1] that the definition of *strongly separable* given in the text is equivalent to the following one:

DEFINITION E.4. The function z is *strongly separable* with respect to the partition if it can be expressed in the form

(E.16) $$z(x) = f[v^1(x^1) + \ldots + v^m(x^m)] \;,$$

where f and v^r are twice differentiable functions.

LEMMA E.3. The Hessian matrix of a strongly separable function with respect to a partition may be expressed as the sum of a matrix of rank one or zero and a block-diagonal matrix.

PROOF. From its definition a strongly separable function is also weakly separable. Hence Lemma E.1 and the statements in its proof also hold for strongly separable functions. Moreover, because of the special additive structure of (E.16) the first derivatives f_r become the same for all r. Call it f'. The second derivatives f_{rs} also become the same for all r and s. Call it f''. The derivatives of the branch functions v^r remain the same as in Lemma E.1. Then (E.8) becomes

(E.17) $$H(x) = f'' \begin{bmatrix} v_1 \\ \cdot \\ \cdot \\ \cdot \\ v_m \end{bmatrix} [v_1' \cdots v_m'] + f' \begin{bmatrix} V_1 & & 0 \\ & \cdot & \\ & & \cdot \\ & & \cdot \\ 0 & & V_m \end{bmatrix} .$$

The product of the two vectors forms a matrix of rank one or zero, and the matrix on the far right is block-diagonal. See also panel C of Figure 10.

LEMMA E.4. The Hessian matrix of a strongly separable function that is also quadratic in x may be partitioned as in Lemma E.2, with the second super-block being of rank one or zero.

PROOF. Immediate from Lemma E.2, which applies to strongly separable functions that are quadratic in x, and from the special structure of the first matrix on the right of (E.17). See also panel D of Figure 10.

E.3. Pearce-Separable Functions

For the present purpose the following definition of Pearce-separability, due to Goldman and Uzawa [1964, p. 388], is used:

DEFINITION E.5. The function z is *Pearce-separable* with respect to the partition if it is weakly separable with respect to the partition, and at the same time each branch function v^r is strongly separable with respect to the partition of its vector of arguments x^r into individual elements.

Note that special additive assumptions are now made regarding the structure *within* subsets of the first partition, rather than between subsets, as was done for strong separability. Thus, strong separability and Pearce-separability are different types of specialization of weak separability.

LEMMA E.5. The Hessian matrix of a Pearce-separable function may be expressed as the sum of a block-homogeneous matrix and a diagonal matrix.

PROOF. From its definition a Pearce-separable function is also weakly separable, and hence Lemma E.1 and the statements in its proof also hold for Pearce-separable functions. Moreover, because of the special restrictions on the branch functions, the branch Hessians V_r are all diagonal. Hence the second matrix on the right of (E.8) is diagonal, and the Lemma immediately follows.

LEMMA E.6. The Hessian matrix of a Pearce-separable function that is also quadratic in x may be partitioned as in Lemma E.2, with the first super-block being diagonal.

PROOF. Immediate from Lemma E.2, which applies to Pearce-separable functions that are also quadratic, and from the diagonal structure of the second matrix on the right of (E.8).

APPENDIX F. MATHEMATICAL SUPPLEMENTS

F.1. Kronecker Products

DEFINITION F.1. Let A be a matrix of size m by p and B be a matrix of size n by q. Then the Kronecker product between A and B is the mn by pq matrix

$$(F.1) \qquad A \otimes B = [a_{ij}B] .$$

Note that $A \otimes B$ and $B \otimes A$ have the same elements, but the elements are arranged differently.

From Bellman [1960, pp. 228, 427, Exercise 1] we have the following propositions:

$$(F.2) \qquad A \otimes B \otimes C = (A \otimes B) \otimes C = A \otimes (B \otimes C) .$$

$$(F.3) \quad (A + B) \otimes (C + D) = (A \otimes C) + (A \otimes D) + (B \otimes C) + (B \otimes D) ,$$

where A and B are of the same size, and C and D are of the same size.

(F.4) $$(A \otimes B)(C \otimes D) = AC \otimes BD ,$$

where the multiplications AC and BD are defined.

(F.5) $$\text{tr}(A \otimes B) = (\text{tr}A)(\text{tr}B) ,$$

where A and B are square.

The following additional propositions are easily derived from the above:

(F.6) $$s \otimes A = A \otimes s ,$$

where s is a scalar.

(F.7) $$(A \otimes B)' = A' \otimes B' .$$

(F.8) $$(A \otimes B)(A^{-1} \otimes B^{-1}) = I_{mn} ,$$

where A and B are nonsingular of orders m and n respectively. Hence, with the same A and B,

(F.9) $$(A \otimes B)^{-1} = A^{-1} \otimes B^{-1} .$$

Then, for a set of nonsingular matrices $A, B, C, \ldots$

(F.10) $$(A \otimes B \otimes C \otimes \ldots)^{-1} = A^{-1} \otimes B^{-1} \otimes C^{-1} \otimes \ldots$$

F.2. Limits on a Valid Correlation Matrix

It is well known, but sometimes forgotten, that an arbitrary set of correlation coefficients, when arrayed in a symmetric matrix, will not always yield a correlation matrix that is valid—that is, that could be obtained from real data. The necessary and sufficient condition is, of course, that if R is the correlation matrix, it be expressible in the form

(F.11) $$R = P'P ,$$

where P is any normalized data matrix. This condition is equivalent to the requirement that R be symmetric positive semi-definite.

Consider now the special case where all of the correlations are identical. Let R be of order n and of the form

(F.12) $$R = \begin{bmatrix} 1 & r & . & . & . & r \\ r & 1 & . & . & . & r \\ . & & & & & . \\ . & & & & & . \\ . & & & & & . \\ r & r & . & . & . & 1 \end{bmatrix}.$$

LEMMA F.1. In order for R as given by (F.12) to be a valid correlation matrix, r must lie within the limits

(F.13) $$-\frac{1}{n-1} \le r \le 1 .$$

PROOF. In order for R to be positive semi-definite, it is necessary and sufficient that every principal minor of R, including $\det(R)$, be non-negative. The most stringent of these requirements is that

(F.14) $$\det(R) \ge 0 .$$

By direct evaluation of the determinant, this becomes

(F.15) $$(1 - r)^{n-1}[1 + (n - 1)r] \ge 0 .$$

The limits are found by using the equality in (F.15), and by solving the resulting equation (F.13) is obtained.

APPENDIX G. PROGRESSIVE MERGER PROCEDURE PROGRAMS

G.1. One-way PMP: Recursive Formulas

LEMMA G.1. *Consequence formula.* Let P and M^{-1} be the matrices that are inputs to any stage K of the procedure, let d_{ij} be as given by (5.8) and let m^{ij} be the typical element of M^{-1}. Let $\bar{M}$ be the reduced M matrix of the stage. Then the consequence of merging points i and j is given by (5.7).

PROOF: By substituting (5.2b), (5.5) and (5.6) into (5.4) with $\bar{P}$ now of size G by $K - 1$, we have

(G.1) $$dc_{ij} = \mathrm{tr}PM[I - T_1'(T_1MT_1')^{-1}T_1M]P' ,$$

where the columns of P and the rows and columns of M have been permuted so that $i = 1$ and $j = 2$. Now define

(G.2) $$U_1 = T_1'(T_1MT_1')^{-1}T_1M ,$$

(G.3) $$T_2 = (1 - 1 \, 0 \ldots 0) ,$$

(G.4) $$U_2 = M^{-1}T_2'(T_2M^{-1}T_2')^{-1}T_2 ,$$

where the row vector T_2 has $K - 2$ zero elements. Then it is seen that U_1 is idempotent of rank $K - 1$, and U_2 is idempotent of rank 1.

It follows immediately from their definition that

(G.5a) $T_1T_2' = 0 ,$ \qquad (G.5b) $T_2T_1' = 0 .$

Then it is seen that

(G.6a) $U_1 U_2 = 0$,   (G.6b) $U_2 U_1 = 0$.

Then $U_1 + U_2$ is idempotent of rank K, since for two idempotent matrices A and B it is true that the sum $A + B$ is idempotent with rank equal to the sum of the ranks of A and B if, and only if,

(G.7) $AB = BA = 0$.

See Chipman and Rao [1964, p. 199, propositions (2a) and (2b)].
   Then

(G.8) $U_1 + U_2 = I$,

since the only idempotent matrix with rank equal to its order is the identity matrix.
   Then the square bracket in (G.1) is exactly equal to U_2, so (G.1) becomes:

(G.9) $dc_{ij} = \mathrm{tr} P T_2'(T_2 M^{-1} T_2')^{-1} T_2 P' = \dfrac{(p_i - p_j)'(p_i - p_j)}{m^{ii} + m^{jj} - 2m^{ij}} = d_{ij}(s_{ij(M)})^{-1}$,

where

(G.10) $s_{ij(M)} = m^{ii} + m^{jj} - 2m^{ij}$,

and which establishes the first equation of (5.7).
   Let M_{ij} denote matrix M with row i and column j removed. Then, by direct expansion of determinants it may be verified that

(G.11) $\det \bar{M} = \det M_{ii} + \det M_{jj} + 2 \det M_{ij}$,

and dividing the above equation by $\det M$ that

(G.12) $\dfrac{\det \bar{M}}{\det M} = m^{ii} + m^{jj} - 2m^{ij}$.

By substituting the left side of (G.12) into the denominator of (G.9), the second equation of (5.7) is established. This establishes Lemma G.1.
   LEMMA G.2. *Revision of the matrix P*. Let the matrices P and M^{-1} at stage K be represented by

(G.13) $P = (p_1 p_2 P_R)$

and

(G.14) $M^{-1} = \begin{bmatrix} m^{11} & m^{12} & m^{1R} \\ m^{12} & m^{22} & m^{2R} \\ m^{R1} & m^{R2} & M^{RR} \end{bmatrix}$, where p_1 and p_2 are G by 1 column vectors representing the two points that are to be merged; P_R is a G by $(K-2)$ matrix representing the remaining points; m^{11}, m^{12}, and m^{22} are scalars; m^{1R} and m^{2R} are row vectors with transposes m^{R1} and m^{R2}, respectively; and M^{RR} is a square symmetric matrix. Let the revised matrix $\bar{P}$ be represented by

$$\text{(G.15)} \qquad\qquad \bar{P} = (\bar{p}_2 P_R) \; ,$$

where $\bar{p}_2$ denotes the new condensed point obtained by merging old points 1 and 2, so $\bar{P}$ has the order G by $(K-1)$. Then $\bar{P}$ is obtained from (5.9), where K is substituted for H.

PROOF: Let

$$\text{(G.16)} \qquad\qquad \tilde{P} = \bar{P} T_1 \; ,$$

where T_1 is defined by (5.6). That is, $\tilde{P}$ is a G by K matrix having the same columns as $\bar{P}$ but with the first column, $\bar{p}_2$, repeated. Then, from (G.16), (5.5), (5.2b), (G.2), (G.4), and (G.8),

$$\text{(G.17)} \quad \tilde{P} = PMT_1'\bar{M}^{-1}T_1 = PU_1' = P(I - U_2') = P - PT_2'T_2M^{-1}(s_{12(M)})^{-1} \; ,$$

in the last step making use of (G.10) with $i = 1, j = 2$.

Formula (5.9) follows from the expansion of (G.17) and from the facts that from the repetitive first column defined in (G.16), we have:

$$\text{(G.18a)} \quad \tilde{p}_1 = \tilde{p}_2 = \bar{p}_2 \; , \qquad\qquad \text{(G.18b)} \quad \tilde{p}_j = \bar{p}_j \text{ for } j = 3, \ldots, K \; .$$

LEMMA G.3. *Revision of* M^{-1}. Let the revised matrix $\bar{M}^{-1}$, of order $K - 1$, be

$$\text{(G.19)} \qquad\qquad \bar{M}^{-1} = \begin{bmatrix} \bar{m}^{22} & \bar{m}^{2R} \\ \bar{m}^{R2} & \bar{M}^{RR} \end{bmatrix} ,$$

where the first row and column is associated with the new condensed point—i.e., the upper left element is a scalar, the upper right a row vector, the lower left a column vector, and the lower right a symmetric matrix. Then these elements are obtained by (5.10), where K is substituted for H.

PROOF: Define

$$\text{(G.20)} \qquad\qquad \tilde{M}^g = T_1'\bar{M}^{-1}T_1 \; ,$$

where T_1 is defined by (5.6). That is, $\tilde{M}^g$ is a K by K matrix having the first two rows and columns identical.[1] Then, using (G.20), (5.2), (G.2), (G.4), and (G.8),

$$\text{(G.21)} \quad \tilde{M}^g = M^{-1}U_1' = M^{-1}(I - U_2') = M^{-1} - M^{-1}T_2'T_2M^{-1}(s_{12(M)})^{-1} \; .$$

----

[1] $\tilde{M}^g$ is the generalized inverse of a $\tilde{M}$ defined as $T_1'(T_1T_1')^{-1}\bar{M}(T_1T_1')^{-1}T_1$. See Appendix D.

Formula (5.10) follows from the expansion of (G.21) and from the relations implied by (G.20):

(G.22a) $\tilde{m}^{11} = \tilde{m}^{12} = \tilde{m}^{22} = \overline{m}^{22}$, (G.22b) $\tilde{m}^{1j} = \tilde{m}^{2j} = \overline{m}^{2j}$,

(G.23) $\tilde{m}^{ij} = \overline{m}^{ij}$ for $i, j = 4, \ldots, K$;

where $\tilde{m}^{ij}$ is an element of $\tilde{M}^g$.

LEMMA G.4. *The case of diagonal M.* When M is diagonal, (5.7), (5.9), and (5.10) become (5.11), (5.12), and (5.13) respectively.

PROOF: When M is diagonal, we have

(G.24a) $m^{ii} = 1/m_{ii}$, (G.24b) $m^{ij} = 0$ for $i \neq j$.

Substituting these values into (5.7), (5.9), and (5.10) produces the needed results.

LEMMA G.5. *Revision of D matrix.* Let the generalized distance $d_{ij(C)}$ be defined as in (5.18) and the revised generalized distance $\bar{d}_{ij(C)}$ be defined by the same formula with bars over p_i and p_j to denote columns of the revised $\bar{P}$. Then $\bar{d}_{ij(C)}$ may be obtained directly from $d_{ij(C)}$ and M^{-1} by

(G.25) $\bar{d}_{ij(C)} = d_{ij(C)} + S_{ij(M)}[d_{1i(C)} + d_{2j(C)} - d_{2i(C)} - d_{1j(C)}] + S^2_{ij(M)}d_{12(C)}$,

where

(G.26) $\qquad S_{ij(M)} = (m^{1i} + m^{2j} - m^{2i} - m^{1j})(s_{12(M)})^{-1}$,

and where $s_{12(M)}$ is given by (G.10).

PROOF: Consider the distance

(G.27) $\qquad d_{ij(C)} = (\tilde{p}_i - \tilde{p}_j)'C(\tilde{p}_i - \tilde{p}_j)$,

where $\tilde{p}_i$ and $\tilde{p}_j$ are columns of $\tilde{P}$ as given by (G.17). Then $\bar{d}_{ij(C)}$ is the desired $\bar{d}_{ij(C)}$ only repeated for the identical points $\tilde{p}_1$ and $\tilde{p}_2$. Now let

(G.28) $\qquad T_{2(ij)} = (0 \ldots 010 \ldots 0 - 10 \ldots 0)$

with $K - 2$ zero elements and the 1 and -1 corresponding to the columns i and j of $\tilde{P}$. Thus $T_{2(12)}$ is the same as our former T_2 from (G.3). Then, from (G.27) and using (G.17), (G.28), and (5.19),

(G.29) $\quad d_{ij(C)} = T_{2(ij)}\tilde{P}'C\tilde{P}T'_{2(ij)} = T_{2(ij)}(I - U_2)P'CP(I - U'_2)T'_{2(ij)}$
$\qquad\qquad = T_{2(ij)}(B - U_2B - BU'_2 + U_2BU'_2)T'_{2(ij)}$.

Then, using (5.18), (5.19), (G.4), and (G.28), (G.29) becomes

(G.30) $\quad d_{ij(C)} = b_{ii} + b_{jj} - 2b_{ij}$
$$- \frac{2\,(m^{1i} + m^{2j} - m^{2i} - m^{1j})(b_{1i} + b_{2j} - b_{2i} - b_{1j})}{m^{11} + m^{22} - 2m^{12}}$$
$$+ \frac{(m^{1i} + m^{2j} - m^{2i} - m^{1j})^2(b_{11} + b_{22} - 2b_{12})}{(m^{11} + m^{22} - 2m^{12})^2} \; .$$

From (5.20) it may be verified that

(G.31) $-2(b_{1i} + b_{2j} - b_{2i} - b_{1j}) = d_{1i} + d_{2j} - d_{2i} - d_{1j}$.

Then, using (5.20), (G.26), and (G.31), (G.30) becomes (G.25).

G.2. One-way PMP: Outline of Computer Routine

Input. It is first assumed that the inputs are the original P, the original M, the terminal number of subsets J, the branch-off stage L, the list of forbidden merger pairs if any, and the number of chains to be run. The M matrix is assumed to be nonsingular, and the C matrix is assumed to be the identity matrix.

Preliminary Operation. Invert the original M matrix if the inverse is not available. After the inverse M^{-1} or its upper triangle is obtained, it is not necessary to retain the original M in storage.

Basic Chain Routine. To obtain an optimal sequence of mergers, yielding an optimal sequence of costs or c values conditional that no pair on the forbidden list be merged. A single merger of two points occurs in a stage.

Routine at Each Stage K. Given as data to stage K the matrices P and M^{-1}, the job of the stage is to find an optimal merger, to make the necessary revisions in the given matrices resulting from the merger, and to pass on to stage $K - 1$ as output the revised matrices $\bar{P}$ and $\bar{M}^{-1}$. In stage L of the first chain, four "near-optimal" mergers are also recorded. These mergers are used to begin new chains. Necessary steps in the routine at each stage are:

1. Test all possible pairs of points, i, j, for possible merger. There are $K(K - 1)/2$ pairs.

   a. Test to see if pair (i, j) is not forbidden.

   b. For each pair that is not forbidden compute dc_{ij} from formula (5.7).

   c. Compare the dc_{ij} and find the minimum. For stage L of the first chain, find also dc_{ij} for the "near-optimal" mergers. Record these dc_{ij}, the indices i and j associated therewith, and the cost c that is effective after an optimal merger takes place.

2. Revise P by formula (5.9). This involves computing and recording $G \times (K - 1)$ new elements. As the new elements are computed and recorded, the old ones may be removed from storage.

3. Revise M^{-1} by formula (5.10). This involves computing and recording an upper triangle of $(K)(K - 1)/2$ new elements counting the diagonal. As the new elements are computed and recorded, the old ones may be removed from storage. (That is, assuming that the new $\bar{P}$ is already recorded from Step 2 above.)

New Chains. At stage L of the first chain there are near-optimal mergers recorded. Go back and start another chain, merging another pair of points. Complete this chain by the routine described above. Form new chains as directed.

Selection of Final Partition for J Subsets. Completion of the preceding steps will result in the recording of one to five partitions of the original points into J subsets, namely, the last partition of each completed chain, and also the c values of these partitions. Compare these c values. A partition having a minimum c value will be deemed to be the desired solution.

Modification for Symmetric input. Assume now that a B or D matrix is input in place of P. D is stored and revised throughout the chain routine instead of P. If the input is B, compute the first D as a preliminary operation using formula (5.8). D is input to each stage K instead of P, and $\bar{D}$ is output.

Step 2 above then should read: "Revise D by formula (G.25). This involves computing and recording an upper triangle of $(K)(K-1)/2$ new elements. As the new elements are computed and recorded, the old ones may be removed from storage."

Otherwise the routine is the same as for P input.

G.3. Lockstep PMP: Recursive Formulas

All of the Lemmas of this section use the following assumptions. The input to stage K is five K by K matrices: P, M^{-1}, C^{-1}, D(col), and D(row), all symmetric except P, where D(col) contains elements $d_{ij(C)}$ given by

$$(G.32) \qquad d_{ij(C)} = T_{2(ij)}P'CPT'_{2(ij)} ,$$

and D(row) contains elements $d_{ij(M)}$ given by

$$(G.33) \qquad d_{ij(M)} = T_{2(ij)}PMP'T'_{2(ij)} ,$$

where $T_{2(ij)}$ is defined by (G.28). The stage consists of two steps. In the column step $S = I$, $T = T_1$ as given by (5.6); P is reduced to size K by $K-1$; and M^{-1} and D(col) are reduced to size $K-1$ by $K-1$. In the row step $S = T_1$, $T = I$; P is reduced to size $K-1$ by $K-1$; and C^{-1} and D(row) are also reduced to size $K-1$ by $K-1$.

LEMMA G.6. *Consequence formula.* The consequence of merging columns i and j of P and also rows i and j of P is

$$(G.34) \qquad dc_{ij} = \frac{d_{ij(C)}}{s_{ij(M)}} + \frac{d_{ij\,(M)}}{s_{ij(C)}} - \frac{q_{ij}^2}{s_{ij(M)}\,s_{ij(C)}}$$

where

$$(G.35) \qquad q_{ij} = p_{ii} + p_{jj} - p_{ij} - p_{ji} ,$$

(G.36) $s_{ij(C)} = c^{ii} + c^{jj} - 2c^{ij}$,

and where $s_{ij(M)}$ is defined by (G.10).

PROOF: Let $dc_{ij}(\text{col})$ denote the consequence after the column step alone. This consequence is given by (5.7) for the one-way case where now the generalized distance $d_{ij(C)}$ is used for d_{ij}, instead of (5.8). The proof is exactly the same as that of Lemma G.1 with the following slight changes: the cost formula (2.39) is used to start with instead of (5.4); a C appears immediately to the right of the tr symbol in (G.1) and in (G.9); in the last equation of (G.9) the numerator of the fraction on the left is multiplied by the matrix C, and the symbol $d_{ij(C)}$ replaces d_{ij} on the right. The resulting consequence may also be expressed as

(G.37) $dc_{ij}(\text{col}) = T_{2(ij)}P'CPT'_{2(ij)}(s_{ij(M)})^{-1}$.

The consequence of the row step alone is obtained by repeating this one-way result, with $\bar{P}'(\text{col})$ and C playing the role just assumed by P and M, and $\bar{M}(\text{col})$ playing the role just assumed by C. Let this consequence be denoted by $dc_{ij}(\text{row})$. Then, making the above substitutions into (G.37),

(G.38) $dc_{ij}(\text{row}) = T_{2(ij)}[\bar{P}'(\text{col})]'[\bar{M}(\text{col})][\bar{P}'(\text{col})]T'_{2(ij)}(s_{ij(C)})^{-1}$.

Using the expressions for $\bar{M}$ and $\bar{P}$ as given by (5.2b) and (5.5), and using also (G.2) and (G.8), the product of the three square brackets in (G.38) becomes

(G.39) $PMT'_1\bar{M}^{-1}T_1MP' = PMU_1P' = PM(I - U_2)P'$.

Using for U_2 its expression given by (G.4), substituting (G.39) back into (G.38), and simplifying, one obtains

(G.40) $dc_{ij}(\text{row}) = \dfrac{T_{2(ij)}PMP'T'_{2(ij)}}{s_{ij(C)}} - \dfrac{(T_{2(ij)}PT'_{2(ij)})^2}{s_{ij(C)}s_{ij(M)}}$.

The complete consequence of the stage is the sum of the separate consequences for the column step and the row step. That is,

(G.41) $dc_{ij} = dc_{ij}(\text{col}) + dc_{ij}(\text{row})$.

Adding (G.37) and (G.40) and using (G.32), (G.33), and (G.35) will produce (G.34), which was to be derived.

LEMMA G.7. *Revision of D(col).* The revised generalized distance $\bar{d}_{ij(C)}$ for the stage may be obtained by

(G.42) $\bar{d}_{ij(C)} = d_{ij(C)} + S_{ij(M)}d_{12,\,ij(C)} + S^2_{ij(M)}d_{12(C)} - \dfrac{(q_{12,\,ij} - S_{ij(M)}q_{12})^2}{S_{12(C)}}$,

where $S_{ij(M)}$ is given by (G.26), $d_{12,\,ij(C)}$ is given by

(G.43) $$d_{12,\,ij(C)} = d_{1i(C)} + d_{2j(C)} - d_{2i(C)} - d_{1j(C)} \ ,$$

and $q_{12,\,ij}$ is given by

(G.44) $$q_{12,\,ij} = p_{1i} + p_{2j} - p_{2i} - p_{1j} \ .$$

PROOF: The revision of $d_{ij(C)}$ after the column step alone is given by (G.25). Call this revised element $\tilde{d}_{ij(C)}(\text{col})$, and call the revised P after the column step alone $\bar{P}(\text{col})$, as before, and its disaggregated version $\tilde{P}(\text{col})$. Call the disaggregated version of $\bar{P}$ after both column and row steps $\tilde{P}$. The effect of the row step on $\tilde{P}(\text{col})$ is equivalent to that of merging two columns of its transpose, $\tilde{P}'(\text{col})$ and this effect is given by (G.17), when we let $\tilde{P}'(\text{col})$ and C play the roles of P and M, respectively, and define the relevant U_2 in the present context, by analogy with (G.4), as

(G.45) $$U_2 = U_{2(C)} = C^{-1}T_2'(T_2C^{-1}T_2')^{-1}T_2 \ .$$

That is to say, in the present notation (G.17) says that

(G.46) $$\tilde{P}' = \tilde{P}'(\text{col})(I - U_{2(C)}') \ .$$

Then the desired revised distance is

(G.47) $$\tilde{d}_{ij(C)} = T_{2(ij)}\tilde{P}'C\tilde{P}T_{2(ij)}' \ .$$

Substituting (G.45) into (G.46), and then (G.46) into (G.47), we obtain

(G.48) $$\tilde{d}_{ij(C)} = \tilde{d}_{ij(C)}(\text{col}) - \frac{[T_{2(12)}\tilde{P}(\text{col})T_{2(ij)}']^2}{s_{12(C)}} \ .$$

Substituting in the square bracket of (G.48) for $\tilde{P}(\text{col})$ the $\tilde{P}$ as given in the original version of (G.17), this square bracket becomes

(G.49) $$T_{2(12)}PT_{2(ij)}' - \frac{(T_{2(12)}PT_{2(12)}')(T_{2(12)}M^{-1}T_{2(ij)}')}{s_{12(M)}} = q_{12,\,ij} - S_{ij(M)}q_{12} \ ,$$

using also (G.43) and (G.44). Then, substituting (G.49) into (G.48), and adding (G.48) to (G.25), (G.42) results.

LEMMA G.8. *Revision of D(row).* The revised generalized distance $\tilde{d}_{ij(M)}$ for the stage may be obtained by

(G.50) $$\tilde{d}_{ij(M)} = d_{ij(M)} + S_{ij(C)}d_{12,\,ij(M)} + S_{ij(C)}^2 d_{12(M)} - \frac{(q_{12,\,ij} - S_{ij(C)}q_{12})^2}{s_{12(M)}}$$

where

(G.51) $$d_{12,\,ij(M)} = d_{1i(M)} + d_{2j(M)} - d_{2i(M)} - d_{1j(M)} \ ,$$

(G.52) $$S_{ij(C)} = \frac{c^{1i} + c^{2j} - c^{2i} - c^{1j}}{s_{12(C)}} \ ,$$

and where $s_{ij(M)}$ is given by (G.36).

PROOF: The same proof as for Lemma G.7, but interchanging the roles of C and M, of the column step and row step, and using P' for P.

LEMMA G.9. *Revision of P.* The revised $\bar{P}$ for the stage has elements given by

$$(G.53) \quad \bar{p}_{ij} = p_{ij} - \frac{(m^{1j} - m^{2j})(p_{i1} - p_{i2})}{s_{12(M)}} - \frac{(c^{i1} - c^{i2})(p_{1j} - p_{2j})}{s_{12(C)}} ,$$

where $s_{12(M)}$ and $s_{12(C)}$ are given by (G.10) and (G.36) respectively.

PROOF: The complete revision is the sum of the revision of each step. The revision after the column step is obtained from (5.9) and is given by the first two terms to the right of the equals sign in (G.53). The revision of the row step is effected by subtracting the left term of (G.53) by means of applying (5.9) to the transpose of P and using C instead of M.

LEMMA G.10. *Revision of C^{-1} and M^{-1}.* For the stage the revised $\bar{m}^{ij}$ is given by (5.10), and the revised $\bar{c}^{ij}$ is given by the same formula, with c substituted for m.

PROOF: In the column step the revision of M^{-1} is given by (5.10). In the proof of (5.10) in Lemma G.3 the presence of non-identity C in the problem makes no difference. Moreover, the merger of the row step does not affect M^{-1}. Likewise, the merger of the column step does not affect C^{-1}, nor does the presence of non-identity M in the problem change the formula for revising C^{-1} in the row step. Hence these formulas give the needed revisions for M and C for the complete stage.

G.4. *Lockstep PMP: Outline of Computer Routine*

Input. Inputs to the computer routine are the original P, the original C, the original M, all square with C and M nonsingular, the terminal number of subsets J, the branch-off stage L, the list of forbidden merger pairs if any, and the number of chains to be run.

Preliminary Operations. Invert the C and M matrices if the inverse is not available and store the upper triangles. Compute the initial $D(\text{col})$ and $D(\text{row})$ matrices, using formulas (G.32) and (G.33), and store the upper triangles. After these computations are performed it is not necessary to retain the original C and M in storage.

Basic Chain Routine. To obtain an optimal sequence of mergers of the rows and columns of P, on condition that the indices of the rows and of the columns merged at each stage are the same, and conditional that no pair of indices on the forbidden list will be merged. In each stage two rows and two columns are merged.

Routine at Each Stage K. The input data to stage K are the five matrices P, M^{-1}, C^{-1}, $D(\text{col})$, and $D(\text{row})$. The job of the stage is to find a permissible and optimal merger, and then make the necessary revisions in each of these five matrices and pass on the revised matrices to stage K 1. In stage L of the first chain, L having been specified by an input parameter, four "near-optimal" pairs of indices are also recorded. These pairs are used to begin new chains. Necessary steps in the routine at each stage are the following:

    1. Test each pair of indices (i, j) for possible merger.

        a. Test whether the pair is forbidden. This is the same sub-routine as in the one-way case.

        b. Compute consequence by formula (G.34) for pairs that are not forbidden. Need D(col), D(row), P, C^{-1}, M^{-1}.

        c. Compare consequences and find the minimum. For stage L of the first chain find also the "near-to-minimum" consequences, and record.

    2. Revise matrices. Store revised, discard old, elements in the indicated sequence.

        a. Revise D(col) by formula (G.42). Need old D(col), old P, old C^{-1}, old M^{-1}.

        b. Revise D(row) by formula (G.50). Need old D(row), old P, old C^{-1}, old M^{-1}.

        c. Revise P by formula (G.53). Need old P, old C^{-1}, old M^{-1}.

        d. Revise M^{-1} by formula (5.10). Need old M^{-1}.

        e. Revise C^{-1} by formula (5.10) with c's. Need old C^{-1}.

New Chains and Selection of Final Partition. This part of the outline is the same as for the one-way case, as described in section G.2 of this Appendix.

INDEX

THE JOHNS HOPKINS PRESS

Designed by Arlene J. Sheer

Composed in Times Roman text and Times New Roman Display
by Monotype Composition Company, Inc.

Printed offset by Universal Lithographers, Inc.
on 60-lb. Perkins & Squier R

Bound by L. H. Jenkins, Inc.
in Columbia Riverside Vellum